799
Wei
Co.

D1251259

Trial and Error

Photo by A. Himmelreich

CHAIM WEIZMANN

TRIAL AND ERROR

THE AUTOBIOGRAPHY

OF

CHAIM WEIZMANN

IN TWO VOLUMES

VOLUME II

Philadelphia

THE JEWISH PUBLICATION SOCIETY OF AMERICA

5709-1949

TRIAL AND ERROR, THE AUTOBIOGRAPHY OF CHAIM WEIZMANN

COPYRIGHT, 1949, BY THE WEIZMANN FOUNDATION
PRINTED IN THE UNITED STATES OF AMERICA

ALL RIGHTS IN THIS BOOK ARE RESERVED. NO PART OF THE BOOK MAY BE REPRODUCED
IN ANY MANNER WHATSOEVER WITHOUT WRITTEN PERMISSION EXCEPT IN THE CASE
OF BRIEF QUOTATIONS EMBODIED IN CRITICAL ARTICLES AND REVIEWS. FOR INFORMATION
ADDRESS HARPER & BROTHERS

Table of Contents

VOLUME II

CHAPTER 24

Cleveland and Carlsbad

My First Visit to America—Its Purpose—Albert Einstein Joins Our Delegation—New York's Reception of Us—The Deeper Meaning of the Split in American Zionism, 1921— "Private Initiative" Versus "National Funds"—"Washington Versus Pinsk"—Break with the Brandeis Group—Cleveland Convention—Fund Campaigning in America—Zionist Educational Work—The Carlsbad Congress—Disappointments in Palestine—Larger Immigration and Colonization Begin—Criticism of Our "Fancy Experiments"—Tug of War between City and Soil.

I HAVE so far indicated only the beginning of the divergence between the Brandeis group on the one hand and the remainder of American Zionism, allied with European Zionism, on the other. It had to do with much more than program and method; its source was a deeper divergence in what might almost be called folkways. It reached into social and historic as well as economic and political concepts; it was connected with the organic interpretation of Zionism. It cannot be described in abstract terms, and its nature will reveal itself gradually as the narrative unfolds.

Some suspicion of this truth was already present in my mind when I made my preparations for the trip to America—for me a *terra incognita*. Shmarya Levin was there, of course; he had been caught by the war and held to the country for four years, during which he had carried on a great educational campaign among Zionists and Jews at large. His work in those early years was to bear fruit for an entire generation, and I knew that at the time of my first visit in 1921 he was doing everything possible to prepare the ground for us. But I still had misgivings about the magnitude of the task before me, and wished to go armed with as much support as I could find.

The immediate purposes of the trip were two; first to found the American *Keren Hayesod* (Palestine Foundation Fund), as one of the two main instruments of the rebuilding of the Homeland—the other, the Jewish National Fund, I have already described; second, to awaken American interest in the Hebrew University. It seemed to us that the foundation stones had been sitting alone on Mount Scopus for quite long enough, and now that we had a civil administration under Herbert Samuel it was time to get on with the job of actually establishing the University. At the back of my mind there was also the intention of taking some soundings as to the prospects of establishing some sort of Jewish council (or agency) with the co-operation of some of the important Jewish organizations engaged in public welfare work.

It was an ambitious program—more so than I quite realized. But I set about the creation of as strong a delegation as possible. From among my colleagues I enlisted Mr. Ussishkin, and Dr. Ben-Zion Mossinsohn, director of the Herzlian Gymnasium in Tel Aviv. I also approached Professor Albert Einstein, with special reference to the Hebrew University, and to my great delight found him ready to help. He brought with him his secretary, Simon Ginsburg, son of Achad Ha-am; my wife and I joined them at Plymouth, to continue the journey on a Dutch boat. Leonard Stein, just released from the army, and recently returned from Palestine, where he had been acting as Military Governor of Safed, came along as my personal assistant. So we were quite a party on the boat.

I remember that we arrived in New York Harbor about noon on Saturday, April 2, 1921, altogether unaware of the extraordinary reception that awaited us. Some half-dozen boats carrying friends and journalists came out to meet us, and for the whole of that afternoon we were subjected to an endless series of grueling if well-meant interviews. Since it was the Sabbath, we could not land until the onset of evening; we simply had "to take it." Einstein was, of course, the chief target; his name was something of a portent in those days, and the journalists were eager to get from him a bright, popular paragraph on the theory of relativity. When they failed in this, they invariably turned to me, saying, "But you're a scientist, too, Dr. Weizmann." In the end, in sheer desperation, we took refuge in an inconspicuous cabin and waited till it was time to go ashore.

We intended, of course, to proceed straight to our hotel, settle down, and begin planning our work. We had reckoned—literally—without our host, which was, or seemed to be, the whole of New York Jewry. Long before the afternoon ended, delegations began to assemble on the quay and even on the docks. Pious Jews in their thousands came on foot all the way from Brooklyn and the Bronx to welcome us. Then the cars arrived, all of them beflagged. Every car had its horn and every horn was put in action. By the time we reached the gangway the area about the quays was a pandemonium of people, cars and mounted police. The car which we had thought would transport us quickly and quietly to our hotel fell in at the end of an enormous procession which wound its way through the entire Jewish section of New York. We reached the Commodore at about eleven-thirty, tired, hungry, thirsty and completely dazed. The spacious hall of the hotel was packed with another enthusiastic throng; we had to listen to several speeches of welcome, and I remember making some sort of reply. It was long after midnight when we found our rooms.

I was the more anxious to come to grips with my task because I knew that this magnificent popular reception was only one part of the story. Before leaving the ship I had received a printed memorandum brought to me by Judge Julian Mack, in which the Brandeis group, which constituted the American Zionist administration, expounded their views and set forth the conditions on which they would be prepared to support my mission. The main points dealt with their conception of the new character of the Zionist Organization and with the economics of the movement. Henceforth world Zionism was to consist of strong local federations, so that the old unity which had been the background of the authority of our Congresses should be replaced merely by co-ordination. In this there was a reflection of the deeper—and less conscious, therefore less overtly formulated— feelings of the Brandeis group about the organic unity of world Jewry. To us who had grown up since childhood in the movement, Zionism was the precipitation into organized form of the survival forces of the Jewish people; Zionism was in a sense Jewishness itself, set in motion for the re-creation of a Jewish Homeland. The World Zionist Organization, the Congresses, were not just *ad hoc* instruments; they were the expression of the unity of the Jewish people. The propositions of the Brandeis group, dealing ostensibly with merely formal matters, with organizational instrumental rearrangements, actually reflected a denial of Jewish nationalism; they made of Zionism simply a sociological plan—and not a good one, as I shall show—instead of the folk renaissance that it was. And then there was the attitude of the Brandeis group on the national funds. It became clear that the opposition to the attempt to raise a large budget really did not spring from a conviction that large sums could not be obtained: the Brandeis group stood for emphasis on "private investment" and "individual project" methods. My colleagues and I knew that "private initiative" would not be feasible to any significant extent before the Jewish people, in its corporate, national capacity, had made the financial effort which would create the foundations of the Homeland.

What we had here was a revival, in a new form and a new country, of the old cleavage between "East" and "West," in Zionism and Jewry; and the popular slogan called it, in fact, "Washington vs.

Pinsk," a convenient double allusion to Brandeis and myself, and also to the larger ideological implication.

There was, in fact, a deep gulf; but I was determined to do my utmost toward finding a compromise solution. The memorandum presented me by Judge Mack, as a condition for the co-operation with me of the Zionist Organization of America, I could not accept. It was in the nature of an ultimatum. Its formal provisions dealt with matters on which only the World Zionist Congress could speak authoritatively; I could not agree to changes which I, as President of the World Zionist Organization, had not been empowered to introduce. And still I hoped that some discreet middle road would be found in practice, and that we would face the world as a united group. I was all the time thinking of the people in Palestine whose hopes were centered on this trip, and of the new High Commissioner, so anxious to see large-scale colonization undertaken in the country. We *had* to have maximum results.

We felt—and the event proved us right—that the great masses of American Zionists resented the attitude of their leaders, but the leaders were powerful, and I foresaw that it would be difficult to do anything substantial without their co-operation. For weeks we discussed the possibility of compromise—greatly assisted by Leonard Stein's conciliatory disposition and drafting abilities. We knew he would go to the utmost limit of possible concession, and that if it were possible to find a "formula" he would find it. On the other hand, there was Ussishkin, who was not prepared to yield a jot on the budget, or on the constitution and functions of the *Keren Hayesod*; at the other end, the Brandeis group was not going to permit us to proclaim the *Keren Hayesod* as a Zionist instrument, and to raise funds for it in America, without an acceptance of the terms of the memorandum.

It was an unhappy situation, with passions mounting on both sides and things being said which added nothing to the substance of the discussion. A whispering campaign was launched against the Executive in Jerusalem, which was accused of consisting of men completely incapable of handling large sums of money : great idealists, of course, but utterly impractical, and given to "commingling of funds". And neither they (the members of the Palestine Executive), nor we (the anti-Brandeisists), had any notion of "American standards"—whatever that might mean. Enough poison was put in circulation to render the collection of any substantial sum of money extremely difficult.

As time went on the ideological controversy also crystallized into a conflict between the mass of American Zionism and a few privileged "Western" Jews who occupied high positions in American society. There was also implied a struggle for the control of the fate of

Palestine, whether it should belong to "America" or "Europe"—a struggle which in turn implied a fatal breach in the unity of world Jewry. All this was further complicated by the fact that some non-Zionist American Jews whom I was intensely anxious to win over for the practical work in Palestine (e.g., Mr. Louis Marshall and his friends) disliked the Brandeis group. Marshall himself, as will be seen, was no fanatical opponent of Zionism, and often acted as our disinterested adviser. Another, darker complication developed during our stay in America—the bitter Jaffa outbreak of May 1921, which led Herbert Samuel to suspend immigration temporarily. Everything during those days pointed to the urgent necessity of proceeding with our work and of getting a firm foothold for the Jewish National Home.

All our endeavors to find a compromise formula led to nothing. Samuel Untermyer, the brilliant lawyer and arbitrator, did his best to find a middle ground for us, but in vain. In the end we were compelled to break off relations with the Brandeis group, and I had to issue a statement to the American Jewish public, that, by virtue of the decision of the last Zionist Conference, and of the authority vested in me as President of the World Zionist Organization I declared the *Keren Hayesod* to be established in the United States. This action provoked violent protest from the other side, mingled with some abuse—all of it played up by the general press, so that the public at large was fully aware of our dissensions. So, of course, was the British Embassy. I remember going to see Sir Eric Geddes in Washington one morning when one of our opponents' pronouncements had appeared in the papers, and he remarked that I had rather placed myself in the position of President Wilson when he appealed to the Italian people over the heads of their constituted Government; he hoped I would not meet with the same fate! I said that my relations with the American Jewish community were, after all, a good deal more organic than Wilson's with the Italians, and I therefore hoped to avoid his failure.

My hope was vindicated when we underwent our formal trial of strength with the Brandeis group. At the twenty-fourth Convention of the Zionist Organization of America—the famous "Cleveland Convention"—of June, in that year, the mass of the American Zionists proved that they understood thoroughly the nature of the issues. The fact was that the American leaders did not want the *Keren Hayesod*, nor did they really want to see the Zionist Organization a world organization. They regarded our political work as ended—this despite the shock of the May riots in Palestine, and Samuel's suspension of immigration—and they had their own views as to the economic upbuilding of the country. All my detailed reports to the American leaders about the attitude of the British administration in Palestine, and about the need for mass colonization, failed to move them. They refused to see the portents, and they insisted that the best plan would be for every separate Zionist federation—the German, the Austrian, the Polish—to undertake some specific task in Palestine, the Executive of the World Zionist Organization having nothing to do but "co-ordinate" the work. This proposal would have meant, in effect, the reduction of the whole World Zionist Organization to the status of a technical bureau with doubtful authority; and the Zionist Congress, which was the forum of world Zionism, its deliberative and legislative body, expressing the will and the aspirations of world Jewry, would—if it did not fall into complete desuetude—become a conference of "experts."

All this was threshed out in Cleveland, in an atmosphere which I could not re-create even if I wanted to. I attended the Convention, together with the rest of the European delegation, but did not think it proper to take part in the proceedings. The issue was fought out between the American Zionists: on the one side the nationally known figures of Judge Mack, Professor Felix Frankfurter, Stephen S. Wise; on the other the relatively obscure but thoroughly representative figures like Louis Lipsky, Abraham Goldberg and Morris Rothenberg. The result was that the administration was defeated by an overwhelming majority. I am afraid that they did not prove very good losers, for the whole Brandeis group resigned from the Executive of the American Organization. Nor did they remain neutral; most of them entered into active and formidable opposition against our work. There is little doubt that our efforts in the first few years after Cleveland— crucial years for Palestine—would have been much more productive if not for the implacable hostility of most of our former colleagues.

We declared the *Keren Hayesod* officially established in America. Samuel Untermyer became its first President, and the job of organizing and popularizing the fund began. We divided the work among us as far as possible—I am speaking now of the European delegation— but I am afraid the lion's share of it fell on my shoulders; first, because I spoke both English and Yiddish, while the others, Ussishkin, Mossinsohn and Shmarya Levin, though excellent Yiddish speakers— Shmarya was, as I have already told, an orator of the very first order—knew but little English at this time; second, because I was urged to take the lead. Thus I found myself committed to visiting most of the principal American Jewish centers.

To anyone who has not actually been through it, it is difficult to convey any idea of what this experience meant. It must not be confused with the round of a lecturer, and not even with that of a political campaigner; I was, if you like, both of these, but I was also out to raise large sums of money. Besides, it was my first visit to the States, and I was completely ignorant of the terrain; I did not know what had to be done or—more important—what could safely be omitted. A typical day's "stand" in American towns worked out something like this:

One arrived by an early train, to be met at the station by a host of enthusiasts in cars, who formed a sort of guard of honor to escort one through the streets of a still half-sleeping town. All advance requests for the omission of this part of the proceedings, all suggestions that it would be helpful and healthful to have an hour or two to oneself on arrival after a night on a train, were completely ignored; one was repeatedly assured that the parade was an essential part of the publicity campaign—indispensable advertisement of coming events. So one submitted, in order not to upset the elaborate arrangements in which the local workers had taken so much pride.

From the station one proceeded to the hotel or to the city hall, to breakfast with anywhere between twenty-five to fifty local notables, including, usually, the mayor. One listened and replied to speeches of welcome. By the time this was over, it would be about ten o'clock, and the cameramen and reporters would be ready, all looking for some particularly sensational pose or statement. No discouragement could put them off. For some unfathomable reason they always billed me as the inventor of TNT. It was in vain that I systematically and repeatedly denied any connection with, or interest in, TNT. The initials seemed to exercise a peculiar fascination over journalists: and I suppose high explosive is always news.

One was lucky to be through with the press by eleven or eleven-thirty, and to find time to sneak up to one's room for a bath and change before the formal luncheon, usually timed for twelve-thirty, and seldom starting less than an hour late. This was a long, grueling affair of many courses and speeches, and the arrangement always was that the guest of honor should speak last, lest the public should be tempted to leave, thus depriving some of the other speakers of their audience. After this performance one was permitted an hour or so of rest, though even this was seldom without its interruptions.

In the late afternoon came the meeting for the local workers, tea—and more speeches; then there was dinner, very like lunch, only more so, and the day usually concluded, officially, with a mass meeting at the town hall or some similar building. From the mass meeting one was escorted by friends and well-wishers to the train, to retreat, with a sigh of relief, into one's sleeper, and one awoke the next morning in the next city on the list, to begin the whole performance all over again.

This went on with astounding regularity for weeks and months, with only minor variations. If I stayed more than a day in any town, I might indeed manage to get a little leisure. Then the local leader was sure to place his car at my disposal "to drive around a bit and see the sights." Being inexperienced, I used to accept, in the earlier days, with alacrity. But when the car arrived it usually contained three or four occupants, all grimly determined to entertain me, or to be entertained by me, as long as the drive lasted. And I had hoped for a little blessed solitude, and fresh air!

Intervals between public functions were usually filled in with private talks with "big donors" (a big donor was anyone whose contribution might be expected to reach about five thousand dollars). Often, alas, the "prospect" turned out to be a gentleman the indefiniteness of whose knowledge about Palestine was exceeded only by the extreme definiteness of his views about it. I would have to listen then to strange versions of the criticisms leveled at us by the Brandeis group, or by non-Zionists and anti-Zionists, to crank schemes for the overnight creation of a Jewish Homeland, to paternal practical advice from successful businessmen, all of which had to be received attentively and courteously.

They were good, kindly, well-intentioned people, some of them intelligent and informed Zionists, but my endurance was reaching its limit. I thought longingly of the ship that was to take us back to Europe. Yet even in Europe—though I did not know it yet—I was never to be free from the consequences of my work in the States. As soon as the summer invasion began, if I happened to be in London or Paris, I had to face the necessity of meeting the friends who had helped me in Boston or Baltimore or Chicago. It was important to show them every courtesy, lest they become offended and decide to take it out of me when I returned to America. It was not that I minded very much giving umbrage on my own account; but I learned that there were people who, having tried to see me in Europe and failed—I am sure through no fault of mine —went back to the States to cancel their pledges to the *Keren Hayesod*!

In the States a big donor would often make his contribution to the fund conditional on my accepting an invitation to lunch or dine at his house. Then I would have to face a large family gathering—three or four generations—talk, answer questions, listen to appeals and opinions, and watch my replies carefully, lest I inadvertently scare off a touchy prospect. I would sit through a lengthy meal and after it meet a select group of local celebrities, and again listen and answer till all hours of the night. Generally, I felt that I had fully earned that five thousand dollars.

On the whole the response of American Jewry was remarkably good, considering their unpreparedness for the burden thrust upon them, and the secession and active opposition of the Brandeis group. The work was vigorously continued after our departure, and the first year's income was about four times the five hundred thousand dollars which Mr. Brandeis had set as the maximum obtainable from the Jews of America, thus proving the tonic effect of setting a fairly high budget. But we still had nothing near the sum required by the program of the Annual Conference. However, we could go ahead with some land purchase, immigration and settlement. The first year or two after the foundation of the *Keren Hayesod* saw the founding of the Agricultural Mortgage Bank, an extremely important institution, the beginning of our payments on the Emek Jezreel purchase, and the founding of Nahalal, the first of our postwar settlements, which became the center of our activity in the Emek, the draining of its swamps, the combatting of malaria, and so on.

As the years passed, and my visits to America were repeated almost annually, a sort of tradition was established and a routine—a policeman's beat between Jerusalem and San Francisco. Gradually the *Keren Hayesod* took hold, became an acknowledged institution, until it was swallowed up in the United Palestine Appeal. The work grew easier, more profitable and more pleasant; visitors began to come to Palestine from America, contacts between the countries became frequent.

But there was something more to all this than political propaganda and money raising. All of us regarded our mission as, fundamentally, education in Zionism, both on its practical and on its theoretical side. On the practical side I sought to explain to American businessmen the reasons why their American experience did not always apply to the Palestinian scene. I said: "When a pioneer comes into Palestine, he finds a deserted land, neglected for generations. The hills have lost their trees, the good soil has been washed into the valleys and carried to the sea. We must restore the soil of Palestine. We must have money to sink in Palestine, to reconstruct what has been destroyed. You will have to sweat and labor and give money on which you will not get any return, but which will be transformed into national wealth. When you drain the marshes, you get no returns, but you accumulate wealth for the generations to come. If you reduce the percentage of malaria from forty to ten, that is national wealth."

And again: "You cannot build up Nahalal and Nuris without national funds. The *chalutzim* are willing to miss meals twice a week. But cows must be fed, and you cannot feed a cow with speeches."

How obvious it all seems now, how new it was then, and for years to come, and how difficult to get the lesson home. I shall show later what a fierce struggle developed in Zionism between what I considered premature emphasis on private enterprise and profits, and the laying of the national foundations. But there was needed, as the background to that understanding which I sought to instill in regard to practical matters, a feeling for the basic elements of the Jewish problem. I said to one meeting:

"Among the anti-Semites none is more interesting than the tender-hearted variety. Their anti-Semitism is always based on a compliment.

They tell us: 'You are the salt of the earth'—and there are Jews who feel themselves extraordinarily flattered. Yet I do not consider it a compliment to be called 'the salt of the earth.' The salt is used for someone else's food. It dissolves in that food. And salt is good only in small quantities. If there is too much salt in the food you throw out the food and the salt with it. That is to say, certain countries can digest a certain number of Jews; once that number has been passed, something drastic must happen: the Jews must go.

"They call us not only salt, but leaven. The Jews are not only the salt of the earth, but also a valuable ferment. They produce extraordinary ideas. They provide initiative, energy; they start things. But this compliment, too, is of a doubtful sort. There is a very fine difference between a ferment and a parasite. If the ferment is increased by ever so little beyond a certain point, it becomes a parasitical growth. So that those who wish to be polite call us 'ferments'; others, less polite, and less scientific, prefer to call us 'parasites.'"

I explained part of the reason for the status of the Jew with a simple simile: "You will always be treated as a guest if you, too, can play the host. The only man who is invited to dinner is the man who can have dinner at home if he likes. Switzerland is a small country, and there are more Swiss outside of Switzerland than in it. But there is no such thing as anti-Swiss sentiment in the sense that there is anti-Jewish sentiment. The Swiss has a home of his own, to which he can retreat, to which he can invite others. And it does not matter how small your home is, as long as it is your home. If you want your position to be secure elsewhere, you must have a portion of Jewry which is at home, in its own country. If you want the safety of equality in other universities, you must have a university of your own. The university in Jerusalem will affect your status here: professors from Jerusalem will be able to come to Harvard, and professors from Harvard to Jerusalem." This is, in fact, what has happened.

I sought to bring inspiration to them from the past. I said: "We are reproached by the whole world. We are told that we are dealers in old clothes, junk. We are perhaps the sons of dealers in old clothes, but we are the grandsons of Prophets. Think of the grandsons, and not of the sons."

It was really moving, the way they listened and took the words to heart. Despite the exhaustion and the discomfort and the occasional tedium, I felt an immense privilege in the work. I told them once: "I cannot think of any man with whom I would change positions. Here I am, without policemen, without an army, without a navy, facing out with a group of fellow-workers a proposition which is really unheard of: trying to build up a country which has been waste two thousand years, with a people which has been waste two thousand years, at a time when one-half of that people, perhaps the best half, has been broken up by a terrible war. And here, at midnight, you are sitting, five or six thousand miles away from Palestine, a country which many of you may never see, and you are waiting to hear me speak about that country. And you know very well that you will probably have to pay for it. It is extraordinary. I defy anyone, Jew or gentile, to show me a proposition like it."

From my first visit to America I went almost directly to the Congress in Carlsbad, the first since 1913 to bring together representatives of Zionists from all over the world.

Herbert Samuel had been High Commissioner for about a year, but there was already noticeable, in the Congress discussions, the beginnings of the disappointment, and even bitterness, which his regime was to inspire. I myself felt that he had not had a real chance yet, but three things had happened which gave rise to uneasiness.

First there had been his handling of the riots of May 1921, which I have already mentioned. Desirous of starting his work as peaceably as possible, Samuel's reaction to the riots had been to stop immigration, and this decision had been announced at a gathering of Arab notables in Ramleh. Both the decision, and the form of its announcement, came as a severe shock to Jews everywhere. Immigrants already within sight of the shores of Palestine were not allowed to land. Samuel disregarded the protests of Dr. Eder, and the interdict stood.

Samuel had also amnestied the two principal instigators of the Jaffa and Jerusalem pogroms, and it was largely due to him that Haj Amin el Husseini later became head of the Moslem Supreme Council and Mufti of Jerusalem (or Grand Mufti), with very considerable powers, and control over large funds—and with results too well known to need mention. In spite of the proverb, poachers turned gamekeepers are not always a success. The Arabs soon discovered that the High Commissioner's deep desire for peace made him susceptible to intimidation, and this discovery led to the third of what we regarded as Samuel's mistakes.

An Arab lawyer in Haifa, Wadi Bustani by name, had succeeded in working up a widespread agitation on behalf of certain Bedouin who had frequented the State lands in the Beisan area. They laid claim, through Bustani, to a large tract of irrigable Government land—about four hundred thousand dunams (one hundred thousand acres); and eventually, after a good deal of argument, their demands were granted, and the land was handed over to them for a nominal fee. One of the most important and most potentially fertile districts of Palestine (and one of the very few such districts which were "State lands") was thus condemned from the outset to stagnation and sterility, and important water resources which could fertilize much larger areas still run to waste today because of the "Beisan Agreement." Except for such portions as the Jews have been able to buy piecemeal from individual Arab beneficiaries, the Beisan lands are still, in fact, not under plow. I believe that Samuel himself later realized that the claims put forward through Bustani had no legal foundation; and the British representative who appeared before the Mandates Commission in 1926 could not defend the action on economic grounds; but all this hindsight did not help us to cultivate the Beisan Valley. We, on the other hand, had to struggle for years, and pay heavily, in order to obtain any share at all in the State lands, and then it was only some seventy-five or eighty thousand dunams, much of it consisting of the sand dunes of Rishon-le-Zion—valueless unless large sums are sunk in their amelioration.

The pogrom, the suspended immigration and the lost State lands were on the record at the preliminary meeting of the Actions Committee in Prague. But what depressed me more than these was my own feeling of helplessness in the face of the lack of understanding which seemed to prevail, even among responsible Zionists. For instance, the Actions Committee adopted a budget of seventeen million five hundred thousand dollars for the coming year, to cover considerable acquisitions of land and the settlement of large numbers of immigrants, as well as of some who had come to Palestine before the war and were still awaiting settlement. But the compilers of this budget unfortunately failed to indicate where the money was to be found. I knew that no such sum was in sight; in the conditions of that time it could not be produced even by superhuman effort. European Jewries had just not got the money; American Jewry had yet to be educated to the assumption of so great a responsibility. True, it was spending a great deal on the relief of distressed Jewish communities in Europe, but there was no sign yet of any readiness to divert even a part of these vast sums to the resettlement of European Jews in Palestine. The Actions Committee budget was, of course, severely criticized in Congress as unreal, and eventually cut down to 15 per cent or 20 per cent of the original figure. But this naturally gave rise to deep disappointment in the ranks of the movement, and we should have known better than to allow such fantastic figures to be dangled before the eyes of our constituents.

The Congress did well to bring the movement down to earth, to some appreciation of the hard facts, and to set our feet on the only path that could lead to success—the path of slow, laborious and methodical work in Palestine. It formally decided to establish the settlements of Nahalal, Kfar Yechezkiel, Ain Harod and Tel Yosef, thus beginning the conquest of the land—and that was worth more than all the rest of the talk. I rejoiced in these decisions because I knew men who were ready and waiting to invade the malaria-infested Emek and establish themselves and their families there, to face all the risks and hardships of a pioneering life. I saw my duty for the next five or ten years very clearly; it was to help these people make a success of their venture. For their success would be of greater political importance than any so-called "political" concession which we might obtain, after heartbreaking negotiations, from a reluctant Government.

The Congress had opened on a depressed note; it ended on a note of optimism. After all, immigration had begun, at the rate of something like ten thousand a year, and though this was not a very imposing figure it was not negligible either, considering the conditions in the country. We knew that a too rapid increase in this stream of immigration would lead to unemployment, of which there were faint but visible signs already on the horizon, and therefore the stream had to be stemmed and regulated.

But it was bringing with it the first *chalutzim*—that new and heartening phenomenon in Jewry. Keen, eager, intelligent, they had trained themselves to do any kind of physical work in Palestine; they were determined to let no one else perform the duties, however primitive and exacting, which attended the laying of the foundations of the National Home. They would build roads, drain marshes, dig wells, plant trees— and they faced all the physical dangers and hardships joyfully and unflinchingly. Of such were the young men and women I had watched, with Mond, breaking stones on the Tel Aviv road the previous year.

Much was heard before, during and after the Congress of the non-rentability of Jewish National Fund land. There was a good deal of criticism of the first co-operative settlements, which were just beginning their work. Again, I felt that time was too young to afford any basis for judgments: these infant enterprises should be given their chance. We faced the task of converting into peasant farmers an urbanized people, completely divorced from the soil for hundreds, if not thousands of years, a people whose physical and intellectual equipment unfitted them for the hardships of an outdoor life in a barren land whose soil was exhausted by centuries of misrule and poor husbandry. Moreover, we had not the means to start our agricultural ventures properly, and our heavily cut budget made no provision for the inevitable percentage of failures which occurs in all colonizing work—such as, to take recent instances, the settlement of British soldiers in Canada or Australia. When we compared our results with those of the British Dominions (which had adequate finances, unlimited virgin soil, familiar climates, a friendly population speaking the same language as the immigrant—and no Arab problem) I think we had, even in those early days, no reason to be ashamed of the Jewish experiment.

Still, the Jews grumbled, and the non-Jews criticized mercilessly. British officials and Zionist visitors to Palestine returned to advise us to put an end to "all these fancy experiments" in agriculture, and concentrate on building up industry and trade—in other words, take the line of least resistance, and relapse into the old Diaspora habit of creating towns to receive an urbanized immigration. I have already said something, and will have more to say, about my views on the subject of premature private enterprise. I resisted all this advice strenuously, and sometimes in my eagerness to defend my point of view I may have been less than just to the lower-middle-class people who came to settle in Jerusalem, Tel Aviv and Haifa, since they too were pioneers, in their own fashion. They built up hundreds of small industries, investing their small lifetime savings, brought with difficulty out of Poland or the Ukraine; and they too were building up the National Home of their people.

Even so, I still believe that the backbone of our work is and must always be agricultural colonization. It is in the village that the real soul of a people—its language, its poetry, its literature, its traditions—springs up from the intimate contact between man and soil. The towns do no more than "process" the fruits of the villages.

So, for more than a quarter of a century now, it has been given to me to watch, with a deep and growing exultation, the steady development of our village life in Palestine. I have watched the Emek's marshes drying out, and gradually growing firm enough to support more and more clusters of red-roofed cottages, whose lights sparkle in the falling dusk like so many beacons on our long road home. The thought of those spreading clusters of lights in the dusk has been my reward for many weary months of travel and disappointment in the world outside.

CHAPTER 25

The Struggle About the Mandate

Drafting the Mandate—"Historic Right" or "Historical Connection"?—Arabs and "Die-Hards" Attack Us—The Haycraft Commission and Report—Lord Northcliffe Turns on Us—Beaverbrook Joins the Assault—The Arab Delegation in Rome, Paris, and London—Counteraction—Italy and the Vatican Have Complaints—"We Fear Your University"—The Remarkable Italian Jewish Community—I am Mistaken for Lenin —Berlin and Walter Rathenau—Parliament Debates the Mandate—The Churchill White Paper—Trans-Jordan Lopped off —Our Own Shortcomings—The Stage Set for Mandate Decision—Miracle from Spain—The Mandate Is Unanimously Ratified.

BY THE autumn of 1921 I was back in London, having surveyed the tasks confronting us in Palestine, in America and in Europe. We were very conscious that though policy had, in principle, been settled for some time past, the situation in Palestine was almost bound to be uncertain and unsatisfactory as long as the Mandate remained unratified by the League of Nations. The ratification did not take place until July 1922, and in the interval a good many unforeseen difficulties arose and had to be overcome—at the cost of numerous journeys between London, Paris, Geneva and Rome. Besides the political work in connection with the Mandate, the other main problem which could never be lost sight of for a moment was the building up of the *Keren Hayesod*, already established in Palestine and America, but either not established at all, or still in embryo, in most of the European countries. My travels in the winter of 1921-1922 had thus a double object.

Curzon had by now taken over from Balfour at the Foreign Office, and was in charge of the actual drafting of the Mandate. On our side we had the valuable assistance of Mr. Ben V. Cohen, who stayed on with us in London after most of his fellow-Brandeisists had resigned from the Executive and withdrawn from the work. Ben Cohen was one of the ablest draftsmen in America, and he and Curzon's secretary— young Eric Forbes-Adam, highly intelligent, efficient and most sympathetic—fought the battle of the Mandate for many months. Draft after draft was proposed, discussed and rejected, and I sometimes wondered if we should ever reach a final text. The most serious difficulty arose in connection with a paragraph in the Preamble—the phrase which now reads: "Recognizing the historical connection of the Jews with Palestine." Zionists wanted to have it read: "Recognizing the historic rights of the Jews to Palestine." But Curzon would have none of it, remarking dryly: "If you word it like that, I can see Weizmann coming to me every other day and saying he has a *right* to do this, that or the other in Palestine! I won't have it!" As a compromise, Balfour suggested "historical connection," and "historical connection" it was.

I confess that for me this was the most important part of the Mandate. I felt instinctively that the other provisions of the Mandate might remain a dead letter, e.g., "to place the country under such political, economic and administrative conditions as may facilitate the development of the Jewish National Home." All one can say about that point, after more than twenty-five years, is that at least Palestine has not so far been placed under a legislative council with an Arab majority—but that is rather a negative brand of fulfillment of a positive injunction. Looking back, I incline to attach even less importance to written "declarations" and "statements" and "instruments" than I did even in those days. Such instruments are at best frames which may or may not be filled in. They have virtually no importance unless and until they are supported by actual performance, and it is more and more to this side of the work that I have tried to direct the movement with the passing of the years.

As the drafting of the Mandate progressed, and the prospect of its ratification drew nearer, we found ourselves on the defensive against attacks from every conceivable quarter—on our position in Palestine, on our work there, on our good faith. The spearhead of these attacks was an Arab delegation from Palestine, which arrived in London via Cairo, Rome and Paris, in the summer of 1921, and established itself in London at the Hotel Cecil. Under the leadership of Musa Kazim Pasha, it ventilated numerous Arab grievances at the Colonial Office, and also in Parliamentary, press and political circles, and seemed to find little difficulty in spreading the most fantastic stories. The delegation served as a rallying point for elements which we should now describe as "reactionary" or "fascist," but which we then spoke of as "the die-hards." Joynson-Hicks led them in the Commons; in the Lords they found able spokesmen in Lord Islington, Lord Sydenham, and later Lord Raglan, effectively supported in the press by the Northcliffe and Beaverbrook papers, with the "Bag-and-Baggage" campaign for reduction of British overseas commitments in the interests of British economy and the British taxpayer. One had the impression that many English people were coming to regard

Palestine as a serious liability, a country where Jews rode roughshod over "the poor Arabs," and charged the British taxpayer several shillings in the pound for doing it. Along with this type of argument went quasi-impartial statements suggesting that the Jewish enterprise in Palestine was utterly unsound and uneconomic, and that the whole thing was being run by a bunch of impractical idealists who did not know the first thing about colonizing or building up a country.

Well, we were idealists, and we knew we had a lot to learn—and much of it we could only learn by making our own mistakes. But we also saw—as our critics apparently did not—that their two arguments canceled each other out: if the Jewish National Home was an impractical dream, incapable of realization, it could hardly present any real danger to Arabs or British, and there would seem to be no need to do anything about it except leave it to die of inanition. But nothing seemed further from our adversaries' intentions.

In November 1921, they found fresh ammunition in the Haycraft Report (the report of the local judicial commission which investigated the riots of May, 1921) which, while condemning the brutality of the rioters, and denying most of the absurd allegations against the Jews in Palestine (e.g., that they were Bolshevists), contrived to leave on the reader's mind the impression that the root of the difficulty was a British policy with whch the Arabs were—perhaps justifiably— dissatisfied. The Haycraft Report also implied that the Zionist desire to dominate in Palestine might provide further ground for Arab resentment. Again there was a curious contradiction: in dealing with the actual facts which the commission was appointed to investigate, the report frankly admitted, for instance, that the particularly savage attack on Hedera was mainly due to the spreading of false rumors by agitators in Tulkarm and neighboring villages; but it made no attempt to indicate how and why and through whom these rumors had been spread. Thus it happened that an important official document could be held—by those interested in such an interpretation—to support some of the accusations made against us. It was a situation which was to recur more than once in the years that followed—in fact, as often as a commission went out to Palestine to investigate and report upon "incidents" or complications on the spot. In a sense, the Haycraft Report contained the germ of very many of our main troubles in the last twenty-five years.

The report was, of course, a gift for our opponents, and they made good use of it. So much confusion was created, so many misstatements of Zionist aims were made, that we felt driven to issue a full reply. This was drafted by Leonard Stein, who had by now become our political secretary in London, and was a most effective piece of work. But I remember feeling at the time that our opponents were unlikely to pay much heed to the marshaled facts and to the arguments advanced with such forceful logic; they were impervious to objective reasoning on the subject. Now I wonder whether the underlying cause may not have been a vague anti-Jewish sentiment rather than any specific anti-Zionist conviction.

Another gift for our attackers was Lord Northcliffe's return to London after a visit to Palestine "to see for himself." His visit was brief, his criticisms sharp. He had, during the war, been inclined to support us, but his Palestine experiences seem to have put him off. He had, it appears, succeeded in impressing himself most unfavorably on the few Jewish settlers he met, and the feeling was mutual. It was told that he happened to arrive in Tel Yosef (then just founded) about lunchtime. Lunch in a new settlement is apt to be a rather sketchy affair: people rush in straight from the fields, collect a snack from the hatch, and dispose of it with small ceremony before rushing back to their jobs. Lord Northcliffe's presence in the dining room passed unnoticed for a time (in itself enough to arouse some resentment), and when it was announced it evoked no great enthusiasm. Whatever it was, Lord Northcliffe came back with the impression that Jewish settlers in Palestine were mostly Communists and/or Bolshevists—and arrogant, aggressive types into the bargain. Still, he did leave us Philip Graves as *Times* correspondent in Palestine, and Graves was a man of much more balanced and moderate views, though his cautious mind was often critical, and the series of articles from his pen which appeared in the *Times* about this period often damned with faint praise. We cannot forget, however, that we owe to him a most able and authoritative exposure of the Protocols of the Elders of Zion.

Once back in London, Lord Northcliffe lost no time in making his views known. I received an invitation—perhaps I should say command—to lunch with him. I found him with Mr. Maxse, to whom he was already representing Zionism as a danger to the British Empire, on the grounds that in his opinion it was a matter of five hundred thousand Jews (at most) against fifty million Moslems— and it was lunacy to upset the fifty million Moslems for the sake of the five hundred thousand Jews. It was useless to challenge this oversimplified version of the facts: Lord Northcliffe had been to see for himself—and had returned not to listen, but to talk. After lunch we adjourned to another room containing a number of very comfortable easy chairs, and one supereasy chair, to which Lord Northcliffe promptly gravitated. He placed me on his right and Maxse on his left, and said: "Now, Maxse represents England; you are a Jew; I am the umpire!" From this we inferred that we were to be asked to state our respective cases—but not at all! Lord Northcliffe proceeded forthwith to tell us all about it. This conception of the functions of an umpire was new to me, and suggested that I was probably wasting my time, so I shortly made my excuses and withdrew. I daresay Lord Northcliffe was not pleased. Anyhow, though the *Times* remained dignified—if mistrustful—on the subject of Palestine, the other Northcliffe papers—*Daily Mail, Evening News,* and so on—launched out into a virulent campaign against us. In particular a certain Mr. J. M. N. Jeffries succeeded, in a series of savage articles, in presenting a wholly distorted picture of Jewish life in Palestine. His conclusion was that the only thing to do was to annul the Balfour Declaration and scrap the whole British Palestine policy.

The Beaverbrook press was conducting a similar campaign from a slightly different angle. They incorporated Palestine in their "Bag-and-Baggage" demand for withdrawal from a number of British overseas commitments primarily on grounds of economy. While using roughly the same arguments as the Northcliffe press, they lumped together the cost to Britain of Palestine, Trans-Jordan and Iraq (Palestine's share was, even at this early stage, insignificant—something like five million dollars annually), and thus suggested that the ordinary British taxpayer was being heavily mulcted in order to enable a few East European Jews to oppress and expropriate the Palestine Arabs. In fact, of course, the upbuilding of Palestine as the Jewish National Home was not costing the British taxpayer a penny. About seven million, five hundred thousand dollars a year was at that time being spent on maintaining the garrison, but that would in any case have had to be maintained somewhere, and probably cost less in Palestine than it would have in Egypt.

Another tempting target for the arrows of the press was, of course, the "Rutenberg Concessions" for the harnessing of the Auja and Jordan rivers, which were made in 1921. All sorts of claimants appeared on the scene, and were sure of good publicity. They were mostly people who had secured "concessions" from the Turkish Government, and felt themselves entitled to have those concessions confirmed by the British. Many of them had friends in Parliament through whom they could bring pressure to bear on the Government on the ground that the Rutenberg Concessions were favors granted to the Jews at the expense of the general interests of Palestine and of Britain. And this, besides holding up the development of Palestine, increased the difficulty of our political task.

Through all this maze we still managed somehow to progress, if with maddening slowness, toward the ratification of the Mandate. We had some good friends, whose help did much to offset the attacks. Among them were Mr. Ramsay MacDonald and Lord Milner, both of whom visited Palestine and returned to speak and write of what they

had seen there: Mr. MacDonald with enthusiasm of the Jewish communal settlements, and Lord Milner with knowledge and sympathy
of the great tasks in agriculture, afforestation, industry, transport,
education, and so on, which awaited the Jews in Palestine, and of
the way in which the Jewish community was addressing itself to
them. Lord Milner, at least, had no fears that the Mandate would
involve any noticeable extra burden on the British taxpayer, and
felt confident that such burden as there was would very soon disappear.

Opposition to the Jewish National Home policy was not confined to
England. On its way to London the Arab delegation had stopped off in
Rome and Paris, and in both cities had proved, as it was to prove in
London, a rallying point for reactionary forces. Pressure on the British
Government was therefore to be anticipated from some, at least, of the
Allied governments—though they had already given their endorsement
of the Balfour Declaration and signified their approval in principle of
the Mandate based upon it.

Partly for this reason, and partly in the interests of the *Keren Hayesod*, I found myself committed to visiting a number of European capitals;
and since the most serious political opposition to the Balfour Declaration
policy seemed likely to emanate from the Vatican, I decided to begin with
Rome.

We knew that the Latin Patriarch in Jerusalem, Monsignor Barlassina, was strongly opposed to Zionism, and that for some reason he
held us responsible for the unsatisfactory settlement of the question of
the Holy Places. It was in vain that we declared that we were completely uninterested in this problem, that we fully realized it to be
something to be settled between the Christian powers and the Vatican,
and that if these could not reach a satisfactory agreement among themselves it was no fault of ours. When I set out on my round of visits in
Rome, therefore, I had it in mind to try and discover what really was
the trouble about the Holy Places, and in what manner it could be considered to concern us.

Signor Schanzer, the then Italian Foreign Minister, was a Triestino,
and probably of Jewish descent. I remember an odd talk with him in
which he urged me to do my utmost to bring about a speedy settlement
of the problem of the Holy Places in the sense desired by the Vatican.
I protested in vain that it might be, to say the least, a little tactless for a
Jew to meddle in such matters, but somehow my protestations seemed
unconvincing to him. He was particularly anxious about the *Cenacolo*—
the Room of the Last Supper—on the outskirts of Jerusalem. My education in Church history having been deficient, I did not know why the
Italians laid such stress on the *Cenacolo*, nor could I understand why
Schanzer, presumably representing a purely secular Italian interest,

should be such an ardent champion of a cause which one would have imagined to be primarily the concern of the Vatican. Clearly I had a great deal to learn in this field, and I decided to prolong my stay.

In due course I received an invitation to call on the Cardinal Secretary of State, Cardinal Gasparri. He had been very well informed by Monsignor Barlassina, who, as I have said, was no friend of ours. It happened that my first talk with Cardinal Gasparri took place the day after an address of mine at the Collegio Romano, which had been attended by representatives of the Italian and international press, as well as by a number of Italian dignitaries—the mayor of Rome, the chief of police, and so on. I had tried at this meeting to explain what we were doing in Palestine, and what our aims and aspirations were. The next morning a full report appeared in the *Osservatore Romano* (the organ of the Vatican); not an unfair report, on the whole, but with a few pinpricks. For instance, my statement that for the moment we were not buying land in Palestine, as we had reserves of land sufficient for the next ten years or so, appeared in the *Osservatore* something like this:

> Dr. Weizmann stated that the Zionist Organization was in possession of vast reserves of land, and would not need to expropriate the Arabs for another ten years.

When I came into His Eminence's room next morning, he said: "You made a very interesting speech yesterday." I replied: "Do you mean my speech at the Collegio Romano, or my speech in the *Osservatore Romano*?" He smiled and said that one must bear with the journalists, who sometimes slipped up, and I said that I thought far too highly of Vatican journalists to attribute to them careless mistakes in reporting. That point dropped, I thought I had better take my opportunity of asking what it was that the Vatican really feared from the Zionist movement; for I remember that Mr. Sokolow had, in audience with His Holiness, given a very full explanation of our aims, and that his explanation had apparently found favor. It gradually became apparent that His Eminence was concerned with matters which had to do with the British administration rather than with the Zionists. He was, for instance, distressed that members of various nursing and teaching Orders, and other Catholic emissaries to Palestine, were finding some difficulty in getting visas. I tried to explain that we had nothing to do with the granting of visas to travelers, but clearly His Eminence still suspected that the Zionist Organization was, in some obscure fashion, a branch of the Palestine Government, and "could use its influence" if it chose. I spent some minutes trying to make the position clear, but I am not at all sure whether I had any success, either on this point, or on the question of the Holy Places.

At another interview with Cardinal Gasparri, when the talk had been on more general lines, and I had been giving some account of the work we were actually doing and preparing to do in Palestine—agricultural settlement, drainage, afforestation, medical work, education—he indicated that the colonization work, and so on, caused him no anxiety, but added: *"C'est votre université que je crains"* (it is your university that I fear). Which gave me food for thought.

I saw a number of Italian statesmen and officials, including the Duke of Cesaro, Signor d'Amandola (the Minister for the Colonies), Prime Minister Luzzati, Signor Contarini of the Foreign Office. I was received in audience by the King, who spoke appreciatively of his acquaintance with Dr. Herzl (whose photograph stood on his desk). But the question I had come to ask: What exactly was the reason for Italian and Vatican opposition to Zionism? remained unanswered. Nor could I discover to my own satisfaction why the purely religious issue of the Holy Places should arouse so much interest in Italian political circles—and in French ones, too. There were no Holy Places in Palestine to which the Jews laid actual physical claim—except, perhaps, Rachel's tomb, which was at no time a matter of controversy. The Wailing Wall we did not own, and never had owned since the destruction of the Temple; controversy was later to arise over the Jewish prayers conducted there, but at this time there was no suggestion even of that. Yet the resentment felt by the various Christian communities in Palestine—and especially by the Catholic communities—at the choice of a Protestant Mandatory Power lent a special edge to the discussion of the question of the Holy Places, and we could not escape from it. Our disclaimers fell on deaf ears.

I can make a happy digression at this point. My stay in Italy brought me, for the first time, into close contact with the Italian Jewish community, and with Italian Zionism. The latter had always held for me the fascination of mystery. None of the motives for Zionism which held good in other countries applied in the case of the Italian Jews. Jewish emancipation in Italy had been complete for generations. The community was a small one, but its members took an active part in Italian life—political, economic, artistic, scientific—and were to all intents and purposes indistinguishable from their fellow-citizens, except that they went to synagogue instead of to Mass. In metropolitan Italy they numbered no more than some fifty thousand of a total population of forty million or so. Of these fifty thousand, some fifteen thousand lived, curiously enough, in a sort of voluntary ghetto in Rome, spoke a language which was virtually Italian, with some Hebrew and Arabic embroideries, and pursued various minor crafts or kept small shops. But the rest of the community was assimilated to a degree.

Yet, under the influence of Peretz Chayes, the brilliant scholar who later became Chief Rabbi of Vienna, a group of young people had founded an Italian Zionist Organization. They had begun in Florence, where lived a young and ardent prophet of Zionism, Arnoldo Pacifici; and when they formed their society they went the whole way: they spoke Hebrew, they began to prepare themselves for life in Palestine; many of them—including Pacifici himself—became strictly orthodox; they edited one of the best Zionist papers of the day—*Israel*. Numerically insignificant, they were by the depth of their conviction and their absolute sincerity a great moral force. And though at first the community at large was inclined to resent them, they were so tactful, and at the same time so transparently honest in their faith, that even convinced anti-Zionists came to look on them as something in the nature of "apostles" of the Jewish revival, and to respect, if they could not understand, them.

Early leaders of this group, besides Pacifici, were men like Dante Lattes, Enzo Sereni, nephew of Angelo Sereni, head of the Rome Jewish community, and David Prato, later Rabbi of Alexandria. With the last named I toured the cities of Italy—Florence, Pisa, Milan, Genoa, Leghorn, Padua. It was a great experience for me to meet ancient Jewish families with a long intellectual tradition (sometimes deriving from Spain), a wide culture, and an exquisite hospitality. Amid all the suffering of the last few years, there is for me a special poignancy in the destruction which has overtaken the Italian Jewish community—though a number of Italian Jews have been fortunate enough to reach Palestine. They had given so much to Italy, and so much to their own people. Before World War I, on my very first visit to Italy, friends had pointed out to me with pride that the Italian cabinet contained four Jews: Luzzati, Ottolenghi, Sonnino, and—I think—Titoni. Then the mayor of Rome was also a Jew. The greatest living Italian mathematician, Levi Civita, was a Jew; the great Italian firm of contractors which was charged with the maintenance of the harbor of Alexandria, was a Jewish firm. In short, the Italian Jewish community seemed to be a community of *sujets d'élite*. And the élite of that community, accustomed to enjoy in Italy every material and social advantage a man can ask, were turning their eyes to Palestine. I could not explain it. I could only thank God.

My tour with Dr. Prato was mainly in the interests of the *Keren Hayesod*, but also a little in the hope of winning at least some sections of Italian public opinion over to a more tolerant view of Zionism. I was beginning to attach considerable importance to Italy; I saw it as a leading Mediterranean Power with extensive contacts in the Levant, under a Government which was taking more than a passing interest in our affairs. Gradually it was becoming clear to me that Italian official circles feared that Zionism was merely a cloak for the creation of a British imperial outpost in the Levant; they were thus very ready to press the Vatican contentions with regard to the Holy Places.

We had a rather strenuous few weeks, and afterward my wife and I took a short rest in Capri. The island was at that time something of a center for Russian émigrés; they frequented the smaller cafés and restaurants on the promenade, and in many of these the only language commonly heard was Russian. One morning, as we walked into one of them, I heard a whispered aside: "Here comes our Minister." I was not as puzzled as I might have been, for it was not the first time I had been mistaken for Lenin: the same thing had happened not long before in Genoa, during the Economic Conference, the first Western European Conference to be attended by representatives of the Soviet Government. I had been walking with a friend—a high official of the Genoa municipality—when we noticed that our footsteps had for some time been dogged by a policeman. My friend stopped, and asked him why we were being followed. The answer was: "We have received instructions, sir, not to let the Russian delegation out of our sight. I believe you have M. Lenin with you." It took quite some time, and all my friend's official authority, to persuade the policeman that I had no connection with Lenin, beyond a remote physical resemblance.

Capri was exquisite, but at the back of my mind were always London and Jerusalem. The reports were disturbing. In London the campaign against the Mandate was in full swing, and from Jerusalem came distressing news of inadequate income, cut budgets, settlers leading lives of incredible hardship—without beds, with insufficient food, without tents in the quagmire that was still the Emek. I had for the time being done what I could on the financial front in America—and anyhow, I could not leave Europe again until the Mandate was ratified. I therefore decided that the *Keren Hayesod* must make a start in the principal European Jewish communities, and my next port of call was Berlin, where a German Zionist Federation was just beginning to make some headway.

My previous contacts with the Berlin Jewish community had been slight, and I was relieved to find a warm welcome, and to hear Herr Dernburg, a former Minister for the Colonies, paying high tribute to our colonization work in Palestine and to the new methods we were developing there. In such an atmosphere I felt that the German *Keren Hayesod* would soon become a real prop to the work—and such, in fact, proved to be the case. From the outset it owed much to the devotion of Kurt Blumenfeld, and to the keen mind and warm heart of Oskar Wasserman.

One of the more vivid impressions I retain of this visit is that of my talk with Walther Rathenau, whom I met one evening at Einstein's house. He plunged at once into eloquent argument against Zionism—much on the lines of his book, *Hear, O Israel*. The gist of what he had to say was that he was a Jew, but felt entirely German and was devoting all his energy to the building of German industry and the redeeming of Germany's political position. He deplored any attempt to turn the Jews

of Germany "into a foreign body on the sands of the Mark of Branden-
burg"—that was all he could see in Zionism. His attitude was, of course,
all too typical of that of many assimilated German Jews; they seemed to
have no idea that they were sitting on a volcano; they believed quite
sincerely that such difficulties as admittedly existed for German Jews
were purely temporary and transitory phenomena, primarily due to the
influx of East European Jews, who did not fit into the framework of
German life, and thus offered targets for anti-Semitic attacks. The "real"
German Jew would be immune from, above, all that. . . . By no stretch
of the imagination could Rathenau be described as an East European
immigrant; all the same, not many months were to pass before he fell
at the hands of "Nazi" assassins. Not even then did his Jewish friends
and followers see the writing on the wall.

From Berlin we went to Paris, again mainly on *Keren Hayesod* business, though I knew that the proceeds from France would not be very
considerable. The Fund there was under the able direction of Professor
Hadamard, Dr. Zadoc Kahn, and one or two other leading French Jews
—by no means all of them Zionists. The Foundation Fund proved from
the beginning a sort of bridge, or halfway house, for Jews who, while
interested in Palestine and anxious to help, hesitated to throw their
whole weight behind the Zionist movement because of its "political implications." They would help pay for the work, but they were not prepared to assume any responsibility for its political, social or moral outcome. With some of these people, in France as elsewhere, there may also
have been the underlying idea that it might be prudent to direct future
Jewish immigration away from the Western countries, lest such immigration provoke a recrudescence of anti-Semitism.

For a French fund—French voluntary funds are seldom very successful
—the *Keren Hayesod* did fairly well, and I was not unduly disappointed
with my visit from the financial point of view. I, of course, profited from
my stay in Paris to see one or two official people—M. deMonzie, and
General Gouraud among them. With the General I discussed the then
vexing question of the northern frontiers of Palestine, though without
conspicuous success, since the French tended to regard Palestine as
"southern Syria," and Syria as a whole as a French sphere of influence,
hence to resent the separation of Palestine, and to regard with special
suspicion any attempt to modify its northern frontier. I tried to convince
General Gouraud of the importance to Palestine of the waters of the
river Litani, but could arouse no interest, and came away with the rather
depressed feeling that for him, as for the Italians, Zionism was nothing
more than camouflage for British imperialism.

From Paris we returned to London, to find debates on Palestine pend-
ing in both Houses of Parliament. Lord Sydenham, Lord Islington and
Lord Raglan led the attack in the Lords, and in spite of a rather lively

debate, their motion for the repeal of the Balfour Declaration won by a substantial majority. In the Commons, with such champions as Mr. Churchill and Major Ormsby-Gore, we had better luck, and a similar motion was heavily defeated. Still, I was greatly distressed by the outcome of the debate in the House of Lords. I went to see Mr. Balfour at Sheringham, and expressed my perturbation. He advised me not to take it too seriously, saying: "What does it matter if a few foolish lords passed such a motion?"

Against this background, the London Zionist Executive was engaged in correspondence and discussions with the Colonial Office on various matters arising in connection with the final text of the Mandate. The volume of criticism directed against the Mandate policy had convinced the Government of the need for a detailed commentary, and this took the form of a White Paper published in June 1922 (the "Churchill White Paper"). The main memorandum, we thought, was probably drafted by Sir Herbert Samuel, though it compared none too favorably with some of his Palestine speeches and was clearly dictated by a desire to placate the Arabs as far as possible. It was as little realized in 1922 as it is today that the real opponents of Zionism can never be placated by any diplomatic formula: their objection to the Jews is that the Jews exist, and in this particular case, that they desire to exist in Palestine. It made, therefore, little difference whether our immigration was large or small: protests were as vociferous over a hundred immigrants as over thousands. This main memorandum was communicated to us in advance of publication, and we were invited to signify our acceptance of the policy defined therein.

The Churchill White Paper was regarded by us as a serious whittling down of the Balfour Declaration. It detached trans-Jordan from the area of Zionist operation, and it raised the subject of a legislative council. But it began with a reaffirmation of "the Declaration of November 2, 1917, which is not susceptible of change." It continued: "A Jewish National Home will be founded in Palestine" and "the Jewish people will be in Palestine as of right and not on sufferance." Further, "Immigration will not exceed the economic capacity of the country to absorb new arrivals."

In short, it limited the Balfour Declaration to Palestine west of the Jordan, but it established the principle of "economic absorptive capacity." In addition, it was also made clear to us that confirmation of the Mandate would be conditional on our acceptance of the policy as interpreted in the White Paper, and my colleagues and I therefore had to accept it, which we did, though not without some qualms. Jabotinsky, at that time a member of the Zionist Executive, was arriving from America on the very afternoon when we had to signify our acceptance of the statement of policy. A messenger was sent to meet the boat at

Southampton with a copy of the document and of our letter of acceptance, in order that his agreement might be obtained in time. I was more
than a little nervous about his reaction, but curiously enough he raised
no serious objection, merely remarking that the White Paper, if carried
out honestly and conscientiously, would still afford us a framework for
building up a Jewish majority in Palestine, and for the eventual emergence of a Jewish State. Subsequent events showed his view to have
been right: so long as, through immigration and the investment of
capital, the Jews were able to develop the country, its "absorptive
capacity" would continue to grow, and immigration would show a
steady rise. It was only when the Government interfered with the activities of the community with the definite intention of hampering such
development that the growth of the National Home was impeded. We
know now, though we were not so sure in 1922, that the principle of
"absorptive capacity" could, if generously applied, have been the key to
the rapid and stable expansion of the *Yishuv*; we also know that it was
in fact applied in such a spirit as to prove a stumbling block to Jewish
enterprise. For "absorptive capacity" does not grow wild on the rocks
and dunes of Palestine; it must be created, and its creation calls for
effort, enthusiasm, imagination—and capital.

It follows that in the expansion of "absorptive capacity" the economic
policy of the Government is no less important than its political policy,
and in the economic field the motto of the Palestine Government was
from the outset "safety first." In fairness I must add that in the early
years after the ratification of the Mandate, great opportunities really
did open out before us in Palestine, but we could not take full advantage
of them while the time served because of lack of really substantial support from the Jews of Europe and America. Two other factors slowed
down our early progress in Palestine. First, as I have already said,
Russian Jewry had for our purposes ceased to exist, and Polish Jewry
was broken and impoverished. Second, our methods of colonization
were still in the experimental stage: we were feeling our way by trial
and error toward a new system, for it was clear that the colonies of
Baron Edmond, and even some of the early Zionist colonies, were insufficient to justify a speedy advance in agricultural colonization. We
were hesitating between the *kvutzah* (communal) and the *moshav* (co-
operative smallholders) settlements. In the Emek we had started with
Nahalal, which is a *moshav*; Ain Harod, which followed shortly afterward, is a large *kvutzah*.

When the signatures of the Zionist Executive were appended to the
letter of acceptance, the stage was set for the formal submission of the
Mandate for ratification; but ratification itself was by no means a foregone conclusion. By the League's constitution, Council decisions had to

be unanimous, and we were not certain of the attitude of the representatives of some of the states which had seats on it.

In states with a fair number of Jews it was possible to enlist their aid in winning over the sympathy of the governments. In the case of France, the Jewish population could argue in our favor. We could turn to the Jews of Italy in the same expectation. But there was Spain. There were practically no Jews in Spain. The story of our relationship with Spain is a long and bloody one. The absence of a significant Jewish community in Spain has something to do with it. There was Brazil. Our numbers in Brazil were insignificant. Yet as far as our fate in Palestine was concerned, the votes of Brazil and Spain were each equal to the vote of England.

The Palestine Mandate came up for ratification only on the last day of the League Council meeting (Saturday, July 24, 1922), in London, and up to the last day we were uncertain of what would happen. We weighed every possibility and looked on every side for help. We remembered then that when, in 1918, we laid the foundations of the Hebrew University in Jerusalem, there came a congratulatory telegram from a professor of the University of Madrid. To this man we turned for help; and he brought all his influence to bear on his friends that they might in turn urge the Government to act in our favor.

This Spanish professor was a marrano (a descendant of the crypto-Jews of the time of the Inquisition), and most of the friends he enlisted were also marranos. Suddenly we discovered a great deal of unexpected and—at the moment—inexplicable sympathy in Spain. Members of the learned societies, the higher clergy, prominent members of the Spanish nobility, received the local delegation in the most friendly fashion. Meanwhile, in London, we called on the Spanish representative on the Council, and it chanced that he was to be the President of the session at which our fate was to be decided. We said to him: "Here is Spain's opportunity to repay in part that long-outstanding debt which it owes to the Jews. The evil which your forefathers were guilty of against us you can wipe out in part." Whether it was our plea, whether it was the pressure from Madrid, the Spanish representative promised us his help, with Brazil as well as with his own country, and kept his word.

At the eleventh hour the Papal Nuncios tried to get the Secretariat of the League to postpone this item on the agenda. I happened to be in M. Viviani's rooms in the Hyde Park Hotel (M. Viviani was the French representative on the Council), when Signor Ceretti called on him, and asked his help in obtaining the postponement. There was, said Signor Ceretti, an important document due from the Vatican. M. Viviani introduced me and said: "As far as I am concerned, I have no objection to the postponement, but it is for this gentleman to decide." I said that there had been delay enough, and if we waited till Monday or later, who knew what differences would arise around the Council table. Signor Ceretti, who did not at all like M. Viviani's trick of making me the responsible party, heard me out, then bounced from the room in high dudgeon. M. Viviani smiled at me and said: *"Quand les prêtres de village se mettent à faire de la politique, ils font des gaffes"* (when village priests take to politics they always make howlers).

So on the Saturday morning Mr. Balfour introduced the subject of the ratification of the Palestine Mandate. Everything went off smoothly, and with the unanimous vote of ratification there ended the first chapter of our long political struggle.

CHAPTER 26

Trial and Error

Realism and Unrealism in the Zionist Debates—Fred Kisch Enters Zionist Work—Ruppin and the Collectives—Chaim Arlosoroff—The Lean Years—Transforming a People—Agricultural Foundations—The Attack on the Kvutzoth*—"Capitalist" Versus "Working-Class" Immigration—I Warn against Economic "Ghettoism" in Palestine—Land Speculation—* Chalutzim *in Tel Aviv for* Rosh Hashanah.

THE Annual Conference of the World Zionist Organization—the smaller representative gathering which met in the alternate years between Congresses—began its sessions in Carlsbad on August 25, 1922, a month after the ratification of the Mandate. Its debates followed a pattern with which I was to become very familiar in the ensuing years, at Conferences and Congresses.

My report was followed, naturally—and properly—by adverse, as well as favorable comment. Criticism of the Churchill White Paper was particularly sharp, but was to a certain extent, I thought, unreal; for it concentrated on its negative and ignored its positive aspects, emphasized the theoretical and minimized the practical. I remember one delegate who compared the White Paper at great length and most unfavorably with "the charter"—that traditional object of Zionist aspiration in Herzlian days, the international document which was to "give us" Palestine. I had to point out the basic difference between the two documents, namely, that the White Paper existed, the charter did not. And the White Paper gave us the opportunity for great creative work in Palestine.

In my report I had to devote much space to conditions in Palestine, and these were not commensurate with the political victory we had just scored. In spite of the smallness of our immigration there were already some fifteen hundred to two thousand unemployed in Palestine—a heavy proportion of our population. It was my painful duty to insist that no amount of diplomatic success could neutralize this fact, and that for it we had no one to blame but ourselves. Constructive criticism was needed: not belittlement of the terms of the White Paper, but indication of methods by which those terms

could be taken advantage of in order to expand the Jewish Homeland.

There were, fortunately, constructive critics, men like Arthur
Ruppin, Shmarya Levin and Chaim Arlosoroff—the last a young
rising force of whom I shall have more to say—who emphasized the
great possibilities of the moment, and stressed the need for con-
centrating on the improvement of the financial resources of the
movement, and for attracting new forces from among those Jews
who had hitherto stood aside. Ruppin put it succinctly as follows:
Zionist work rested on three pillars: the sympathy of the enlight-
ened world, an understanding with the Arabs, and the devotion and
single-mindedness of the Jewish people itself. While we might have
little control over the first two, the last depended entirely upon
ourselves.

I left the Conference more than ever convinced that for many years
to come my life would be divided between Palestine, where the
actual work had to be got under way as soon as possible, and the
great Western communities which would have to provide the bulk
of the funds for it.

The Palestine Executive was by that time gradually consolidating
its position, but it was sadly weak in its contacts with the administration. Until August 1922, our mainstay on this front had been the
invaluable Dr. Eder, but he told us at the Conference in Carlsbad
that he would shortly have to return to his medical work in London,
which he had neglected too long. There, he promised, he would
give us such help as he could, and up to the time of his death his
wise and experienced mind was at the service of the London Executive. To replace him in Palestine was not a simple matter.

In this difficulty I turned to General Macdonogh of Military Intelligence, a devoted friend of the Zionist movement, in the hope that he
might be able to suggest someone shortly to be released from his department. It was General Macdonogh who had arranged my trip to Gibraltar
described toward the end of Book One of these memoirs. I explained
to him the complicated nature of the proposed assignment: we needed
a man belonging to both worlds, English as well as Jewish; and on the
Jewish side he had to be willing and able to understand and co-operate
with the Eastern Jews who would form the bulk of our immigrants as
well as with the Westerners who would supply most of the funds for
the work. The General brought up the name of Colonel Fred Kisch, with
whom I had had fleeting contact precisely in connection with my Gibraltar trip. During most of the war Kisch had been with the engineers
in Mesopotamia, but during a brief convalescence had been attached to
intelligence. After the war, Kisch was stationed in Paris, and his work

was connected with the drafting of some of the peace treaties. Macdonogh recommended him warmly.

In my first long conversation with Kisch I realized at once that his
chief had been right in thinking that he had many of the qualities needed.
He was completely British in upbringing, but came of a family which
already had some connections with Zionism. His father, Hermann
Kisch, was an old *Chovav Zion*. He was therefore not entirely a
stranger to our problems, even though his life as an engineer officer
had so far lain apart from us. I explained frankly to him the scope, the
difficulties and the complications of the task which would lie before
him if he came to us, and made no secret of the fact that he might
easily fall between two stools: the Jews might not accept him because he
was too much of an Englishman, while the British might come to
regard him—in spite of his distinguished military career—as an Englishman "gone native." I told him that he would need a lot of courage,
self-discipline and self-sacrifice, and would most probably get little
satisfaction out of it. I also advised him not to decide until he had
actually seen Palestine and got to know some of the people with whom
he would have to live and work for years to come in a rather narrow
circle.

Kisch made only one condition: that I should personally initiate him
into his work. So it came about that we set out for Palestine together
in November 1922, and I was able to watch over his first steps in the
new environment. They were very cautious. I soon saw that I had made
an excellent choice. Some of his senior colleagues, particularly Mr.
Ussishkin, did little to make the job easier for him, but Kisch, once he
had seen the country and the people, was so fascinated by the possibilities of the job that he was not to be deterred. Almost his first act on
settling in Palestine was to make arrangements for a daily Hebrew
lesson, so as to understand the Palestinians and be able to make himself
understood without an interpreter. His next was to make a careful
survey of the country. He had the advantage of being well acquainted
with Sir Herbert Samuel, on whose warm support and encouragement
he could count, and thus started on his new career under favorable
auspices. For the first few months he served as political officer to the
Executive, without formal status, but at the thirteenth Congress, in the
summer of 1923, he was elected to the Executive, and continued to
serve on it until he resigned in 1931, following my defeat at the Congress of that year.

The story of those nine years he has told for himself in his *Palestine
Diary*. They were years of absorbing interest and very considerable
difficulty—years of foundation laying. Kisch showed himself to be
devoted, painstaking and resourceful to a degree, and made a great
contribution to the development of the Jewish National Home in its

early formative stages. As time went on, the Jews of Palestine, and of the movement outside, came to know him and to appreciate him. But in proportion as his authority grew with the *Yishuv*, it diminished at Government House, and, more especially, among the lower strata of British officialdom in Palestine. But this in no way impaired Kisch's morale; he was not to be deflected from his chosen road. After his resignation from the Executive he settled in Palestine, and only left his beautiful home on Carmel to rejoin the Royal Engineers at the outbreak of the Second World War. He served with great distinction as chief engineer of the Eighth Army, and died in the front line before Tunis on April 11, 1943.

Kisch's arrival in Palestine meant much to me personally. For the first time there was somebody with whom to share the work which, since Eder's resignation, had been my own responsibility; someone who could also go to America and talk to the assimilated Jews there as man to man—and from them get the respect due to an officer high in the British military hierarchy. Indeed, he was better able to talk to them than I was, for he did not bear the stigma of being an East European Jew; and his work with the Western assimilated Jews was always eminently successful.

It was a good thing that it was so, for the years 1923-1924 saw the beginning of Palestine's first postwar depression and, as I have already recounted, our travels to America and various European capitals took place against a background—of which we were ceaselessly conscious— of inadequate income, unpaid teachers and officials in Palestine, settlement work held up for lack of funds, settlers short of the most elementary necessities, and the ever-present threat of serious unemployment. Gradually, as the various branches of the Fund got under way, larger amounts trickled in; but the increase in those early years was very slow, and anxiety lest the utmost we could do should prove "too little and too late" dogged our every footstep.

Another man who carried a heavy burden at that time, and carried it magnificently, was Arthur Ruppin. He helped found our colonies in a manner which set an example not only for Palestine, but for many other countries. The human problem that faced us was the highly complex one of absorbing into agriculture immigrants who were by nature and training urban, and who had been divorced all their lives, like their ancestors for hundreds of years, from agricultural pursuits and traditions. Our material was, in fact, what our enemies sometimes called "the sweepings of the ghetto."

These men and women had to be trained, and prepared to lead new lives in a strange climate, on a soil neglected and abused for centuries. And this had to be done at a time in human history when the prevailing tendency everywhere was in the opposite direction—a marked drift away from the village and into the town. So we were working against the stream—"trying to set the clock back" (another favorite phrase of our opponents). And our income was both limited and uncertain. At best the results of agricultural colonization are slow to mature; faced with the task of the rapid absorption of considerable numbers of people, one would naturally turn to urban industrial development as the easier course. I have already told of the conflict which therefore developed between those of us who thought that the first task of the Zionists was to create industries and develop towns, and those who, like myself, were convinced that without a solid agricultural basis there could be no firm foundation for a Jewish culture, or for the Jewish way of life, or even for a Jewish economy. As immigration into Palestine proceeded, this difference of outlook became more acute; by 1923-1924 the debate was in full swing.

It was Ruppin who, undaunted by the storm of polemics which raged about him, and the abuse to which he was subjected, calmly pursued his agricultural program in the teeth of every difficulty. If today Jewish Palestine can proudly review the sons and daughters of some three hundred agricultural settlements, this is largely due to Ruppin's foresight and obduracy, and his profound understanding of the East European Jew. Himself a Westerner, his sympathetic insight enabled him to find ways and means of adapting the East European mentality to the hard conditions of Palestine agriculture.

It was in the collective settlement, in the *kvutzah*, that Ruppin found the form that best served both as training ground for newcomers to the land and as a unit able to establish and maintain itself in remote and unsettled parts of the country. Roads were few and bad in those early days, and new settlements had to face months and years of virtual isolation. The solitary settler, or the small village of independent farmers, could not have existed in the conditions then prevailing.

But the "collectives" had to face an extremely hostile section of Zionist and general public opinion. A great deal of nonsense was talked and written about them by opponents, both within the movement and outside of it. We were told that they were "Communist" (i.e., Bolshevist) cells; that men and women were herded together in them, leading lives of sexual promiscuity; that they were irreligious, atheistic, subversive—in short, sinks of iniquity scattered up and down the Holy Land. Such "criticisms" could only come from people who had never been inside a *kvutzah*, or what was worse, had been inside one for half an hour. With the passing of years, and the gradual increase in the number of people who *had* visited them, ideas began to change. Travelers returning from Palestine had, and have, nothing but praise for the communal villages, the life their members lead, and the work they are doing. These units are based on the principles of co-operative buying and selling, self-labor and the national ownership of land. Fifty years ago all these ideas sounded like dreams; today, in Palestine, they are solid economic reality. The settlements are firmly rooted, conveniently as well as pleasantly designed; the settlers are robust, cheerful, keen on their jobs. They love the country, and are bringing up a young generation proud of their agricultural skill, eager, upstanding, independent—young men and women who have shed all the attributes of the ghetto and acquired those of a normal, healthy, self-respecting peasant class.

The way has not been easy. For lack of funds the work was prolonged and made more costly, and much unnecessary suffering was caused. Often on my early visits to new settlements my heart ached with the knowledge that the settlers were doing their utmost to spare me any real perception of their daily difficulties. I heard no word of complaint, but I read in the eyes of settlers more than they could have put into words. I was particularly touched by the efforts they made—for instance in Nahalal and Ain Harod—to comfort *me*, and to assure me that "better times would surely come."

What made things harder still was the accusation that Ruppin and the settlers were doctrinaires, interested more in proving a theory than in getting results. The opposite was the truth; Ruppin was interested precisely in practical results. It was his contention that the *kvutzah* cost less per settler than any other form of colonization. It was also more useful as a training school for men and women new to the land and to the village life. It met to a very great extent one of the principal difficulties in adapting town dwellers to rural life, namely, the loneliness in the early stages. It was, in addition, more capable of defending itself when new settlements had to be established in isolated areas. Twenty-five years have proved that Ruppin was right.

Together with Ruppin worked Elazari-Volcani, who is still at the head of the Agricultural Experimental Station in Rehovoth. Between them and their colleagues they elaborated, after many trials and errors, and in the face of innumerable difficulties, the most suitable type of agriculture for Palestine, namely, mixed farming.

There was an organic connection between Ruppin's outlook on practical matters and his association with me in the "parliamentary" struggle in the Congresses. Shmarya Levin's support of me was equally consistent and effective, but had other roots. In the years which elapsed since my student days in Berlin, I had grown to love and admire his great personality and apostolic devotion to Zionist work. Somehow, without words, without preliminary agreement, we always found ourselves, by instinct, on the same side of the fence. It was so in the days of the great controversy with Herzl on what was then called "political Zionism"—and it was so in the Zionist Congress debates for many years after the ratification of the Mandate. Still another pillar of strength

on our side in this struggle was Eliezer Kaplan, who in later years
became the treasurer of the Jewish Agency and exercised a powerful
influence in the ranks of labor.

Chaim Arlosoroff, whom I have mentioned as another stanch supporter of my view of Zionist work, was by far the youngest of us. He
was a man of brilliant mind, and he was particularly fitted to present
our philosophy of Zionism to the younger generation. He did it with
great zest and power and with indefatigable energy. It was a privilege
to watch him at work. He became later the political officer of the
Executive—this was in the time of the Wauchope administration—but
already at the Congresses and Conferences of 1922 and on, he was one
of the leading spirits. He was merciless in his attacks on the extremist
group, which later crystallized into the Revisionist faction.

Arlosoroff had received an excellent education, and his Jewish background was solid. He was one of the few who knew the East and the
West equally well, and was therefore most suitable for the office which
he filled. He was fundamentally good natured, but did not suffer fools
gladly, and was severe in his attacks on his opponents. But he took as
well as gave. His brilliant career was cut short in 1933 by an assassin.
He was murdered in dastardly fashion late one night on the seashore
of Tel Aviv. His death left a gap which has not been adequately filled
until the present.

The controversy had not yet reached, in 1922 and 1923, the fury
which was to characterize it later, but it was already very lively. The
year 1923 saw the beginnings of a change in the character of our immigration. The early immigrants had been preponderantly of the *chalutz*
type. In 1923 a new regulation offered settlement visas to anyone who
could show possession of twenty-five hundred dollars—this was called
"the capitalist" category—and gave a much needed opportunity to
many Russian Jews stranded in Poland after the war. These new immigrants were permitted over and above those who received "labor
certificates." And so the immigration figures rose month by month.
So, unfortunately, did the unemployment figures, though much more
slowly. I was uneasy. True, a considerable amount of capital was being
brought into the country by these small capitalists, but openings in
industry, trade and commerce were as yet limited, and the numerous
small shops which seemed to spring up overnight in Tel Aviv and
Haifa caused me no little worry. These people were, as I have indicated,
not of the *chalutz* type, and some of them were little disposed to pull
their weight in a new country. A few, in their struggle for existence,
showed antisocial tendencies; they seemed never to have been Zionists,
and saw no difference between Palestine as a country of immigration
and, for instance, the United States. Many of them had no knowledge
of Hebrew, and it was soon being said, rather ruefully, that at this rate

Tel Aviv would soon be a Yiddish-speaking town. Even to the casual observer, the new immigration carried with it the atmosphere of the ghetto. In the end, I felt that I had to give warning. I had to give it many times, in fact; and its character may be gathered from a speech I made in Jerusalem in October 1924.

I said, among other things: "When one leaves the Emek and comes into the streets of Tel Aviv, the whole picture changes. The rising stream of immigration delights me, and I am delighted, too, that the ships should bring these thousands of people who are prepared to risk their life's savings in the Jewish National Home. Nor do I underrate the importance of this immigration for our work of reconstruction. Our brothers and sisters of Djika and Nalevki"—I was referring to typical ghetto districts of Warsaw—"are flesh of our flesh and blood of our blood. But we must see to it that we direct this stream and do not allow it to deflect us from our goal. It is essential to remember that we are not building our National Home on the model of Djika and Nalevki. The life of the ghetto we have always known to be merely a stage on our road; here we have reached home, and are building for eternity."

This speech earned me the hatred of a great many Polish Jews, particularly of the *Mizrachi* type—a hatred which I have never lived down. I daresay I might have put it more tactfully, but I felt too strongly to mind. Naturally, such statements got me into hot water: the new immigrants, with their three or four or five thousand dollars each, considered themselves just as good as the men from Daganiah and Nahalal, and I was accused of taking sides, and discriminating between one type of immigration and another. It was not that I did not realize the importance of the small capitalist for Palestine's economy; their industry, diligence and frugality were invaluable assets. But I feared that in the early stages of our growth a too-high proportion of them might unduly weight the balance. I feared that too many of them would meet with disappointment in an unfamiliar country, lose their small savings, and be driven to return to Poland or Rumania. And that would have been a catastrophe. In fact, something of the sort did happen, though on a small scale; but small as it was, we were not to escape its dire consequences.

The most vicious of the forms in which the "ghetto" influence found expression was land speculation. We had to struggle very hard to suppress this type of activity, which cut at the very root of our land system and hence of our whole work. But the prospect of quick gain was a powerful attraction for many people, and the only way to combat it was to concentrate the acquisition of land in the hands of the Jewish National Fund. This, however, meant much more money than the Jewish National Fund had, or could expect, at the time. So we had to stand by and watch the rise in land prices which we knew must inevitably lead to a slump, to failures, to re-emigration, with all the attendant sufferings and difficulties. There were some land speculators who never even came to Palestine. Bogus land companies sprang up, and parcels of Palestine land were hawked on the markets of Warsaw, Lodz and Lemberg, changing hands with bewildering rapidity. We knew that such speculation carried its own nemesis, but it was hard to convince the small man who saw a chance of doubling his life's savings at one stroke. After all, he always knew of someone who had made a fortune that way: why not he?

All this was the more painful to watch because most of the human material of the new immigration was extremely fine. I came again to Palestine in the autumn of 1924, and spent the High Holidays in Tel Aviv, where my mother then lived. This gave me the opportunity to see some of the various small industries which were being created by the new immigration. Often I would go to a dwelling consisting of one biggish room, with an annex. In the big room one would find a loom, and the head of the family—often a man of advanced age—together with his son or daughter, working it. I asked more than once whether such home industries were providing even a modest livelihood for the family. The reply was almost invariably something like this: "Dr. Weizmann, don't you worry about the economic side. *We* shall manage to pay our way here. You'll see. What *you* have to do is see that more Jews come into Palestine." One way or another we came through the period of trial; some of those little industries are big industries today. The process of overexpansion was arrested in time, and later we established a sort of industrial bank to give credits to small shopkeepers and industrialists in the towns. The Anglo-Palestine Bank also extended assistance to the same type of immigrant. All the same, they had, I am afraid, some reason to be dissatisfied with the Executive and myself. There was a time when the agricultural settlers were getting the advice and support of the Zionist Organization, while the urban settlers were left to their own devices. But the fact was that it was impossible to satisfy everybody, and we—particularly I—believed the agricultural side to be the more important.

The experience of the great festivals of the New Year and the Day of Atonement in Tel Aviv was a great one for me, and left a deep impression. The atmosphere was so different from that of a Russian or Polish town—or even an English one. As soon as the hour of sunset approached, the Great Synagogue—at that time still unroofed, and covered with some sort of makeshift tarpaulin arrangement—began to fill with a mass of young men who had marched into Tel Aviv from the neighboring villages. They were sturdy, bronzed, healthy-looking specimens, in everyday clothes (they had no other), some even in shorts, but all very clean, and somehow festive looking. Their presence in the synagogue belied all the rumors that the people of the *kvutzah* were atheists, disregarding all the traditions and tenets of the Jewish religion. Chaim Nachman Bialik and I stood watching them throughout the service, thinking the same thoughts: these were men and women who served God with spade and pick and hoe on weekdays, and came at the High Festivals to the synagogue to thank God for permitting them to do so, for bringing them out of the hell of the ghetto, and setting them on the threshold of a new life.

TREE OF LIFE CONGREGATION

Wilkins & Shady Avenues

Pittsburgh 17, Pa.

CHAPTER 27

The Jewish Agency

Non-Zionist Jewish Leaders and Philanthropists—Anything rather than Jewish Nationalism—Russian Colonization Plans —Zionist Division on the Agency—Louis Marshall—Felix Warburg—Philanthropy and National Regeneration—Zionist Educational Work Continues—Western Cities—Samuel Zemurray—The Constituent Assembly of the Jewish Agency, August 1929—The Triple Setback.

SEVEN years lay between the ratification of the Mandate—July 1922 —and the founding of the Jewish Agency—August 1929. Amid the varying fortunes of the Zionist movement, I did not once, during that period, forget the need for the Agency. I had, in fact, been preoccupied with the idea in preceding years.

Article IV of the Mandate reads: "An appropriate Jewish agency shall be recognized as a public body for the purpose of advising and co-operating with the administration of Palestine in such economic, social and other matters as may affect the establishment of the Jewish National Home. . . . The Zionist Organization . . . shall be recognized as such agency. It shall take steps in consultation with His Britannic Majesty's Government to secure the co-operation of all Jews who are willing to assist in the establishment of the Jewish National Home." The words "Jewish Agency" as used in my narrative, mean, specifically the Agency in the extended or enlarged form contemplated by the Mandate.

Chiefly, though by no means exclusively, I had in mind the leaders of the American Jewish community, the mainstay of the Joint Distribution Committee. Their philanthropies were manifold and generous, and Palestine might occasionally be included among them as a peripheral interest. They had done and were doing magnificent relief work for European Jewry during and after the First World War, but for one who believed that the Jewish Homeland offered the only substantial and abiding answer to the Jewish problem, their faith in the ultimate restabilizing of European Jewry was a tragedy. It was heartbreaking to see them pour millions into a bottomless pit, when some of the money could have been directed to the Jewish Homeland and used for

the permanent settlement of those very Jews who in Europe never had
a real chance. They accused us Zionists of being doctrinaires, of being
more interested in creating a Jewish homeland than in saving Jewish
lives. Actually the shoe was on the other foot. They were too often the
doctrinaires who gladly supported any worthy cause as long as it did
not involve them in what they called Jewish nationalism.

An outstanding instance was the project for the creation of an auton-
omous Jewish settlement in Soviet Russia, which began with the
Crimea as the chosen area. It was, of course, a reasonable scheme,
though it was confined to Russian Jewry, and could have no effect on
the Jews of Poland, Rumania, etc. I believe the Crimea scheme was a
sincere attempt on the part of the Russian Government to "normalize"
certain Jewish elements which did not fit into the reorganized economic
life of Soviet Russia. They consisted of middlemen and small traders
who would be condemned to starvation under the new regime unless
they could change their means of livelihood. Though the project entailed
certain risks, no one would have felt justified in opposing a scheme so
well intentioned. There was no need for Zionists to support it actively,
but there was equally no need for violent opposition. But for a great
many non-Zionists, at that time at any rate, the peculiar merit of the
Crimea scheme was precisely that it had nothing to do with Palestine
and Jewish nationalism, and could in fact be used to deflect from
Palestine the attention of Jewish groups. This attitude, in turn, gave
a handle to certain Zionist groups which were not particularly keen—
for reasons I shall shortly give—on seeing the enlarged Jewish Agency
materialize.

Nor was it only to Jewish causes that these men were generous
donors—to the practical exclusion of Palestine. Mr. Julius Rosenwald,
of Chicago, for instance, was a universal philanthropist. For a Negro
university, for a *Volksmuseum* in Munich, for a Berlin school of den-
tistry, his purse seemed bottomless. But the only Palestinian institutions
to share in his benefactions were the Teachers Seminary in Jerusalem
and the Agricultural Station in Athlit. What seemed odd to me, in these
circumstances, was his continued and apparently quite lively interest in
all that went on in Palestine. He read most of our material, and his
stock remark whenever I met him was: "If you can convince me that
Palestine is a *practical* proposition, you can have all my money." But
nothing could convince him. Personally he was most friendly to me
and to Shmarya Levin. To Levin he once said: "Look, my villa in the
suburbs is called 'Tel Aviv.' What more do you want?" Levin answered:
"Only that you should build a house in the suburbs of Tel Aviv and call
it 'Chicago.'"

In most countries, as I have pointed out, the *Keren Hayesod* provided a sort of bridge for those people who were interested in Palestine

and who were ready to help the work as long as it did not commit them in the political field. But this was not enough. The Mandate referred to a "Jewish Agency" which would in fact speak for all Jews interested in the building of the Homeland. The Fund was an instrument, not an agency. It did not provide for the degree of participation which the phrase in the Mandate contemplated and which I was eager to obtain.

Among the Zionists the opposition to the Agency was of two kinds. There was, it will be remembered, the Brandeis group, which wanted the Zionist Organization to remain as the Agency since, in their opinion, it was no longer essentially a political body, and non-Zionists no longer needed to shy away from it. But since the Brandeis group had more or less withdrawn from organizational work, its opposition was not important. Much more important was the second type of opposition, which sprang from precisely the opposite point of view.

Many of the European Zionists, and some of the American Zionists, did not want to have the rich Jews of America, the so-called "assimilationists," in an Agency which would have a controlling voice in the affairs of the Jewish Homeland. These Zionists were afraid of an emasculating influence in the direction of philanthropy; and I was accused of trying to drag those rich Jews into Zionist work against their will and better judgment. "If they want to co-operate," said those Zionists, "the doors of the Organization are open to them. They can become Zionists." Which of course begged the question; such men were not ready to join the Zionist Organization any more than the PICA was ready to give up its individuality and merge with us. Moreover, the difference between them and the Zionists was not only political; it was also social.

Among those American Zionists who were strong advocates of the Agency idea were men like Louis Lipsky—whom I have already mentioned—the late Jacob Fishman, and Morris Rothenberg. Fishman, who will long be remembered as one of the ablest Jewish journalists in America—he was for many years editor of the *Jewish Morning Journal*, and conducted a widely read column on current affairs—had a special insight into the public mind. There were very few in America, or for that matter anywhere else, to whom I stood nearer, and with whom I could discuss Zionist affairs in a more intimate way. He made his paper a powerful influence for the good; his calm, level-headed comments helped to maintain an informed point of view during times of crisis, like the struggle with Brandeis, and the struggle round the Jewish Agency. Jacob Fishman died in harness—attending the Zionist Congress at Basle in 1946. It was a great loss to the Zionist movement, and to his friends.

Morris Rothenberg belonged to the younger set, and has played a considerable role in many phases of American Zionism as a clear, cool-headed and judicial mediator between various contending parties. In spite of this role, which often exposes a man to attacks from both sides, he always enjoyed the respect of divergent elements. He was, and remains, an extremely valuable counselor, especially to one like myself who only comes for short periodic visits and is likely to commit grave errors if not loyally guided by advisers fully conversant with the scene and with the *dramatis personae.*

The idea of the Jewish Agency was debated at our Actions Committee meetings, our Conferences and Congresses, as stormily as our relations with Great Britain. But shortly before I left for America in February 1923, a session of the Actions Committee, held in Berlin, adopted a resolution approving in general terms the idea of the Jewish Agency, and laying down as a guiding principle for our negotiations "that the controlling organ of the Jewish Agency shall be responsible to a body representative of the Jewish people." This beautifully vague statement, though it left me free to make a start, also left the door open to the partisans of the "World Jewish Congress" idea.

There were, it might seem, two ways of drawing into the work of Palestine those Jews who were not prepared to declare themselves Zionists—two ways of creating the Agency. One was to organize a full-fledged "World Jewish Congress" with elected delegates from every Jewish community. Theoretically this was correct enough; but in practice the calling of a World Jewish Congress encountered insuperable difficulties—foremost among them the fact that the very elements in Jewry which we wanted to bring in would have nothing to do with the idea! So that, even if and when achieved, such a congress would amount to little more than a slightly enlarged Zionist Organization.

There were other grounds for the rejection of the World Congress idea in this connection. To the people whose co-operation we sought, the ultrademocratic machinery of Congresses was wholly unattractive. They were reluctant even to meet the Zionists and discuss with them the possibility of a covenant. It was therefore clear to me that the only practical approach was to invite the various great organizations already at work in other fields to join with us without forfeiting their identity. This second way was the one I proposed and ultimately carried into effect.

It was a curious fact that while the plan was attacked by ultra-Zionists as "antidemocratic," the most democratic body in Palestine itself, the labor organization, was wholly in favor of it. At the various meetings of the authoritative Zionist bodies the Palestine laborites stood behind these efforts because they were men of practical experience; they knew how badly we needed new sources of income and new forces in order to get on with the job; and though they may have seen certain dangers in the plan, they agreed with me that it would be a grave mistake to exclude from our work, on grounds of purely formal "democracy," those powerful and responsible groups of American Jews.

So much for internal Zionist opposition to the Agency. There remained still "the party of the second part." Within the non-Zionist groups too there was opposition to the proposed match. The Joint Distribution Committee suffered, moreover, from a great weakness: it had very few men to give us who could participate in executive work on the level of their Zionist opposites in the Agency. Whereas the Zionist men of the Executive were elected at Congresses after a severe struggle, which more or less assured a high level of quality, the executives of the Joint were appointees. I do not say that they did not do their work very well, but when the Agency was in fact constituted their position in the mixed Executive was somewhat precarious. And before the Agency was constituted they did whatever they could to prevent the merger, fearing that in it they would lose their privileged position.

My acquaintance with Louis Marshall began in 1919, when he came to Paris as the head of the American Jewish Delegation to the Peace Conference. I saw little of him, for I did not take part in their work; the whole fight for minority national rights seemed to me to be unreal. But I was greatly impressed by Marshall's forceful personality, his devotion to Jewish matters and the great wisdom he brought to bear in the discussions. Although counted among the "assimilationists," he had a very clear understanding of and a deep sense of sympathy for the national endeavors of the Jewish communities in Europe who were struggling for cultural minority rights. He had learned Yiddish and followed the Yiddish press closely, showing himself very sensitive to its criticism. Of a naturally autocratic habit of mind, firm if not obstinate on occasion, impatient of argument, he was, I felt, a man who, once convinced of the rightness of a course, would follow it unswervingly. The main difficulty in working with him lay in his tendency to procrastinate—mainly due to his preoccupation with his profession and his various public activities. One had always to be at his elbow to make sure that the particular business in hand had not been snowed under by other urgent duties. This naturally added to the delays in our negotiations—the more so as the opponents of the Agency idea made use of this weakness in Marshall. I countered by maintaining such pressure as I could. Unable always to be in America, I sent out others; once Leonard Stein, and on another occasion Kisch. Morris Rothenberg acted as a sort of permanent liaison officer.

It was a profound mistake to think, as some Zionists did at the time, that Marshall was not "representative" because he had not been elected, like members of the Zionist Executive. As one traveled up and down the States one could not but be impressed by the extent and power of his influence. The most important Jewish groups in every city in

America looked to him for the lead in communal matters, and his attitude went a long way, in fact was often decisive, in determining theirs.

And yet in one sense he was not representative of his following. He was much nearer to Jews and Judaism; nearer, in fact, than Brandeis, an ardent Zionist, ever was. For Brandeis Zionism was an intellectual experiment, based on solid foundations of logic and reason. Marshall was hot blooded, capable of generous enthusiasms as well as of violent outbursts of anger—though it was seldom long before his cooler judgment reasserted itself.

I found him at first completely skeptical as to the possibilities in Palestine, knowing next to nothing about the country and about our work. But he had such a great fund of sympathy and was so warm-hearted, that it compensated for his ignorance of the subject. I remember how, at the end of a long conversation on our prospects, he suddenly burst out in his temperamental way: "But Dr. Weizmann, you will need half a billion dollars to build up this country." To which I calmly replied, "You'll need much more, Mr. Marshall," and that completely disarmed him. He was so baffled that he stared at me for a long time, and I said: "The money is there, in the pockets of the American Jews. It's your business and my business to get at some of it." I think that from that moment on he began to understand the magnitude—and the appeal—of the problem.

Of an entirely different character was Felix Warburg, whom I did not meet until the spring of 1923. He was a man of sterling character, charitable to a degree, a pivotal figure in the American Jewish community, if not in very close touch with the rank and file. There was something of *le bon prince* about him. But he was susceptible to gossip, and readily believed—or at least repeated—what his satellites told him about Palestine.

Shortly after my arrival in the spring of 1923, I was somewhat surprised to receive an invitation to lunch with him at the offices of Kuhn, Loeb and Company in William Street. Enthroned in one of the more palatial rooms of that palatial building, I found an extremely affable and charming gentleman, very much the *grand seigneur*, but all kindness. I decided that my lunch with him was going to be quite as much pleasure as duty. I judged too soon. We spent about an hour and a half together, and almost the whole time was occupied by Mr. Warburg's account of what, according to his information, was happening in Palestine. A more fantastic rigmarole, I have, to be honest, never heard from a responsible quarter: bolshevism, immorality, waste of money, inaction, inefficiency, all of it based on nothing more than hearsay. I listened with what patience I could muster—it seemed to me then a good deal—to this tirade, and felt a little embarrassed at the thought of replying. I could not leave his statements unchallenged, but as his guest I found it difficult to frame the flat contradictions which they called for.

I let him talk himself out, and then I said: "You know, Mr. Warburg, I am really quite well acquainted with Palestine and with the work there; I have been there every year since the end of the war, the last time only a couple of months ago. I have been present at the inception of almost every enterprise of ours. But as to these stories which I hear from you—I must suppose at second, or third, or even fourth hand—I cannot deny that there may be some particle of truth in the accusations —'no smoke without fire' and so on—but so far it has escaped my attention. I think you have not yet been in Palestine yourself, and I am frankly not prepared to accept your sources as unimpeachable." I then asked if I might put a plain question to him: "What if things were the other way round? Suppose I came to you with a collection of all the tittle-tattle and backstairs gossip that circulates, I have no doubt, about Kuhn, Loeb and Company? What would you do?"

He laughed and answered: "I should probably ask you to leave."

I said: "I can hardly ask you to leave, for I am your guest."

He at once realized that he had gone too far, and he was ready to make amends by offering me a contribution, I forget whether to the *Keren Hayesod* or the Hebrew University. I did not accept, saying: "Mr. Warburg, it will cost you much more than you are likely to offer me now. The only way you can correct this painful interview is by going to Palestine and seeing for yourself. If your information is confirmed at first hand I shall have no more to say, for I must respect your views when based on personal experience."

To my astonishment he took me up! "Your suggestion is the right one," he said. "I will talk it over with my wife, and if possible go to Palestine at once." To my further astonishment he was as good as his word, and left for Palestine, together with Mrs. Warburg, within a fortnight of this first conversation. I wired to Kisch to show them around.

The next news I had of Warburg was a post card—still in my possession—in which he wrote that he had been going up and down the country and felt like doffing his hat to every man and every tree he saw! He was deeply moved by every phase of our work, settlements, schools, hospitals, and most of all by the settlers themselves. He and his wife returned to the States—I was still there—eager to help in every way they could. I was again invited to lunch, this time at their home. Again I sat and listened, and what I heard now was nothing but praise of Palestine and of our enterprises. I have seldom witnessed a more complete conversion.

Yet somehow it left me cold. Warburg noticed this, and said I did not seem very pleased. I tried to explain: "You see, you went to Palestine convinced that of every dollar collected here in America some ninety cents was being wasted. Probably you had a pleasant surprise to discover in Palestine that, as far as you could see, only fifty cents was being wasted. Perhaps, if you take a genuine interest in the work— enough to lend a hand—you may one day discover that not one cent is wasted. We have our difficulties; sometimes the progress is very slow, sometimes it picks up a little speed; but ours is a living organism, afflicted with all the diseases and complications that commonly beset living organisms. If you want to understand it, it will take more than one visit to Palestine. I am sure you will go again, and yet again—and not merely as a tourist; and in the end we shall understand each other."

This talk was the real beginning, I think, of Warburg's participation in our work. Incidentally it laid the foundations of a lifelong friendship which stood the strain of a good many differences of opinion. These arose from the fact that we looked at Palestine from different angles: for us Zionists it was a movement of national regeneration; for him it was, at any rate in the early stages of his interest, one among the fifty-seven varieties of his philanthropic endeavors—perhaps bigger and more interesting than some others, but not different in essence. His whole upbringing militated against his taking the same view as we did; besides, his co-workers in the innumerable other causes to which he was committed no doubt constantly warned him against the danger of identifying himself too closely with the Zionists. Warburg was one of their most valuable assets in communal work, and they greatly feared to lose him under the impact of a new idea which by its very radicalism might capture his imagination. Particularly was this the case with a certain Mr. David A. Brown, a typical American go-getter with a noisy technique for conjuring millions from the pockets of wealthy American Jews. People used to tell me wistfully that if we could only get for Zionism the whole-hearted support of Mr. David A. Brown, all our troubles would be over.

Warburg made several more trips to Palestine, where he was usually under the guidance of Dr. Magnes or of some member of the Executive. He really learned to know Palestine. The Hebrew University was his chief interest; he contributed large sums to it and became a member of its Board of Governors. Later the Dead Sea project and the Rutenberg development also attracted him.

The weight of Marshall's and Warburg's influence made things easier for me in the States. Even before the Agency was officially founded American non-Zionists began, under this influence, to co-operate in the *Keren Hayesod* and in other instruments for the building of Palestine. The fact that Marshall spoke from the same platform with me on March 13, 1923—it was my first American meeting of that visit—gave

the *Keren Hayesod* campaign a new impetus. Subsequently Marshall
and Oscar Strauss, the former Ambassador to Turkey, called together
a number of their friends with the purpose of founding a new investment corporation for Palestine. They did not achieve this object, but
they did bring new support to what is now the Palestine Economic
Corporation, which was able greatly to increase its investments in
various Palestinian enterprises.

In the fall of 1923, when I came for the second time that year to
America, after attending the Thirteenth Zionist Congress in Carlsbad,
Mr. Warburg initiated a half-million dollar fund for the Hebrew University through the medium of the American Jewish Physicians Committee. A first tentative sketch of the Jewish Agency constitution—
half a dozen headings on a few quarto sheets—which we had worked
on in the spring, was being elaborated; its development and ramifications were to keep us all busy at intervals for the next six years.

During all this period I carried on, throughout my American visits,
and side by side with my Agency conferences, my direct Zionist activities, which I have already described. American Jewish communities
were not of a uniform pattern. Chicago was a difficult city for us,
because of Rosenwald's influence. Still more difficult was Cincinnati,
where the community consisted mainly of Jews of German extraction—
and assimilated at that. There was a comparatively weak Russo-Jewish
colony, and some of its members worked hard to maintain some sort of
Zionist movement in the face of stony opposition. Generally speaking
our difficulties increased as we moved westward. California was a different world, remote from the Jewish interests of the eastern states, and
practically virgin soil from the Zionist point of view.

There were a few clearings, or oases, here and there. In Chicago,
there were, among others, two able, hard-working Zionists, Albert K.
Epstein and Benjamin Harris, whose lives were saturated with Zionist
thought and feeling. It was a particular pleasure to work with them
because there was more than a coincidence of Zionist feeling; they
were both industrial chemists, and they had practical plans for Palestine.
Some of these are now being put into effect, and I have a large file of
letters from them dealing with both Zionism and chemistry.

I made an unusual "find" in New Orleans, where lived a very remarkable personality in American Jewry—Samuel Zemurray, the
"Banana King." I paid my first visit to New Orleans specially to meet
him. He had been told of my arrival and postponed his own planned
departure from the city for several days—days which I found not
only extremely interesting, but also profitable for the Funds.

Zemurray had come to America from Kishinev as a very young man,
and his early years in the New World had been filled in by all manner
of occupations, which somehow had successively brought him a little

further south. His first venture to prove even moderately successful
was peddling bananas from a barrow; this had paid his way down as far
as New Orleans, where he arrived with a small surplus in hand. He
decided to continue in the line which had brought him his first credit
balance. By the time I met him he was the "Banana King"—the owner
of vast plantations in Honduras, with their warehouses, packing sheds,
and so on, as well as of his own fleet of refrigerator ships. Today he
is the head of the United Fruit Corporation, one of the most powerful
American produce companies. Throughout all this record of success
Zemurray retained his simplicity, his transparent honesty, his lively
interest in people and things, and his desire to serve. His chosen
studies in leisure hours were mathematics and music, and he got a
great deal of satisfaction out of them. It was said of him that his success in the Central American republics was mainly due to the fact that
he was deeply concerned for the welfare of the peons he employed—
which was by no means the case with most of his competitors. He built
schools, hospitals, recreation grounds and model villages, and generally
made his work-people feel that he had a genuine interest in their condition. His building operations resulted incidentally in the excavation
of some remarkable relics of the Maya culture, and his great collection
of these antiquities is now one of the show pieces of the New Orleans
University.

Zemurray was one of the highlights of my visit to the States in that
year; and I never missed an opportunity of seeing him on later visits.
He did not take a public part in our work; but his interest has been continuous and generous. I found him, at the outbreak of the war, depressed
by the White Paper of 1939—depressed, yet hopeful of the ultimate
outcome. Despite his distress over the White Paper, he handed over the
greater part of his fleet of ships to Great Britain at the beginning of the
war.

I have said enough, I believe, concerning the obstacles, the delays,
the opposition, the internal and external complications which make up
the story of the creation of the Jewish Agency. Seven years and more
of my life were consumed by it, and the most shattering blow of all was
reserved for the hour of our triumph.

In August 1929, immediately after the Zionist Congress of that year,
the Constituent Assembly of the Jewish Agency met at last, in Zurich,
Switzerland. Zionist opposition had been overcome, external opposition
had been soothed: a genuine assembly of Jewish leaders in the non-
Zionist world declared its intention to stand side by side with the Zionists in the practical work in Palestine. All sections of the Jewish people
were represented and every community of any size. I have described in
this chapter only the American scene in the history of the Agency; in
Poland, England, Holland, in every country with a Jewish population,

the same story had played itself out. And it was not only the wealthy heads of the large philanthropic organizations who had been drawn into the partnership. The Jewish Agency brought together as distinguished a group of Jews as we have witnessed in our time; all classes and fields of achievement were represented, from Léon Blum, the great socialist leader, to Marshall and Warburg on the right; from Lord Melchett, one of England's leading industrialists, to Albert Einstein the scientist and Chaim Nachman Bialik the poet.

At the end of the meeting I had a long talk with Marshall and Warburg. They assured me that now my financial troubles were over; it would no longer be necessary for me to go up and down America—and other countries—from city to city, making innumerable appeals and addresses in order to help create the means for the limited budget of the Zionist Organization. This prediction or promise of theirs represented, I am sure, their sincere belief.

A few days after the Constituent Assembly had dispersed amid mutual felicitations, and while Zionists and non-Zionists all over the world were congratulating themselves on the creation of this new and powerful instrument of Jewish action, the Palestine riots broke out on August 23. On September 11, Louis Marshall, the mainstay of the non-Zionist section of the Agency, died after an operation. And within a few weeks there came the great economic crash of 1929, to be followed by the long depression—perhaps the severest in modern history—which struck hard at the sources of support which the Agency had planned to tap.

It would be quite wrong to say that this last series of blows undid the work of the preceding years. To begin with, the educational achievement of the long effort could never be undone. Its effects continued to grow, the breach between the Zionist and non-Zionist sections of public opinion continued to narrow. The very negotiations produced, before the Agency was completed, a more sympathetic response on the part of the non-Zionists. The notion that the building of the Jewish Homeland was a fantastically Utopian dream, the obsession of impractical, Messianically deluded ghetto Jews, began to be dispelled by the participation of prominent men of affairs with a reputation for sober-mindedness and hard-bitten practicality. Today as I write, nearly twenty years after the official founding of the Jewish Agency, the presence of such figures in the work for Palestine is a commonplace. The dark events of recent years have had a good deal to do with winning them over. But the first steps were taken, the pattern was created, during the long period of persuasion and negotiation which I have described in this chapter.

CHAPTER 28

Foundations

A Decisive Decade—Progress of the Hebrew University— What Were to Be Its Functions?—Inauguration Set for April 1, 1925—Lord Balfour Agrees to Preside—Preparations—An Unforgettable Ceremony—Balfour Tours Palestine—A Loving Reception—Significance of the Opening of the University— Rising Anti-Semitism in Europe, Political Setbacks in Palestine —The "Duality" of the Mandate—The Mandates Commission of the League of Nations—Criticism within the Movement— Jabotinsky Founds Revisionist Party—Ussishkin Resigns from Executive—But the Work Goes on, the Foundations Are Laid.

THE years between 1920 and 1929 were for the Zionist movement and the National Home years of alternating progress and setback, of slow laborious achievement sown with recurrent disappointment, and of the gradual emergence in Palestine of foundations whose solidity was to be demonstrated in the time that followed. For me they were years of hard work and frequent anxiety, of much wandering in many lands, and of continuous effort within the Zionist Organization to keep our activities and methods in line with the views which I have set forth in the preceding pages. Those were also the years that witnessed the rise of the new anti-Semitism in Europe generally and of Nazism in Germany, imparting new and desperate urgency to our task.

One event stands out in the decade of the twenties on which I linger with pleasure, because of both its practical and its symbolic significance, and that is the opening of the Hebrew University. If I give it a special space in these memoirs it is not only because of the peculiar relationship that I had and have toward that institution, but because it represents the fulfillment of my particular dream of the early days of the movement.

The first step toward the realization of the dream, the reader may remember, was the acquisition of Grey Hill House on Mount Scopus in the very midst of the war. The second was the erection of the library building—the Wolffsohn Memorial—near by, to house the large collection of books already existing in the Jewish National Library in Jerusalem. Our first librarian was Dr. Heinrich Loewe, an old Zionist comrade-in-arms of my student days, who had in the interim become a librarian of the Berlin University Library. To Dr. Loewe we owe the establishment of a sound bibliographical organization and tradition. Once the work was launched, we found books pouring in from all corners of the earth; the Oriental section was particularly fortunate, and rapidly assumed real importance in its field. The opening of the School of Oriental Studies followed closely on the completion of the library building, and was for some time accommodated in a private house rented for the purpose.

In 1923 Professor Patrick Geddes was invited to Jerusalem to assist in the replanning of the city. We asked him to undertake the design and layout of the university buildings, and after a study of the site he prepared some magnificent sketches which delighted all of us. Unfortunately none of them has been actually carried out, though the general plan has been followed, and for myself I still hope before I die to see the great assembly hall which Geddes designed rising on the slopes of Scopus.

Grey Hill House was rebuilt completely, to house the two institutes of microbiology and biochemistry, the first under Professor Saul Adler, formerly of Leeds, the second under Professor Fodor, who devoted much time to the acquisition of equipment and the adaptation of the building to laboratory use. The American Jewish Physicians Committee supplied much of the money for this beginning, and covered the budget of the two institutes for the first three years. We now felt that we had at least the nucleus of a faculty of sciences.

Most popular of the faculties was, of course, the Institute of Jewish Studies, which was endowed by Sol Rosenbloom of Pittsburgh. Baron Edmond de Rothschild, Felix Warburg and other friends took a personal interest in this branch of the University, and, indeed, there was a stage when I felt there was some danger in the enthusiasm which it aroused. There were too many who thought of the institute romantically in terms of a great center of Hebrew learning and literature; it was placed under the patronage of the Chief Rabbis of London and Paris, and its council included Dr. Magnes. It ran the risk of becoming a theological seminary, like those of London, Breslau or Philadelphia, instead of the school of "literae humaniores" of a free university. Happily the danger was averted when the council of the Institute of Jewish Studies was merged into the general structure of the University.

Somehow few people in those early days gave much thought to the possibility of developing a great scientific faculty at the Hebrew University. I was repeatedly told that we could never hope to compete with Cambridge or London or Paris or Harvard in chemistry, physics or mathematics. I felt this to be an erroneous conception—anyhow, on a long view. True, for the first few years we might not amount to anything in this field, but if the University was encouraged to develop freely, who could tell what young new forces we might attract from the scientific world? I felt, too, that the sciences had to be encouraged at Jerusalem, not only for their own sake, but because they were an integral part of the program for the full development of Palestine, and also because opportunities for Jewish students in the leading universities of Europe were becoming more and more restricted. The last consideration was at the time no more than a vague uneasiness, even in my own mind. Events in recent years have made it only too bitterly specific.

In addition to the institutes already described, we had, in Jerusalem, the great Rothschild Hospital, which we felt might well be used for research, and later on for teaching. We also had a Jewish Agricultural Experimental Station, with quite a number of research workers, and this might make the beginning of an agricultural faculty.

Altogether, we thought all the foregoing a fair start. Everything was of course on the most modest scale, but it seemed to us to contain much promise. We realized that the process of building up a university was bound to be a slow one, even apart from the fact that limited finances (in relation to the task in hand) imposed on us the utmost caution. But I had never believed that such things as universities could spring into being overnight, particularly in a country still struggling to provide itself with the bare necessities of life. Nor did I believe that everything would—or even ought to be—plain sailing for the infant university. Such institutions, like men, are often none the worse for having experienced poverty and adversity in youth: if they survive at all, they are the stronger, the more firmly rooted, for it.

What seemed important was to make a start with the materials in hand, and to put them to the best possible use. To this we applied our minds in 1923 and the following years, to such purpose that by the spring of 1925 we could look at "our University" and feel there really was enough of it to justify a formal "opening ceremony." Of course at that early stage no students had been accepted, but a body of research workers was gradually assembling and the various institutes were taking shape. After much discussion and heart-searching, therefore, we sent out invitations for an opening ceremony to be conducted by Lord Balfour on April 1, 1925. I need not say how much his instant and enthusiastic acceptance of the invitation meant to us.

I therefore found myself, in the middle of March 1925, setting forth with my wife and our son Benjy, to join the Esperia in Genoa. On board we found Professor Rappard, permanent secretary of the Mandate Commission, who was representing the University of Geneva at the opening. The Balfour party—Balfour himself, his ex-secretary, Edward Lascelles and Mrs. Lascelles, Balfour's niece—came on board at

Naples; Balfour, being an indifferent sailor, had wished to curtail the sea passage as much as possible. Other friends—notably the Sokolows —were also on board, so that there was plenty of company. As far as Sicily the weather held, but after Syracuse the wind sprang up and the sea became choppy, and the Balfour party was out of action for three days. It is rare for the Mediterranean to misbehave so late in March, and I suppose more than one of us muttered *"absit omen"* under his breath. Lord Balfour did not emerge again until we docked in Alexandria. It was still blowing half a gale, and a heavy shower of cold rain met us as we walked down the gangway. Mrs. Lascelles' ironical remarks about the wonderful weather in the Mediterranean and the blue skies of Egypt left me with an uncomfortable impression that I was perhaps being held responsible for the misconduct of the elements.

The Balfours went on to Cairo, to stay with Lord Allenby, who came with them a couple of days later to Kantara and accompanied us up to Jerusalem.

The situation in Palestine was at the time somewhat tense, but the security officers assured us that apart from a fairly peaceable demonstration in the form of a strike, and the closing of a few Arab shops in Jerusalem, Haifa and Jaffa, nothing untoward was happening. Which was just as well, as our guests were beginning to arrive in considerable numbers: representatives of universities and learned societies from all over the world, not to mention a great influx of tourists. It was not easy to find rooms for all these people in Jerusalem, for hotel accommodation was still scarce, and not of the best. Still, our reception committee did its work well, and I was not aware that any complaints were made. Every resident who had an appropriate house had placed it at the committee's disposal, and one way or another we managed to see to it that our guests enjoyed reasonable comfort.

The Balfour party and the Allenbys stayed of course at Government House. Kisch, Eder and I lived through some days of rather severe tension, with the responsibility of so many distinguished people on our hands under rather difficult conditions. There was, for instance, only one road from the city to the University on Mount Scopus, and that a narrow one, with little room for cars to turn. Control of traffic was a rather alarming problem, for the number of cars traveling to and fro was a record for Jerusalem at that time. Another purely physical difficulty was the actual site chosen for the opening ceremony. There was as yet no hall which could accommodate anything approaching the number of our guests and visitors—we expected some twelve thousand to fourteen thousand people. The only place, therefore, where we could stage the ceremony was the natural amphitheater facing a deep wadi on the northeast slope of Scopus. Round this amphitheater we arranged tiers of seats, following the natural rock formation. Everything was rather rough and ready, but the setting had such natural beauty that no art could have improved on it.

The snag was that, to face the audience in this amphitheater, the platform had to be on a bridge over the wadi itself. The gorge was deep, sheer and rocky; the bridge was an improvised wooden affair which inspired—in me at least—little confidence. I was told that it had been repeatedly tested, but my blood ran cold at the thought that something might give way at the crucial moment. . . . The builders, however, were convinced that the platform could safely bear two hundred or two hundred and fifty people. However, two hundred of our sturdiest young *chalutzim* volunteered to dance an energetic *hora* on the contraption. Nothing happened—except a great deal of noise—and I felt a little easier. Minute inspection of the platform failed to reveal any damage.

One final problem remained: the guarding of the tested platform during the night before the opening. Again our young *chalutzim* (members of the Haganah this time) came to the rescue: they established a sort of one-night camp in the wadi, and conducted frequent inspections, the last only a few minutes before the guests began to arrive.

Though the accommodation might be simple, even primitive, the surroundings—the austere magnificence of the landscape which opens out before one from this part of Scopus—more than made up for it. I doubt if anyone who made the pilgrimage to Mount Scopus that day, and the arrivals began before dawn, regretted the nonexistence of the Central Hall. Apart from our foreign visitors, people came from all over the country, people of every class and age and type. Only the three or four front rows of the amphitheater were reserved; the rest were open to the public, and needless to say were thronged hours before the ceremony began. I noted with some pride the discipline and good humor shown by the crowds.

Half an hour or so before the opening time the speakers and other platform guests assembled in the Grey Hill House to don their academic robes; then they passed, a colorful little procession, through the University grove on to the platform. The party from Government House approached direct, from the opposite side. Lord Balfour's appearance set off a tremendous ovation, which was hushed into complete stillness as he took his place on the platform.

The ceremony itself is a matter of historic record, and I need not describe it here. Many of the speakers were deeply moved. One or two of them were, as was only to be expected, rather long winded. I remember thinking at the time that Bialik (of all people!) was rather straining people's patience: he spoke in Hebrew, which to many of those present was a strange tongue. Moreover, I knew that at sunset the air would cool rapidly, and I was afraid that Lord Balfour (who was a man of seventy-seven) and some of the others might suffer, since all were

bareheaded and without overcoats. However, we did finish before sun-
down; the crowds dispersed in orderly fashion; the guests departed to
rest before the dinner party arranged for the evening; and the various
committees responsible for the arrangements heaved a sigh of relief
that everything had gone off without a noticeable hitch.

At dinner that evening my wife sat next to Lord Allenby. She was
moved to ask him: "Did you think my husband completely harebrained
when he asked your permission for the laying of the foundation stones
in 1918?" He thought for a moment and replied: "When I project my
mind back to that day—as I often do—I come to the conclusion that
that short ceremony inspired my army, and gave them confidence in
the future." He repeated this statement in the short speech which he
made after the dinner.

Before Lord Balfour came to Palestine, it had been our idea to spare
him as much as possible. We had planned a short drive through the
country to show him one or two places in which we thought he might
be specially interested, but nothing at all tiring. We had, however,
counted without our guest, who refused to be spared. He liked the look
of the country, and wanted to see as much as he possibly could of it. We
were also very anxious that he should not speak too much, especially in
the open. But here again, when it came to the point, there was no holding him back. He was warmly received wherever we went, and naturally
the man in charge would say a few words of welcome (which I tried,
with varying success, to keep as few as possible). Lord Balfour clearly
liked replying. He said on one occasion that it reminded him of a general election tour—but with everybody on the same side!

The most impressive feature of his trip was to Tel Aviv. I had been
a little uneasy about this beforehand. It was a biggish town, and there
were bound to be all sorts of people among its crowds. Anyone who
wanted to work mischief could easily do so. Security measures were, of
course, stringent. We traveled down by car from Jerusalem one morning, and stopped for lunch at Mikveh, the Agricultural School a couple
of miles this side of Tel Aviv. There we had a light lunch, and left Lord
Balfour to rest, while we went ahead to reconnoiter. The crowds I met
both impressed and terrified me. The main streets—Allenby Road and
Herzl Street—were lined with solid blocks of people: not only were the
pavements a living wall, but every balcony, every window, every roof-
top, was jammed to capacity. These crowds had been waiting for some
hours. I went to see Mr. Dizengoff, the mayor, who assured me that
there was every reason to be satisfied with the measures taken for the
maintaining of order, and then we returned to Mikveh to pick up the
rest of the party.

So we came into Tel Aviv in the early afternoon, in an open car. The
enthusiasm with which Lord Balfour was received was indescribable.

In Herzl Street stood a group of Jewish women from Poland, weeping for joy; now and again one of them would press forward and gently touch either the body of the car or Lord Balfour's sleeve, and pronounce a blessing on him. He was obviously deeply affected. The car moved forward slowly; complete order prevailed; and in due course we reached "Balfour Street," which Lord Balfour was to open. Here he was greeted by representatives of the municipality, and the short ceremony followed. Then we moved on to the Herzliah High School, where the students staged a gymnastic display which greatly impressed the Balfour party. With one voice they made two comments: "These boys might have come from Harrow!" And "Mr. Dizengoff might easily be the mayor of Liverpool or of Manchester!" Both remarks were intended—and taken—as the highest compliments.

After tea we adjourned to the quarters prepared for the party in Shmarya Levin's old house, which had been vacated for the purpose. Everything was ready there, including a staff of servants and a guard, and we left Balfour and his party to recover from a rather strenuous day. I arranged to call on them in the morning.

Later in the evening I thought I would like to see how things were round about the Levin house, and strolled in that direction. But a cordon of young men, on guard, shut off the whole neighborhood. Even I could not get within three hundred yards of the gate. This was only in part for security reasons; the idea was mainly to keep off the noise of the crowd, which showed little disposition to go home to bed. Balfour told me the next morning that he had had a quiet night, so the precautions seem to have been effective.

We set out that day on a short tour of the Judaean colonies—Rishon and Petach Tikvah—then turned north to Haifa, where Balfour had another wonderful reception at the Technical Institute (opened almost simultaneously with the University). We went on into the Emek. On the way to Nahalal we passed a hill crowned with a newly erected barracks, round which clustered a number of people who looked like recently arrived refugees. They made a striking group. We discovered that they were *Chassidim*, who, led by their Rabbi (the Rabbi of Yablon) had landed in Palestine only a few days before. Many of them had since then been compelled to sleep in the open, which in spite of the light rains still to be expected in April, they were finding a wonderful experience. Balfour alighted from the car and went into the barracks to receive the blessings of the Rabbi. I told him that if he would come again in a year or two he would find quite a different picture: he would find these people established on their own land, content, and looking like peasants descended from generations of peasants.

The tour prolonged itself to include a number of places not originally contemplated. Balfour talked to the settlers everywhere—at least to

those who could understand English. He also met some of the Arab
sheikhs who came in from near-by villages. He was impressed by the
looks and bearing of the settlers: upright, sunburned, quiet, completely
self possessed—entirely different from the nervous deportment of the
urbanized Jew. The children, too, were obviously village children, sons
and daughters of the soil, simple, modest, without affectation, and of an
infectious gaiety. Lord Balfour showed a lively interest in everything
and everybody. He wanted to understand these people, their lives, their
requirements, their budget, how they managed without money or personal possessions, how they kept their relations with the outside world
so simple, how they managed to live in virtually self-contained villages,
what sort of intellectual life they had, what music they played, what
books they read. Toward the end of the trip he said to me: "I think the
early Christians must have been a little like these men." He added:
"They fit quite remarkably into this landscape."

The trip ended in Nazareth, into which we came one glorious evening
under a full moon. The Balfour party was leaving the next morning for
Syria, and I was returning to Haifa to join my mother for Passover,
so this was really farewell. I remember walking that last night with
Edward Lascelles along the road out of Nazareth, and our being accosted
by two or three Arab youths anxious to offer their services as guides
to the city. As it was night, we said we would perhaps meet them the
next day. They then entered into conversation with us, and told us in
their rather curious English that there had just arrived in Nazareth a
very great Jew, Mr. Balfour. We tried to persuade them that they were
mistaken in this, but they were quite sure that he was a Jew, and had
come to "hand over" Palestine to the Jews. It was all said quite without
bitterness, indeed lightly, and half-banteringly. One could only reflect
that Arab propaganda had already made considerable progress.

At dinner that evening a discussion arose as to whether Lord Balfour
should go to Damascus by car, or take the train as had been arranged.
I protested vigorously against the suggested change. I did not think it
safe for him to travel by car to Syria; besides, the French authorities
under Sarrail had given every guarantee for the train journey, and the
train would be waiting at the frontier. It had been hard enough in Palestine to take all the measures needed for security, and there we had regular
co-operation with the authorities, in addition to thousands of young men
prepared to maintain order both in the towns and on the roads. Nothing
of this applied in Syria. Quite an argument developed between Mrs.
Lascelles and me, and once or twice she hinted that I was exploiting her
uncle for purposes of propaganda. This was just what I had been doing
my level best to avoid. I had all the time been trying to protect him
from such "exploitation"—it was he who had objected to my well-meant
efforts at restriction. In the end Mrs. Lascelles appealed to Balfour

himself, who had listened to the whole conversation without giving the slightest indication of his own views, and he said: "Well, I suppose we shall have to obey Weizmann's orders; after all, we must be imposing a great strain on him." So the original program was followed.

I had sent my secretary, Miss Lieberman, on to Beyrouth ahead of the party, to report to me how things were going there. The next morning I heard from her on the phone, and received the whole story of the violent demonstration which brought the Balfour visit to an abrupt end almost before it began: how crowds tried to storm the Victoria Hotel; how Sarrail had had to smuggle the party away, and send it by fast car to the boat.

We were deeply chagrined that the visit which had gone off so harmoniously in Palestine should have closed so unpleasantly in Syria, but were thankful that nothing worse had happened than the cancellation of the party's plans. I went down to Alexandria to meet the *Sphinx* and to tell Lord Balfour how sorry I was about the incidents in Beyrouth. He replied placidly: "Oh, I wouldn't worry about that—nothing compared with what I went through in Ireland!" From Alexandria, too, he wrote me a charming letter of thanks for the Palestine visit. In it he said: "The main purpose of my visit was the opening of the Hebrew University. But the highest intellectual and moral purposes can be only partially successful if, parallel with them, there is not a strong material development. This is why I was particularly happy to see the flourishing Jewish settlements which testify to the soundness and strength of the growing National Home."

In the weeks that followed I thought over the question of the opening ceremony, and the criticisms which it had provoked, both before and after. Even Dr. Magnes, about to become the head of the University, inclined to deprecate the ceremony as too much of a "political act." I did not see why it was a "political act" or, if it was, why it should lose any value thereby. It may be that the creation of any great institution in Palestine—or anywhere else, for that matter—is always a political act. The very existence of the Jewish National Home was a political act. But I gathered from Dr. Magnes that the words had a derogatory meaning. Other critics said that there was not enough of the University to justify this "enormous display" and the "solemnity" of the inauguration. Up to a point I agreed. In fact, we had not a real university; we had the germ of a university. It was like the Jewish National Home itself: small, but with great potentialities. It had seemed to me that what was needed was some strong stimulus to galvanize the whole thing into new life, and that the formal opening had something of the effect intended was shown by the fact that funds began to flow in very shortly afterward from all quarters—sometimes from quarters till then indifferent to Palestinian affairs. Externally, too, the opening ceremony made a profound impression. Scientists and scholars from abroad had traveled through the country and seen for themselves what was being done there. Many who had previously been skeptical had revised their views in the face of the facts. Among them were Rappard and Allenby. Though by no means unfriendly, Rappard had on the whole been critical, and it was certainly a surprise to him to find so marked a revival, both of the people and the land, within so short a period. Allenby was, if anything, even more deeply impressed. He had said openly at the beginning that he had been rather against the whole enterprise as impractical; now he had come to believe both in the Jewish National Home and also in its importance to the British Empire.

Again, the ceremony had served as a link with friends, Jewish and non-Jewish, in the Diaspora. Many non-Jewish learned societies held meetings on the same day: in Paris, for instance, a distinguished gathering, headed by Léon Blum, Painlevé and others, sent us messages of greeting; others came from New York, Chicago, Stockholm and—unthinkable as it may seem today—from Berlin, Frankfurt and Leipzig.

Today, less than a quarter of a century after the opening ceremony, we have on Scopus a full-fledged University, comparable in most respects with the ancient homes of learning of Western Europe. It is rapidly approaching completion, insofar as a university may ever be said to approach completion, and if not for the war would already have gained for itself no small reputation. Looking back now, I really believe that this rapid development would not have come to pass without the great impetus given to the idea on April 1, 1925, when Balfour stood, like a prophet of old, on Mount Scopus, and proclaimed to the world that here a great seat of learning was being created—seeing far beyond the few small buildings which then formed the skeleton of the university of the future.

I have said that for me the opening of the Hebrew University was the highlight of a period of labor and anxiety, of alternating disappointment and achievement, during which the foundations of the Jewish National Home were being laid. The more dramatic events, and the more spectacular achievements, of later years have dimmed the memory of the era preceding 1929 and obscured its significance; but if there is today a powerful *Yishuv* in Palestine and a great Zionist movement in the world, their existence and character can be understood only against the background of the early struggle.

The first shadows of the eclipse of Jewish life in Europe were already visible. Hitler made his brief and inglorious debut on the German scene in 1923; in 1924 *Mein Kampf* was published, with its outright declaration of war on the Jewish people. Similar stirrings were noticeable in

Rumania, Hungary and Poland. Most of us have since forgotten these earlier manifestations, and few of us gave them their proper evaluation at the time. But a handful of persons—these mostly in our movement— gave warning even then. Sokolow's speech at the 1923 Congress was devoted mainly to the rise of the new anti-Semitism, and we all knew that he was very far from being a scaremonger.

Side by side with these portents, there was a general diminution in the political status of the Jewish National Home. In England the attacks on the Mandate policy for Palestine continued, both in the Lords and in the Commons. The policy naturally had its defenders, too, but what disturbed us most was the evidence of a constant tendency on the part of the British Government to shift the emphasis from the dynamic aspect of the Mandate to the static. Instead of viewing the Jewish National Home as an institution in the making it seemed to be placing increasing emphasis on the status quo in Palestine. The White Paper of 1922, which removed Trans-Jordan arbitrarily from the operation of the Mandate, proposed for Palestine "a Legislative Council with a majority of elected members." Carried out to the full, this would have meant handing over Palestine to the Arab majority and excluding world Jewry, the partner to the Balfour Declaration, from a say in the destinies of Palestine. The legislative council was never set up; but in 1923 we faced another proposal of the same kind. The British Government offered the Arabs an "Arab Agency," presumably intended as a sort of counterpoise to the "Jewish Agency" provided for in the Mandate. It was difficult to see what functions such an agency would discharge, for it would clearly not represent anyone but the Arabs of Palestine (if them), but it may have been felt that it would please the Arabs to feel that they had, at least in name, equal status with world Jewry, in respect to Palestine. The Government had informed us that they would proceed with this offer of an Arab Agency only if both parties, the Arabs and the Jews, agreed to it. As it happens the Arabs turned it down on sight.

In all these actions we were placed in the curious position of seeming to oppose democratic rights to the Arabs. Only those who had some notion of the structure of Arab life understood how farcical was the proposal to vest political power in the hands of the small Arab upper class in the name of democracy. But of this I shall have much more to say further on. What mattered more, at the time, was the insidious exclusion, by implication, of the relationship between Palestine and world Jewry.

The notion of the "duality of the Mandate," of equal weight being given to the Arabs of Palestine as against the entire Jewish people, crept into the reports of the Mandates Commission, too. In October 1924, the Mandates Commission issued this statement:

. . . the policy of the Mandatory Power as regards immigration gives rise to acute controversy. It does not afford entire satisfaction to the Zionists, who feel that the establishment of a Jewish National Home is the first duty of the Mandatory Power, and manifest a certain impatience at the restrictions which are placed in the way of immigration and in respect of the granting of land to immigrants. This policy is, on the other hand, rejected by the Arab majority of the country, which refuses to accept the idea of a Jewish National Home, and regards the action of the Administration as a menace to its traditional patrimony . . .

The implication here is that the policy in regard to Palestine should include only the Arab minority and the Jewish minority confronting each other in the country—a policy which would have completely nullified the Balfour Declaration.

The attitude of the Mandates Commission undoubtedly owed something to its President, at that time an Italian, the Marquis Theodoli, a definite opponent of the Zionist movement, who had married into an Arab family. However, that first report of the Mandates Commission was for us a warning of how little Zionist aims and aspirations were understood even by those called upon to supervise the administration. It was obvious that a special task lay before us, namely, to explain to the League of Nations, its members, and its organs in Geneva, the fundamental principles, political, ethical and historical, which guided the Zionist movement. We decided to open an office in Geneva, under the guidance of Dr. Victor Jacobson. Gradually succeeding sessions of the Mandates Commission were to show traces of its effect. My own contacts with the leading personalities of the Mandates Commission were, I believe, also of value.

These external difficulties were reflected in the internal stresses of the Zionist Organization which, as a democratic institution, gave full play to the possibilities of an opposition. I faced prolonged and often bitter attacks at the Conferences and Congresses; and I used to complain, half-seriously, that if our movement had no other attribute of a government, it had at least the first prerequisite—an opposition.

Jabotinsky withdrew from the Executive shortly after the issuance of the White Paper of 1922, which he denounced, though he had, like the rest of his fellow-members, signed the letter of acceptance. He proceeded to establish the Revisionist Party, which ultimately became "The New Zionist Organization," to provide the necessary platform. He attacked me for what he called my "Fabian" tactics, and insufficient energy and enterprise: "We have always to fight the British Government." It was rather odd that he should also have attacked me for arranging the opening ceremony of the Hebrew University. He accused me of throwing dust in the eyes of the public, and described it as a tawdry performance

—an "imitation whale made of wood." It was, according to him, a combination of political arrogance and sickening hysteria. Strong words—but not quite in keeping with the other accusation of lack of energy and enterprise.

Ussishkin, too, went into opposition. At the Actions Committee meeting which preceded the Congress of 1923, he subjected the conduct of our affairs to an extremely critical review, and marshaled a series of facts concerning the attitude of the British administration in Palestine and the difficulties resulting from it—all of which he laid at my door. Kisch, Sokolow and I could only urge in reply that we were quite as aware of all this as Mr. Ussishkin, and had taken every possible step both in London and Jerusalem to improve matters. Sometimes we had succeeded, sometimes not; but we were certainly not conscious of any sins of omission in this respect. When we asked what Mr. Ussishkin and his friends would have done in our place, the reply was: "Protest! Demand! Insist!" And that seemed to be the ultimate wisdom to be gleaned from our critics. They seemed quite unaware that the constant repetition of protests, demands and insistences defeats its own ends, being both futile and undignified. I emphasized once more that the only real answer to our difficulties in Palestine was the strengthening of our position by bringing in the right type of immigrant in larger numbers, by acquiring more land, by speeding up our productive work.

I realized, even then, that I had to argue in a vicious circle: in order to get the good will of the Government we had to hasten the work of development; but in order to hasten the work of development we desperately needed the active good will of the Government. This dilemma has faced us, from one angle or another, throughout the last thirty years, and I have often thought how much easier life would be if one had to deal only with single-pronged problems, and not with the twin horns of a dilemma.

The very painful debate with Ussishkin ended in his resignation from the Executive and Kisch's appointment in his stead. We were all deeply sorry about it, and I was much distressed to hear later from Kisch that Ussishkin's comment had been: "I am going now—but I shall come back as President of the Organization." This did not in fact happen, but Ussishkin continued to play a prominent part in our councils, and later accepted the Presidency of the Jewish National Fund; as time went on, the breach between us slowly healed.

These, then, were the struggles I faced within the Organization. They centered on relations with England, relations with the non-Zionist groups of the Agency-in-the-making, methods of colonization, the co-operative versus the individualist colonies, private enterprise versus the national funds, urban versus rural growth. And throughout it all the foundations of the National Home were slowly being laid. We went through very hard times in 1926, 1927 and part of 1928. The big influx of 1925, with its large proportion of small capitalists, produced the crisis which I had feared and warned against. The signs were there by the end of that year; by 1926 there were six thousand unemployed in Palestine, and by 1927 a thousand more. There were strikes, lockouts and clashes between employers and workers. And always there was the shortage of funds, the failure of the wealthier elements in Jewry to respond. But underneath it all there was a steady organic growth, often invisible at first. When the economic crisis came to an end in 1928 the Jewish population had tripled since the close of the war; it stood at close to one hundred and seventy thousand. Unemployment had vanished. The lands of the Jewish National Fund had increased until they had the lead over the old, rich PICA. The most dreadful feature of the depression had been a reversal in the migratory movement; in 1927 there were three thousand more emigrants than immigrants—a startling portent. By 1928 the stream had again been reversed, and it continued to swell. We could begin to draw breath.

Our relations with the Arabs were, on the surface at least, not altogether unsatisfactory. The small upper level which constituted the backing of the so-called Arab Executive continued its protests and propaganda abroad; within Palestine there was quiet. Thousands of Arab workmen were employed by Jewish farmers, and thousands more made a good livelihood selling produce to the Jews.

Sir Herbert Samuel relinquished his post as High Commissioner in 1925, and was succeeded by Field Marshal Lord Plumer, whose prestige and authority did much to discourage any mischief which the Arab agitators were planning. Typical of his attitude is the following story.

During Plumer's High Commissionership the Jewish community decided to transfer the regimental colors of the Jewish Battalion of World War I from London to Jerusalem. The colors arrived in due course, and permission was granted by the High Commissioner to carry them in solemn procession to the Great Synagogue of Jerusalem. As soon as the Arab leaders heard of this, they became greatly agitated and betook themselves in a crowd to see Lord Plumer and to remonstrate with him. His ADC reported to him that there was a biggish crowd of Arabs in the hall, waiting to see him, to which Plumer said: "Will you kindly tell the Arab gentlemen that I have twelve chairs, and they might elect twelve speakers. Then I could see them in comfort." This was done, and the speakers entered. In their usual manner the Arab leaders began to protest and threaten, saying that if the procession took place they could not be responsible for order in the city. To which Plumer promptly remarked: "You are not asked to be responsible, gentlemen; I shall be responsible—and I shall be there."

It was done in the grand manner, and it was effective. This is how a determined administrator speaks politely and firmly to political mischief makers, and thwarts their intentions without resorting to a display of force. Of course one has to be a Plumer to carry it off, and Plumer remained with us less than three years—all too short a period. He was succeeded by Sir John Chancellor, a man of much smaller caliber.

. During all those years I spent the bulk of my time traveling, sometimes accompanied by my wife, sometimes alone, when she did not feel she could leave the children, who resented my constant absence. I was actually at home only for short intervals between trips to America, Palestine, Germany, France, Holland and Belgium, not to speak of my attendance at various international conferences. I was trying to build up the movement, making contacts with governments and Jewish communities, and in the process acquiring a good many friendships in political, literary and scientific circles in different countries. I came to feel almost equally at home in Brussels or Paris or San Francisco. But in the late summer or early autumn of every year there were a carefully engineered few weeks which I spent with my wife and family on holiday.

They were quiet holidays, and always much the same: a village in the mountains of Switzerland or the Tyrol, long walks in the hills among the rocks and glaciers, till I felt I knew almost every stone and rock by name; and then, as the weather in the heights deteriorated, we would go down for a few days to Merano, to a small sanatorium. Merano had an attraction of its own; in those days it was off the beaten track, never overrun with tourists, enjoying an almost perfect climate, especially in the autumn. It was beautiful, too, full of orchards and vineyards. Moreover, it had admirable funicular railways, by which one could reach altitudes of five or six thousand feet in a short time. So most of my days were spent there walking in the mountains, enjoying the pure air and the wonderful scenery, and returning at sunset to the sanatorium, refreshed and invigorated.

Thus I managed to get a few weeks off for real rest and relaxation with my family every year. Often attempts were made to get me back to London or elsewhere before the allotted time was up, but I always refused to budge. My holiday was sacrosanct, devoted entirely to my wife and children, and I grudged every interruption, however urgent. I still believe that without these few weeks of absolute quiet I would never have been able to carry the burden during the rest of the year. Very occasionally I would also manage a break of a week or ten days in the winter, spent as a rule in Switzerland; but this, when I got it, was much more subject to interruptions. Most winters I spent in America or Palestine, hard at work.

CHAPTER 29

Attack and Repulse

The Riots of 1929—Their Political Significance—Death of Louis Marshall—The Shaw Commission Report Whitewashes the Palestine Administration—The Simpson Report and the Passfield White Paper—Warburg, Melchett, and I resign from Jewish Agency—The Struggle with the Colonial Office—We Receive Strong Non-Jewish Backing—Misinterpreting the Mandate to Exclude World Jewry—The Pose of Neutrality —Retraction of the White Paper in Ramsay Macdonald's Letter —Sir Arthur Wauchope Appointed High Commissioner— Consequences—Failure of Arab "Strategy."

THE first constituent meeting of the Jewish Agency opened in Zurich on August 11, 1929, and the agreement between the Zionists and the non-Zionists was signed on the fourteenth. This meeting followed close on the Sixteenth Zionist Congress, held in the same city; its opening, in fact, coincided with the close of the Congress, which had lasted from July 28 to August 11. By the time the last business of Congress and Agency had been cleared away I was quite exhausted, for I had come to Zurich still suffering from the aftereffects of a protracted illness.

I was exhausted but happy. What the founding of the Agency meant to the Zionist movement, what hopes I reposed in it, what labor I had put into its creation, has already been indicated. I looked forward to, and I needed, one of those holidays which I have described at the end of the last chapter; and on August 23 my wife and I left Zurich for Wengen, in Berner-Oberland, Switzerland to join our son Michael. I remember well the happiness which I felt during the three-hour ride, and the sense of peace and achievement which filled me. I felt free from care, I anticipated confidently a future which would witness a great acceleration in the upbuilding of the National Home.

We reached Wengen in the evening, and for the whole of the following day I rested. I tried not to think of the hard years through which we had passed. I did not even look at a newspaper. On the second morning I was awakened by the hotel boy, who brought me a telegram. The envelope was bulky, and I had an instant premonition that it brought bad news. I did not expect any business telegrams. I had separated from my friends less than two days before, and I knew they had all dispersed for their holidays. What could this bulky telegram mean? Only bad news from Palestine. For several minutes I refused to open it, and then I gave way. It began with the words "The Under Secretary of State regrets to announce . . ." and brought me the first news of the Palestine pogroms of 1929, in which nearly a hundred and fifty Jews were killed, hundreds more wounded, and great property damage done.

I was struck as by a thunderbolt. This, then, was the answer of the Arab leadership to the Congress and the Agency meeting. They had realized that our fortunes had taken an upward turn, that the speed of our development in Palestine would soon follow the same curve. The way to prevent that, they thought—wrongly, as we all know now—was a blood bath. The means used to precipitate the riots, the appeal to religious fanaticism, the whipping up of blind mob passions, the deliberate misrepresentation of Zionist aims—all this I shall not dwell on here. It is in the record. In the record too is the story of that mixture of indifference, inefficiency, and hostility on the part of the Palestine administration which had helped give the Arab leaders their opportunity.

I began telephoning to London, but all my friends were away. I could only reach Mrs. Philip Snowden, wife of the Chancellor of the Exchequer, who tried to comfort me. I felt I could not stay on in Wengen. We made arrangements for the care of the children, and left for London. On the day of our departure we learned that Louis Marshall, who was still in Zurich, was gravely ill and would have to submit to a dangerous operation. Soon after our arrival in London we received the news of his death. This was the second blow.

It is difficult to convey the state of depression into which I was cast. The Colonial Secretary of that time, Lord Passfield (the former Sidney Webb) had shown extremely little sympathy for our cause, and was very reluctant to see me on my arrival in London. I had a conversation, at his house, with Lady Passfield (the former Beatrice Webb), in the presence of Josiah Wedgwood who, in those days, as always, stood stanchly with us. What I heard from Lady Passfield was: "I can't understand why the Jews make such a fuss over a few dozen of their people killed in Palestine. As many are killed every week in London in traffic accidents, and no one pays any attention."

When at last I managed to see Passfield and his friends in the Colonial Office I realized at once that they would use this opportunity to curtail Jewish immigration into Palestine. I tried next to see Ramsay MacDonald, the Socialist Prime Minister, but in spite of the efforts of his son, Malcolm, who was extremely sympathetic to our cause until he in turn became Colonial Secretary—a familiar story, this—no interview could be arranged. In fact I did not see Ramsay MacDonald until much later, when he was attending a meeting of the League Council in Geneva.

Meanwhile the machinery was set in motion for the political attack on our position in Palestine. First came the Shaw Commission, sent out to Palestine two months after the riots, to inquire into their "immediate causes" and to make recommendations for the future maintenance of peace. The report which it brought in some months later merely conceded that the Arabs had been the attackers; but it said nothing about the strange behavior of the Palestine administration which during the attacks had issued one communiqué after another representing the riots as "clashes" between Jews and Arabs. From these communiqués it was made to appear that there were two peoples at war in Palestine, with the British administration as the neutral guardian of law and order. Apart from the gross misrepresentation of the Jewish attitude which such utterances impressed on the world, the implied exoneration of the Arab mobs and their inciters boded ill for the future. I have said that the Haycraft Report of 1921 contained the seed of much of our later troubles. Here were some of the fruits.

Then came the Simpson Report. Sir John Hope Simpson and his commission were sent out to Palestine in May 1930, to look into the problems of immigration, land settlement, and development. But before the report was issued, together with what is now called the Passfield White Paper, the Government declared publicly that it intended to suspend immigration, introduce restrictive land legislation, curtail the authority of the Jewish Agency and in general introduce in Palestine a regime which made the appointment of the Simpson Commission either a superfluity or a propaganda instrument for the Government's predetermined policy.

I managed at last to see the Prime Minister. My wife and I had gone to Geneva. During the channel crossing we met Lady Astor, whose attitude toward our work was at that time friendly. I put our case before her, and expressed my desire to see MacDonald, in the hope of obtaining from him a promise that the proposed negative legislation should not be put into effect. In Geneva an interview with the Prime Minister was arranged, and in a long conversation with him I did obtain what seemed to be a satisfactory statement. I saw other statesmen in Geneva, Briand among them, and many of them promised me their support.

There was another meeting with the Prime Minister that spring, with the late Lord Reading, Lord Melchett, Pinchas Rutenberg and myself for our side, and Mr. MacDonald, Lord Passfield and a group of senior officials for the Government. I came to that meeting with a special grievance, the nature of which indicated the depth and persistence of Passfield's hostility. He had promised to have Simpson see me before he left for Palestine, and then had broken the promise deliberately. In a very polite way I charged Passfield openly with a breach of faith. His Lordship never said a word or moved a muscle. I added one strong sentence. I said: "One thing the Jews will never forgive, and that is having been fooled." The Prime Minister smiled, and it also brought out a broad grin on the faces of the officials. Thereupon I turned to them and said: "I can't understand how you, as good British patriots, don't see the moral implications of promises given to Jews, and I regret to see that you seem to deal with them rather frivolously." The grin disappeared.

It was curious to see how little the Prime Minister seemed to realize the inconsistency of the new course with the letter and spirit of the Mandate. And curious too was the spate of reassurances which he offered us—as he offered them to Mr. Felix Warburg in a meeting they had at Chequers. If either of us took those assurances seriously, he was doomed to be bitterly disappointed. On October 21, 1930, the Government published, simultaneously, the Hope Simpson report and the White Paper.

This is not the place for an analysis of the Passfield White Paper. Suffice it to say that it was considered by all Jewish friends of the National Home, Zionist and non-Zionist alike, and by a host of non-Jewish well-wishers, as rendering, and intending to render, our work in Palestine impossible. There was nothing left for me but to resign my position as the President of the Jewish Agency. In this drastic step I had the complete support of Lord Melchett and of Felix Warburg, who also resigned, the former as the chairman of the Council of the Agency, the latter as a member of the Jewish Agency Administrative Committee.

Then began an intense struggle with the Colonial Office which, having been unable to guarantee the security of the Jewish community in Palestine, having ignored our repeated warnings concerning the activities of the Mufti and of his friends of the Arab Executive, having made no attempt to correct the indifference or hostility of British officials in Palestine, now proposed to make us pay the price of its failure. We realized that we were facing a hostile combination of forces in the Colonial Office and in the Palestine administration, and unless it was overcome it was futile to think of building on the foundations which we had laid so solidly in the previous years.

There were, of course, great protests throughout the Jewish world; they were backed by powerful figures in the non-Jewish world. Stanley Baldwin, Sir Austen Chamberlain, Leopold Amery, General Smuts, Sir John Simon, and a host of others, all from various points of view, attacked the Passfield White Paper as inconsistent with the Mandate which Great Britain had been given in Palestine. Apparently the Prime Minister had anticipated an unfavorable reaction, but not the force and volume of it. A few days before the issuance of the White Paper he had, perhaps with the idea of heading off my protests, invited the

Jewish Agency to appoint a committee which should consult with a special Cabinet Committee on the Palestine policy. We accepted—but that did not prevent my resignation, nor the resignations of Lord Melchett and Mr. Warburg.

On the Cabinet Committee there were, among others, Arthur Henderson as chairman, and Malcolm MacDonald as secretary. On our side, besides myself, were Leonard Stein, Harry Sacher, Harold Laski, James de Rothschild, Professor Brodetsky and Professor Namier. On this joint committee we fought back and forth throughout that winter. There were two major points which we sought to establish as the firm basis of all future action on the part of the British Government. The first was intended to counteract the growing tendency to regard the Mandate as something applying only to the Jews in Palestine as against the Arabs in Palestine. I put it thus: "If the obligation of the Mandatory is reduced to an obligation toward one hundred and seventy thousand people as against seven hundred thousand people, a small minority juxtaposed to a great majority, then of course everything else can perhaps be explained. But the obligation of the Mandatory Power is toward the Jewish people of which the one hundred and seventy thousand are merely the vanguard. I must take issue, as energetically as I can, with the formulation of the obligation of the Mandatory Power as an obligation toward both sections of the Palestine population." The second point issued from the first, and was directed against the conception that the Jewish National Home could be crystallized at the stage which it had then reached.

A third point might be considered as having been raised by the first. I quote again from the minutes of one of the sessions: "In paragraph ten of the White Paper," I said, "it is stated that 'incitements to disorder or disaffection will be severely punished in whatever quarter they may originate.'" I saw in that paragraph the influence of the Palestine administration, with its attitude of "neutrality" between two hostile and two equally guilty sections of the population. I said: "Obviously the intention of the author of the White Paper was to balance his statements. If anything is said against the Arabs, something must be said against the Jews, or vice versa. I think His Majesty's Government must be well aware that there is only one quarter from which disaffection, disorder, violence and massacre have originated. We do not massacre; we were the victims of a murderous onslaught. Not one Arab leader has raised his voice against the inhuman treatment meted out to the unfortunate victims."

Lord Passfield was present at some of the committee sessions and proved to be the head and fount of the opposition to our demands. What effect our arguments had on the Government, and how much the change was due to the pressure of an adverse public opinion in England and elsewhere I cannot say. But on February 13, 1931, there was an official reversal of policy. It did not take the form of a retraction of the White Paper—that would have meant a loss of face—but of a letter addressed to me by the Prime Minister, read in the House of Commons and printed in Hansard. I considered that the letter rectified the situation —the form was unimportant—and I so indicated to the Prime Minister.

I was to be bitterly attacked in the Zionist Congress of that year for accepting a letter in place of another White Paper. But whether I was right or not in my acceptance may be judged by a simple fact: it was under MacDonald's letter to me that the change came about in the Government's attitude, and in the attitude of the Palestine administration, which enabled us to make the magnificent gains of the ensuing years. It was under MacDonald's letter that Jewish immigration into Palestine was permitted to reach figures like forty thousand for 1934 and sixty-two thousand for 1935, figures undreamed of in 1930. Jabotinsky, the extremist, testifying before the Shaw Commission, had set thirty thousand a year as a satisfactory figure.

The first indication that I had of the seriousness of MacDonald's intentions was when he consulted me with regard to the appointment of a new High Commissioner to replace Sir John Chancellor. He said he realized how much depended on the choice of the man, and added, "I would like to appoint a General, but one who does it with his head, not his feet." The next High Commissioner for Palestine was Sir Arthur Wauchope, who assumed office in 1931, and under whom the country made its greatest advance.

Two remarks may be added regarding the riots of 1929 and the Passfield White Paper. The riots were the strongest effort made up till that time by the Arab leaders to frighten us, by mob action, from continuing with our work in Palestine. They failed. And if the riots were intended, whatever their effect on our nerves, to overthrow the structure of the National Home, they came too late. We had built too solidly and too well.

Similarly, the Passfield White Paper may be regarded as the most concerted effort—until the White Paper of 1939—on the part of a British Government to retract the promise made to the Jewish people in the Balfour Declaration. That attack, too, was successfully repulsed. The solid structure of the National Home in the making was paralleled by the solid support we had in public opinion. That there is an organic relationship between the two is the essence of my "political" philosophy. Had we, in the years between 1922 and 1929, concentrated on obtaining statements, declarations, charters and promises, to the neglect of our physical growth, we should perhaps not have been able to withstand the sheer physical shock of the riots. Then the political assault would have found no resistance either in us or in public opinion. The dismal incidents of 1929 and 1930 were a severe test of our system and methods, which emerged triumphant.

CHAPTER 30

Demission

Zionist Congress of 1931—Revisionists and Mizrachi *Head Opposition—Vote of No Confidence—The Meaning of the Struggle—"Short Cut" Versus Organic Growth—Sokolow Elected President—I Return to Science—Richard Willstatter's Kindness—Scientific Work for Palestine—The Laboratory in Holborn—No Getting Away from Zionist Work—Colonial Trust in Difficulties—I Accept Presidency of English Zionist Federation—Other Obligations—Refugee Work and Youth Aliyah—Sir Arthur Wauchope.*

I COME now to an incident in my life on which I look back with little pleasure, and write about with some distaste: my demission from the Presidency of the Zionist Organization at the Congress in July 1931.

In spite of the fact that the Ramsay MacDonald letter had restored our political position and initiated a period of peace, prosperity and great immigration into Palestine, the excitement originally created by the Passfield White Paper continued to exercise the minds of the Zionists, and particularly of the Revisionists, led by Jabotinsky. The latter spoke of the letter contemptuously, in part because it was only a letter; they demanded British official endorsement of a clear-cut Revisionist policy, and the acceptance of anything short of that maximum—which meant a Jewish State on both sides of the Jordan, with all that this implies—they declared to be political weakness, cowardice and betrayal. As the Congress of 1931 approached I became the butt of ever-mounting attacks, and the occasion for a pernicious extremist propaganda. I held my ground and continued to point out that in a movement like ours the center of gravity is not an exaggerated political program, but work—colonization, education, immigration, and the maintenance of decent relations with the Mandatory Power. Important, too, was the enlightenment of public opinion in Britain, America and the rest of the world as to our aims and aspirations; this could not result from confusing the issues by impractical demands which excited the Arabs and helped to precipitate troubles which affected the attitude of the Mandatory Power.

My admonitions were in vain. The politicians at the Congress were determined to initiate a debate on "the ultimate aims of the Zionist

337

movement" as if that had any relevance at the moment, and as if any sort of declaration would increase our strength or achievements by one iota. It is difficult to say if this debate was meant sincerely, and was the expression of a desire to fix the Zionist program for all time, and to provide guidance for future generations, or whether it was simply a means to provoke my opposition, and thus facilitate my resignation from office. If the latter, it was the more unjust—I permit myself to say even indecent—in that I announced, in my opening address, my intention of resigning because of the precarious state of my health, which was patent to everybody. My doctors had, in fact, remonstrated with me severely on the dangers of even attending the Congress.

In spite of this, the Congress insisted on going through the motion of passing a resolution of nonconfidence in my policy by a roll-call vote, in which the Revisionists under Jabotinsky took the leading part, with the *Mizrachi*, the religious wing of the movement, strongly supporting.

The conflict which thus reached an unnecessary denouement had of course been going on in the movement for years: It was the conflict between those who believed that Palestine can be built up only the hard way, by meticulous attention to every object, who believed that in this slow and difficult struggle with the marshes and rocks of Palestine lies the great challenge to the creative forces of the Jewish people, its redemption from the abnormalities of exile, and those who yielded to those very abnormalities, seeking to live by a sort of continuous miracle, snatching at occasions as they presented themselves, and believing that these accidental smiles of fortune constitute a real way of life. I felt that all these political formulas, even if granted to us by the powers that were, would be no use to us, might possibly even be harmful as long as they were not the product of hard work put into the soil of Palestine. Nahalal, Daganiah, the University, the Rutenberg electrical works, the Dead Sea Concession, meant much more to me politically than all the promises of great governments or great political parties. It was not lack of respect for governments and parties, nor an underrating of the value of political pronouncements. But to me a pronouncement is real only if it is matched by performance in Palestine. The pronouncement depends on others, the performance is entirely our own. This is the essence of my Zionist life. My guiding principle was the famous saying of Goethe:

Was du ererbst von deinen Vätern,
Erwirb es, um es zu besitzen.

The others believed only in the *Erbe*, and therefore were always claiming their rights; they wanted the easy road, the road paved with the promises of others. I believed in the path trodden out by our own feet, however wounded the feet might be.

I said to the Congress: "The walls of Jericho fell to the sound of shouts and trumpets. I never heard of walls being raised by that means."

Of course it was not only a theoretical political opposition which I faced. It was also the disappointment of middle-class groups which really believed that but for me they would quickly have transformed Palestine into a land of golden economic opportunity for themselves and thousands of others. To me this too was utter lack of realism. I said to the Congress: "I have heard critics of the Jewish Agency sneer at what they call the old '*Chibath Zion*' policy of 'another dunam and another dunam, another Jew and another Jew, another cow and another goat and two more houses in Gederah.' If there is any other way of building a house save brick by brick, I do not know it. If there is another way of building up a country save dunam by dunam, man by man, and farmstead by farmstead, again I do not know it. One man may follow another, one dunam be added to another, after a long interval or after a short one—that is a question of degree, and determined not by politics alone, but in a far greater degree by economics." And to those critics I again said: "Private capital can establish individual enterprises, but it is for national capital to create conditions," and, "But for the work of the Jewish Agency and the National Funds there would even now be no suggestion of a 'business basis' for the development of Palestine by the operation of natural economic laws, and no prospect of such a development within any measurable period of time."

At this Congress I found myself in a minority, with only the laborites and a few of the general Zionists understanding me. I sat through the whole performance, until the last man had voted. When it was finished, and some tactless person applauded my so-called downfall, the feeling came over me that here and now the tablets of the law should be broken, though I had neither the strength nor the moral stature of the great lawgiver.

I left the hall with my wife and a handful of close friends and went for a stroll in Basle. I was immediately joined by Bialik, very tense and very depressed. He said: "I've been watching the hands which were lifted against you. They were the hands of men whom you have not invited to your house, whom you have not asked to share the company of those you cultivate, the hands of people who have not sat at your dinner table—the hands of those who never understood and never will understand the depths that separate you from them. Don't be sad. What they have done will disappear, what you have done will stand forever." We parted with a friendly embrace and Bialik added: "I have nothing more to do in Basle. I leave the city today."

The curious outcome of the Congress was the election of Sokolow to the Presidency: curious because Sokolow (like Brodetsky and others who were re-elected) had been closely identified with me since 1916, not only in the general line of work but in almost every detail. Jabotinsky had resigned, Dr. Soloveitchik, the Lithuanian delegate, had re-signed: Sokolow had co-operated in loyal agreement. To create an antithesis between Sokolow and me was the height of inanity and showed up the artificiality of the setup. But if I was wryly amused, Jabotinsky was bitterly disappointed. He had always lived in the illusion that I was the one who stood in the way of his ascent to the Presidency. After the vote was taken Jabotinsky sent my wife a little scribble, "I am proud of my friends," meaning us both. My wife wrote back on the scribble: "Thanks for condolences; we are not dead yet." It was Jabotinsky's belief that if I went down, he would go up. And it must have been galling to him to see the election go to Sokolow, for whom he had very little respect—if he did not actually despise him. It was, I think, the feeling of my opponents that the pliability of Sokolow would make it easier for them to give the movement the direction they had in mind.

The break in my life, produced by my demission, was not without its blessings. It was not a complete break, as will soon be evident, but it did relieve me of a vast burden of labor. I tried to fill the vacuum as quickly as possible. I directed my attention to other matters; I felt it would be dangerous for me to indulge in contemplation and resentment and become bitter. I fought against such emotions, though they continued to well up in my subconscious.

I was particularly sorry for my children, who took the turn of events as a bitter affront to their father, who in their opinion had given up the whole of his life to the movement, to their detriment. They had become resigned to a situation which deprived them of my company for long stretches every year, but they were deeply shocked by what they regarded as the ingratitude with which I was rewarded; and they were extremely happy when I announced to them my intention of opening a laboratory in London, and going back to my chemistry, which I had neglected for so many years.

It was, by the way, not an easy decision. I was now in my fifty-eighth year. I had not been in a laboratory—except on a chance visit—for about thirteen years. The science of chemistry had made enormous advances in that time, and I had followed the literature only in a desultory fashion. It was a psychological effort to revert to quiet laboratory work after the stormy and adventurous life of the preceding thirteen years. And if I did know something about the latest developments in science, I had lost contact with practical work and had to become accustomed afresh to manipulating chemical apparatus and carrying out the usual operations. It is difficult to explain to a layman how painful and arduous a task it is to restart this sort of professional occupation in one's mature years, and to refind one's way in the literature of the profession, which in the interval had grown to an immense volume.

But, quite suddenly and unexpectedly, there came to my assistance a guide who, by his authority and kindness, made the transition as pleasant and easy as possible.

It happened that at about that time Professor Richard Willstätter, one of the greatest modern chemists, came to London to receive the Gold Medal of the Royal Society. I had met him only once before, and fleetingly. I discovered in him now a delightful companion and a true friend. His knowledge of chemistry and chemical problems was encyclopedic, and as unlimited as the kindness he showed me. I had been told that he was pedantic and rather *geheimratisch*; he did not make me feel that at all, and I confessed to him all my difficulties. After a severe cross-examination of me, he agreed that we should collaborate on a piece of work in a field which was very familiar to him and on which he had done extensive work. I took over only a small corner of this vast field, and was able after a few years to make something practical of it—a vegetable foodstuff which is now being produced on a considerable scale in America and may shortly be produced in other countries.

Willstätter was consistently helpful to me, and his collaboration not only helped to set me on my feet again, scientifically speaking, but enabled me to see him whenever I was in the vicinity of his city, Munich.

There were two factors which urged me on in this change. First, my intrinsic relation to science, which had been part of my life since my boyhood; second, my feeling that in one way or another it had something to do with the building of Palestine. I was already thinking, then, of a research institute which should work in combination with the Agricultural Experimental Station at Rehovoth—and of something larger, and of wider scope, too. And it was during the period when I was out of office that the Daniel Sieff Research Institute was founded, to be followed many years later by the Weizmann Institute of Science.

The break, I said, was not a complete one. It could not be, of course. There was only a considerable shift of emphasis. I opened up a modest laboratory at 6 Featherstone Buildings, Holborn, in an old house belonging to a friend who had been my patent agent for many years. The laboratory was not particularly well fitted out, but it served my purposes, at least at the beginning. I also linked up again with an old friend and assistant, Mr. H. Davies, who had been with me in Manchester and who had worked with me during the first years of World War I. It began to look again like old times. I enjoyed immensely going to the laboratory every day and returning home in the evening. It reminded me very much of my years at Manchester University. My existence was —at least by comparison with the in-between years—unshackled and untrammeled. The echoes of Zionist problems penetrated only faintly the walls of my laboratory and visitors from the nonscientific world who descended on me there usually got a cold reception. Gradually the useful rumor got around that to visit me in my lab was not the way to get anything out of me.

However, there were plenty of visits from Zionist friends at our home, and plenty of pressure to keep me at Zionist tasks. Indeed, only a few days after the Congress, when we were resting at Bad Gastein, a delegation of the laborites visited me, and urged me to take up the leadership of the opposition. This I refused categorically. But a plea of another kind I could not turn down.

We had spent about two weeks in Bad Gastein, and had gone with the children on to Karersee, a charming spot in the Italian Tyrol above Bolzano. No sooner had we settled down there than I began to receive alarming telegrams from the directorate of The Jewish Colonial Trust in London, the bank of the Zionist Organization, which indicated that it was in an extremely precarious position. It was the middle of the world depression and the bank had practically no liquid assets; if a run came, it might mean ruin, and the majority of the depositors were poorer Jews of the East End of London.

It was suggested to me that I go to Paris and talk to Baron Edmond de Rothschild, urging him to extend a helping hand. I felt I had no right to worry the old gentleman, but it was impossible to refuse the plea of the bank for assistance, and there was no one else to turn to! So I left my holiday resort and traveled a long way to Paris. I went in vain. The Baron said: "All banks are at present in a critical condition. The difference between our bank and others is that ours has no friends to help it through." He pointed out that when we had come to him two years previously asking him to help us meet the educational budget in Palestine, he had given us something like one hundred fifty thousand dollars. But he was not prepared to support a financial instrument which was perhaps being mismanaged. All I got from him on this occasion was the advice to sell whatever securities could be sold—for instance some shares of the Rutenberg Concession—and thus increase the liquidity of the bank.

But my visit was not a dead loss. I discovered while in Paris that the Baron's organization, PICA, owed the Colonial Trust a sum of one hundred thousand dollars, about which the Trust had completely forgotten! Between that and the sale of some securities a margin of liquidity was created for the bank.

Back I went to my family, and we decided to go to Jugoslavia and see the Dalmatian coast. We started out in our car, and got as far as Abbazia, on the Jugoslav frontier. There I found another series of frantic telegrams, imploring me to return to London and take counsel with the directors—or such of them as were not *hors de combat*; for some had fallen ill and others had lost their heads.

I gave way again, and persuaded my family to abandon the Jugoslav tour and go instead to Spain. We knew of a nice, quiet place, Sitges, on the coast near Barcelona. There they would be safe and comfortable, and there I would join them as soon as possible. Meanwhile I set off for London.

There we were able to float a loan on the basis of securities, and another liquid fund of about three hundred thousand dollars was created which enabled the bank to ride out the depression. Today the Jewish Colonial Trust is more secure than it ever was.

I have put in the foregoing incident as a sort of first corrective for any reader who might be under the impression that stepping out of office meant a repudiation of Zionist responsibilities. Actually I had plenty to do outside the laboratory; and my laboratory work, too, soon suffered long interruptions, to the great distress of my children, who considered my absences as dangerous bits of backsliding.

I found it impossible, in those years of crisis—as in fact I had found it impossible in an earlier crisis, that which followed the Kishinev and other pogroms thirty years before—to abstract myself even temporarily from Jewish life. In those days I had no sooner settled to my laboratory work at Manchester University, than I began to seek out the local Zionists. Now, in 1931, and the following years, I had no sooner got into the swing of laboratory routine, than I found myself loaded with outside obligations. I could not refuse the request of the British Zionists to accept the Presidency of their federation. Still less was it possible to withhold my assistance from the Central Bureau for the Settlement of German Jews, created by the Jewish Agency. I became the chairman of that body, and President of Youth Aliyah. In the summer of 1932 I interrupted my scientific work for five months in order to tour South Africa for the Zionist Funds; the Executive was passing through a financial crisis and here again I felt that I could not evade my duty.

Another, shorter interruption occurred the following year. In the spring of 1933 I received a number of urgent telegrams from Meyer W. Weisgal, who was then arranging "Jewish Day" at the Century of Progress Fair in Chicago, offering me one hundred thousand dollars for the refugee funds. All he wanted in exchange was that I should deliver a single address at the celebrations in Chicago. I was very much tempted, both for the sake of the Funds and out of regard for the man.

Weisgal is the foremost of the younger friends I have in America. A man of outstanding ability and integrity, with a phenomenal capacity for work, he finds nothing too difficult to undertake when there is service to be rendered to the movement. In these enterprises he spends himself recklessly, and his loyalty and friendship are equaled only by his energy. He has been a moving spirit in the Zionist movement for many years, and at present is one of the chief initiators of the Weizmann Institute of Science in Palestine. I accepted his offer in 1933, made the round trip of

some eight thousand miles for the sake of a single appearance, and
returned with the addition of one hundred thousand dollars to refugee
funds.

Now I am not going to pretend that all of these assignments were
merely chores. Some of them were, of course; others were not. Our
visit to South Africa, for instance, to which I devote a brief chapter, had
other compensations besides the sums it brought in for the *Keren
Hayesod*. Then there were types of work which, being an amalgam of
Zionist work, German refugee settlement work and scientific work, could
not be wholly described as "interruptions" of the last of these. Such, for
instance, was the creation of the Daniel Sieff Research Institute in
Rehovoth, which I shall describe at some length further on.

I took no part in the inner political struggles of the Zionist Organization and did not even attend the eighteenth Congress, that of 1933.
I was extremely chary of lending color to any accusation that I was
"planning a return," or that I was in any way hampering the activities
of the Executive then in power.

It was with a certain discomfort that I even went to see Sir Arthur
Wauchope, the new High Commissioner for Palestine, before he left to
take up his post in the autumn of 1931, and I did so only at his invitation. I went to him, and later corresponded with him, in my private
capacity as one who had paid more than twenty visits, of varying dura-
tion, to Palestine in the preceding thirteen years, and had some knowledge of the country. After 1935, the year of my return to office, our
contacts were official; but during the period now under review, 1931 to
1935, I saw him either in a private capacity, or as the head of the Sieff
Institute; and it is pleasant, in spite of strong differences which developed between us toward the end of his regime, to pay wholehearted
tribute to him. Sir Arthur was a distinguished administrator and
scholar, perhaps the best High Commissioner Palestine has had, and I
believe, a proof of Ramsay MacDonald's serious effort to undo the harm
of the Passfield White Paper. I cannot doubt that he was given the right
sort of send-off by the Prime Minister, and he happened to be the kind
of man who could be influenced in the right direction. In contradistinc-
tion to previous High Commissioners, he really tried to understand the
moral and ethical values underlying the Zionist movement and the work
in Palestine. He was deeply moved by many features of the life there,
such as the *kibutzim*, and even after he left office he gave frequent
expression to his feelings in England, praising the *kvutzoth* and *kibutzim* as a new way of life which should be emulated in other countries,
England included, even if it meant adapting it to specific English conditions. He was much attracted by certain leaders in the movement, like
young Arlosoroff, and the older Shmarya Levin. He valued greatly the
scientific approach to our agricultural program, and used to be a fre-

quent visitor at the Agricultural Experimental Station in Rehovoth, where he helped endow a laboratory for plant physiology which bears his name.

I believe that the differences which did develop between him and the Zionists toward the end of his regime were owing to the great deterioration in the general policy of England, and in the increasing tendency toward appeasement which set in with the Abyssinian war in 1935, extended to Spain and then reached Palestine. I do not believe that of his own accord Wauchope would have taken the stand he did in certain matters which will be related in their turn. We remember him in Palestine as a friend, an intellectual, a soldier, an administrator, and a statesman.

CHAPTER 31

A Strange National Home

Visit to South Africa—Its Jewish Community—The Remarkable Game Reserve.

SOUTH AFRICA was a new experience for my wife and myself. We were attracted by the idea of a visit to the country of Smuts, who had played such a noble part in the first stages of our movement and whose generous interest had, and has, continued unabated. The official attitude toward us was thoroughly cordial. Smuts and Hertzog and their colleagues received us most kindly. Hertzog was perhaps more formal, Smuts—who was not then in power—treated us as old, trusted friends.

I found myself in an unusual Jewish community scattered over a wide subcontinent in small groups, but united in Zionist spirit. South African Jewry was singularly free from the so-called assimilationist taint. There were practically no German Jews in the country, and the few exceptions were mostly diamond or gold magnates who were isolated or had isolated themselves, and had little or no contact with the majority of Jewry. The Jews of South Africa were preponderantly—in fact almost exclusively—from Kovno, or Vilna, or Minsk and the little places in between these Jewish centers. The townlet of Shavli seems, for some unknown reason, to have provided South Africa with great numbers of Jews—it was a puzzle to me how such a small place could have produced such a large emigration.

The South African Jews were kindly, hard-working, intelligent people, and what one may term organic Zionists. If Russian Jewry had not had its life interrupted by the advent of bolshevism, it would probably have developed on the pattern of South African Jewry. It was a pleasure to watch and hear those Jews. Remote as they were from the great stream of Jewish life, the arrival of a visitor from Europe was a tremendous occasion, and the whole life of the community revolved about the event.

I met many types of modest, quiet workers to whom Zionism was the whole of their existence. There were not too many wealthy individuals, but the average level of prosperity was fair. There were not too many intellectuals among them, either, but the few that one met were genuine and attractive. One found both hospitality and comfort in their company.

From the technical point of view the trip was well organized but extremely trying, as one had to visit small communities scattered over a vast subcontinent. Still, we went religiously through our duties, and at the end were satisfied with the results, which were financially quite considerable.

We had few pauses or relaxations in those five months, but there was one which calls for special and somewhat detailed mention, and that was a visit to the famous game reserve. This is a unique institution. It was founded by Kruger, who had been greatly concerned over the rapid disappearance of the South African fauna due to the habits of the early Dutch settlers, who used to kill wild and tame beasts indiscriminately. He had therefore decided to set aside a territory amounting to something like eight thousand square miles for the preservation of animal life. Within that area the shooting of animals, or their molestation in any way, was forbidden, and they lived a free and unmolested life. And the animals knew their privileges! They walked about in the presence of human beings freely and unconcernedly, and driving through this vast place was one continuous excitement.

Naturally one had to have guides and guns—our guide, and a great expert, was a Lithuanian Jew—but the danger was slight if one did not interfere with the animals. There were no roads in the real sense of the word, but there were so-called summer tracks, and as you drove along casually you could meet anything from a specimen of the famous South African springbok to a python curled up on a tree, or a pride of lions. Or suddenly there would break on your ears the ringing and thundering noise of a herd of elephants on the march. If one was particularly observant one saw something of the social life of the jungle.

So, for instance, I once noticed in passing an old wildebeest, squatting abandoned under a tree. It looked dejected and crestfallen, the very personification—if I may use that word—of melancholy. Struck by its appearance, I asked the guide for the meaning of the phenomenon. He told me that this was an old bull who until a little while ago had been the leader of his herd. He had grown old, and had been ousted by a younger and more energetic successor. He had had to leave the herd, and he lived now in absolute isolation, waiting for the lions to come along and tear him to pieces. It all sounded so human.

We spent three days on the game reserve, and it so happened that during our visit the lions—they were always the high point of a visit—were making themselves scarce. We traveled about a good bit, but they did not put in an appearance and we thought we were going to be disappointed. I was ready to give up, but my wife was a little more persistent. Late in the third night we were awakened in our hut by a sound of prowling and growling, and at about 4 A.M. excited Kaffir boys crowded about our entrance, conveying the news that lions were in the vicinity.

We promptly put on our clothes, threw ourselves into the car, and drove in the direction indicated. Sure enough, before long, we came across a magnificent-looking lion standing in the middle of the road like a bronze statue, and occasionally throwing a contemptuous glance at our car. We were admonished not to let our rifles protrude from the car —the lions do not like the sight of them. We could not move forward, so we stood still about twenty yards away from the lion and awaited his pleasure.

About ten minutes passed and the lion decided to leave the middle of the road; he went into the grass which screened him almost completely from our sight, its color being the same as that of his tawny skin. Looking more attentively we suddenly noticed two lionesses crouching there, with the male lion circling about them, looking occasionally in our direction and emitting a growl. After observing this scene for about fifteen minutes we backed away and drove off. We had had a good view of lions and could leave with a clear conscience.

It must be of particular interest—and a source of enormous satisfaction—to a naturalist to spend some time in the reserve and to observe all this animal life, in a state of nature, at close range. As for myself, I could not help reflecting about something else; here were these wonderful animals with a beautiful home reserved for them, with trees, water, grass, food, going about unmolested, as free citizens, establishing their own laws, habits and customs, knowing their way about, probably having their own language, and wise to the natural dangers of their environment. I was told, for instance, that a tiny springbok would approach a lion quite freely when it happened to know—as it could by instinct—that the lion had had his fill, and therefore would not attack it. Not so, however, with the leopard, which kills for the sake of killing, and is therefore always shunned by the springbok. This and more I heard from my guide on the habits of the animals in the reserve.

Here they were, I thought, in their home, which in area is only slightly smaller than Palestine; they are protected, nature offers them generously of her gifts, and they have no Arab problem. . . . It must be a wonderful thing to be an animal on the South African game reserve: much better than being a Jew in Warsaw—or even in London.

CHAPTER 32

Scientists—and Others

*Hitler's Advent to Power—The Tragedy of German Jewry—
My Work with the Central Bureau for the Settlement of
German Jews—The Ousting of the Scientists among Others—
Richard Willstatter Opens Sieff Institute in Palestine, Refuses
Post with Us, Returns to Germany—Is Expelled—Fritz
Haber's Brilliant Career—His Expulsion from Germany—
Turns to Us, too Late—German Jewish Scientists and Pales-
tine—Jewish Tradition and Science—Dr. David Bergmann
Joins Us—The German Jews and Palestine—Their Contri-
bution to the Homeland.*

THE year 1933, the year of Hitler's advent to power, marked the
beginning of the last frightful phase in the greatest catastrophe that has
ever befallen the Jewish people. We did not anticipate the full horror
of the episode; but enough was already happening, even in the preceding
years, to spur us to the most strenuous efforts.

When I accepted the chairmanship of the Central Bureau for the
Settlement of German Jews, I had no particular qualifications for the
work. But the need was so urgent, the human suffering so great, and
the men and women who sought help so pathetic in the misfortune
which had come over them like a tidal wave, that there could be no
question of preparing oneself specifically for the job. One just did the
best one could; and I found that my best would be connected with
Palestine. So my work was divided into two parts, one general, the
other specifically Palestinian. The pressure of need and the development
of circumstances brought a welcome unity into the work.

My work ran parallel with that of the Youth Aliyah, which was
headed by one of the most remarkable figures in modern Jewish history—
Henrietta Szold. She was seventy-three years of age, and her life had
been filled with many labors—literary, educational and Zionist. In the
founding of Hadassah, the American Women's Zionist Organization, she
had made an immense contribution to the social and political development of the Jewish Homeland; and to climax her work and that of her
organization, she had settled in Palestine, where her energy, wisdom
and devotion were an inspiration to the community. At an age well

beyond that of usual retirement from public life, she undertook and carried through with magnificent effectiveness the direction of Youth Aliyah, one of the most important Zionist tasks of the last fifteen years. She carried on virtually to the day of her death, in 1945.

To return to my particular task in that period of calamity: The catastrophe in Germany had of course destroyed the careers of a great many brilliant young scientists who were, almost at a moment's notice, uprooted from their positions and thrown into the street. Nor was this true of the younger people alone. Men of outstanding reputation and achievement, who had rendered invaluable service to science—and to Germany—were forced out one after the other; and often it was difficult to say which was the deeper, the external and physical tragedy, or the internal and spiritual. Two such men stand out in my mind, not because their fate was exceptional, but because of my more intimate contact with them. They are Richard Willstätter and Fritz Haber.

Of Willstätter's kindness to me in 1931, when I opened my little laboratory, I have already told. He was by that time no longer on the faculty of Munich University, but not because of governmental action. At a meeting of the university senate some time in 1928 a discussion had arisen about the appointment of a mineralogist. A candidate was proposed, a front rank mineralogist by the name of Goldschmidt. As soon as the name was mentioned a murmur arose in the meeting and someone remarked: *"Wieder ein Jude!"* (another Jew). Without saying a word Willstätter rose, collected his papers and left the room. He never crossed the threshold of the university again, this despite the repeated entreaties of his colleagues and of the Bavarian Government. It was felt—this was still 1928—that he was too valuable a man to lose, that his withdrawal was a severe blow to the prestige of the university.

It was a tragedy for Willstätter to be deprived of the laboratory in which he had been accustomed to work, but he found a place in the Munich Academy of Science. Not that he ever entered that place either! He directed the work from the outside, and as he told me with a sad smile in 1931, he would be on the telephone with his assistant for between an hour and two hours every day. I could just about see it in my mind's eye. He was extremely exact and attentive to the slightest detail, and although laconic in speech and writing his explanations were always lengthy because of their completeness. He missed the laboratory work all the more because his manipulative skill was magnificent, just as his methods were interesting, original, exact, and always directed toward the clarification of some important problem. Such was, for instance, his classical research on the constitution and function of chlorophyll in plants and its relation to the hemoglobin of the blood. Although his reputation was immense, and he was a Nobel prize winner, he was modest, unassuming and retiring in character; he often reminded me of the old-time venerable type of great Jewish Rabbi.

For a long time Willstätter refused—in spite of his experience in 1928 and his violent reaction to it—to understand what was taking place in Germany. I saw him in Munich, at the end of 1932, and again in Zurich and Paris, in 1933, after Hitler had come to power; but though deeply disturbed, he would not believe that the German people and government would go any further in their anti-Jewishness. We discussed the Daniel Sieff Research Institute, which was then in process of construction; he was immensely interested and generous with his advice. He readily accepted my invitation to preside at the opening, but to my repeated and insistent pleas that he leave Germany and come to us in Palestine, he turned a deaf ear. He came to the opening of the Institute and returned to Germany (in 1934!). He still felt that he was protected by his reputation and by the devotion of the Munich public.

I was not the only one to plead with him to stay with us. I remember how Simon Marks, among others, urged him to accept the directorship of the new Institute, assuring him of a first-class laboratory, all the buildings and apparatus he wanted, and a staff of eager and able assistants. Some of his pupils were already with us. No, he was not to be moved.

The opening of the Sieff Institute coincided with the Passover, and I took Willstätter up to Haifa to attend the Seder at my mother's house. Our Seder was always a rather lively performance, very jolly and unconventional, with some thirty-odd members of the family at table. The celebration reached its critical point when our house was suddenly surrounded by a tremendous crowd of workers, men and women—there must have been over two thousand of them—who had come from their own Seders to greet us for the festival. They filled the whole street, singing Hebrew songs and dancing the *hora*. Willstätter and I were half-pulled, half-carried down from the balcony on which we stood watching, and forced into the dance. Very curious indeed it was to watch the old German professor trying to dance a *hora* surrounded by *chalutzim* and *chalutzoth* singing and clapping their hands. I know he enjoyed the experience. But nothing of all this induced him to change his mind. His last word on the subject was: "I know that Germany has gone mad, but if a mother falls ill it is not a reason for her children to leave her. My home is Germany, my university, in spite of what has happened, is in Munich. I must return."

He actually stayed on in Germany until the outbreak of the war in 1939. Then he was expelled, and took up his residence in Locarno, in near-by Switzerland. There he found a small apartment of two or three rooms, and there he lived in complete isolation. I visited him several times. Of his possessions nothing was rescued but his library, which his old housekeeper had carried off to Stuttgart. He occupied himself, during the closing years of his life, with the writing of his autobiography, and died toward the end of the war. His obstinacy in not acceding to our request was a great loss to Palestine and, I think, a great loss to science.

Fritz Haber's was the second case. Haber was a great friend of Willstätter, though by nature and temperament very different from him. He too was a Nobel prize winner, and responsible for one of the biggest technical successes of the age, namely, the conversion of the nitrogen of the air into ammonia and nitric acid. These two chemicals are essential ingredients in the making not only of explosives, but also of artificial fertilizer, which thus became accessible in large quantities at a low price. Unlike Willstätter, Haber was lacking in any Jewish self-respect. He had converted to Christianity and had pulled all his family with him along the road to apostasy. Long before I met him I had other reasons to feel prejudiced against him. It will be remembered that when I made my first visit to America, in 1921, I had been fortunate enough to enlist the co-operation of Einstein. I learned later that Haber had done all he could to dissuade Einstein from joining me; he said, among other things, that Einstein would be doing untold harm to his career and to the name of the institute of which he was a distinguished member if he threw in his lot with the Zionists, and particularly with such a pronounced Zionist as myself.

I therefore had no desire to meet Haber; nor was there any occasion of an impersonal kind since his field of chemistry—chiefly that of in-organic materials—was remote from mine. But as it happened Haber's son, who was also a chemist, was employed by my brother-in-law, Joseph Blumenfeld, a distinguished industrial chemist in Paris, and once, during a visit to London, Blumenfeld brought the Habers, father and son, to see me. I was already busy—at any rate in my mind—with the founding of the Sieff Institute, and by that time Haber's anti-Zionist prejudices must have been wearing off, perhaps under the influence of developments in Germany. I found him, somewhat to my surprise, extremely affable. He even invited me to visit him at his research institute, which had the high-sounding name of Kaiser Wilhelm Forschungs Institut, in Dahlem, which I did toward the end of 1932, on one of my visits to Berlin.

It was a magnificent collection of laboratories, superbly equipped, and many sided in its program, and Haber was enthroned as dictator. He guided me through building after building, and after the long tour of inspection invited me to lunch with him at his villa in Dahlem. He was not only hospitable; he was actually interested in my work in Palestine. Frequently, in the course of our conversation on technical matters, he would throw in the words: "Well, Dr. Weizmann, you might try to introduce that in Palestine." He repeated several times that one of the greatest factors in the development of Palestine might be found in tech-nical botany. This is a combination of plant physiology, genetics and kindred sciences, which was represented in Dahlem both by great labora-tories and by first-class men conducting them. I was comparing in my mind those mighty institutions which served the agriculture of Germany with our little Agricultural Research Station at Rehovoth, and hoping that the new Institute which I contemplated might help to fill some of the gaps in our reconstruction.

I left Dahlem heavy hearted and filled with forebodings, which I remember communicating to my wife on my return to London.

Not long afterward, I received a telephone call at my home in London from Haber. He was in the city, staying at the Russell Hotel. He had had to leave Berlin precipitately, stripped of everything—position, fortune, honors—and take refuge in London, a sick man, suffering from angina pectoris, not quite penniless, but with very small reserves. I went to him at once, and found him broken, muddled, moving about in a mental and moral vacuum.

I made a feeble attempt to comfort him, but the truth is that I could scarcely look him in the eyes. I of course invited him to the house, and he visited us repeatedly. He told me that Cambridge was prepared to provide him with a laboratory, but he did not think he could really settle down. The shock had been too great. He had occupied too high a position in Germany; his fall was therefore all the harder to bear.

It must have been particularly bitter for him to realize that his baptism, and the baptism of his family, had not protected him. It was difficult for me to speak to him; I was ashamed for myself, ashamed for this cruel world, which allowed such things to happen, and ashamed for the error in which he had lived and worked throughout all his life. And yet it was an error which was common enough; there were many Jews with his outlook—though not with his genius—who had regarded us Zionists as dreamers or, worse, as kill-joys, or even as maniacs, who were endangering the positions they had fought through to after many years.

I began to talk to him then about coming out to us in Palestine, but did not press the matter. I wanted him first to take a rest, recover from his shock and treat his illness in a suitable climate.

He went south, and that summer (1933), following my hasty visit to America, we met again in Switzerland. I was staying in Zermatt, at the foot of the Matterhorn, and Haber was somewhere in the Rhone valley and came over to see us. We dined together that evening. I found him a little improved, somewhat settled and past the shock. The surroundings in the Rhone valley had had a beneficent effect on him.

During the dinner, at which my wife and my son Michael were also present, Haber suddenly burst into an eloquent tirade. The reason was the following: the eighteenth Zionist Congress was then being held in Prague. I had refused to attend, not wishing to be involved in any political struggle. During the dinner repeated calls came from Prague, and frantic requests that I leave Zermatt at once and betake myself to

the Congress. I persisted in my refusal, and though I said nothing to
Haber about these frequent interruptions, except to mention that they
came from Prague, he guessed their purport from something he had
read in the papers, and he said to me, with the utmost earnestness:

"Dr. Weizmann, I was one of the mightiest men in Germany. I was
more than a great army commander, more than a captain of industry. I
was the founder of industries; my work was essential for the economic
and military expansion of Germany. All doors were open to me. But the
position which I occupied then, glamorous as it may have seemed, is as
nothing compared with yours. You are not creating out of plenty—you
are creating out of nothing, in a land which lacks everything; you are
trying to restore a derelict people to a sense of dignity. And you are, I
think, succeeding. At the end of my life I find myself a bankrupt. When
I am gone and forgotten your work will stand, a shining monument, in
the long history of our people. Do not ignore the call now; go to Prague,
even at the risk that you will suffer grievous disappointment there."

I remember watching my young son, as he listened to Haber, who spoke
a halting English which his asthma made the more difficult to follow.
Michael was literally blue to the lips, so painfully was he affected, so
eager was he to have me take Haber's advice, even though it meant my
leaving him in the middle of his holiday.

I did not go to Prague, much to Haber's disappointment. But I made
use of the opportunity to press upon him our invitation to come out to
Palestine and work with us. I said: "The climate will be good for you.
You will find a modern laboratory, able assistants. You will work in
peace and honor. It will be a return home for you—your journey's end."

He accepted with enthusiasm, and asked only that he be allowed to
spend another month or two in a sanatorium. On this we agreed—and in
due course he set out for Palestine, was taken suddenly ill in Basle, and
died there. Willstätter came from Munich to bury him. Some ten years
later Willstätter too died in Switzerland, like Haber, an exile from
Germany.

These were two of the men whom I sought to attract to our institutions in Palestine, both for their sake and for ours. There were others,
of course. I felt it would be a great accession of moral strength, and a
valuable source of technical knowledge if we could offer to the Hebrew
University, or to the Sieff Institute, Albert Einstein the physicist, James
Franck of Goettingen, the mathematician Hermann Weyl, the physicist
Placzek, the chemist Wiegener, to mention but a few names. But somehow I failed to convince them. Some of them found homes in England,
at Oxford, Cambridge, Manchester, Birmingham; others, as we have
seen, in America. That was comprehensible; but there were other places
chosen in preference to Palestine which were utterly beyond me.

Zurich was the center which dealt with academic refugees, and thither

I went to consult the members of the Swiss committee. There I learned early one morning that James Franck was in the city, a refugee—and that he and his wife were breakfasting with my friend, Professor Richard Baer, the physicist. Without waiting for an invitation I barged in on them and found the two gentlemen and Mrs. Franck immersed in a discussion about the merits of going to—Turkey! Whether Franck was considering the idea for himself, or whether he was recommending it to others, I couldn't make out, but at that moment I entirely lost my good manners. I could not contain myself, and exclaimed: "I can understand it if you want to go to Oxford, Cambridge, New York or Chicago. But if you go to Turkey, you will find the scientific conditions there much worse than in Palestine—you might as well accept our invitation to go to Palestine." Franck objected that there was no security of tenure in Palestine, to which I promptly replied that tenure in Palestine would be more secure than in most other countries—not excluding the Western ones. "It is true," I said, "our University has not got government support, but if men like you came out, a great physics institute would be built round you, and after a certain time you would not lack for anything."

It was interesting to watch Mrs. Franck during this conversation. She was a Swedish Jewess, very blonde, and obviously very proud of her "Nordic" descent. She thought that I was trying to reduce her husband to a condition too awful for words. She kept looking daggers at me, and I had to give up the consultation. I felt then as I had felt in the early days of Zionism. Just as the rich Jews never came to us until we were a "practical" proposition, so these intellectually rich Jews thought that Palestine would be detrimental to their careers. True, the German catastrophe had greatly altered the situation, and Palestine was absorbing more refugees than all other countries combined; yet the inertia, the weight of prejudice, was such that many of them preferred Turkey to the Hebrew University in Palestine.

I had an opportunity of seeing some of the scientists who went to Istanbul and Ankara when I visited those cities a few years later. They were a sad lot, bewildered, lost, waiting for their contracts to expire, and knowing that in most cases they would not be renewed. To each scientist had been attached a few young Turkish students who were supposed to learn from him the tricks of the trade, so as to replace him at the end of a few years. In this policy, if it can so be called, the Turks of course miscalculated. It is not enough to learn a few facts from a professor in order to become a scientist. It is background that makes a man a scientist, and that is not to be acquired in a few years; it is a matter of tradition and of generations of endeavor. The Turks still had to learn this elementary truth.

It was a truth I had borne in mind when the foundation stones of the Hebrew University were laid. I knew it was not going to be easy to create a model national university with human material which had to be brought together from the various countries of the Dispersion. There is an ancient saying of the Hebrew sages that to make a pair of tongs one needs a pair of tongs. But we, at least, had had our institutions and traditions. Something of the latter was rescued out of the general destruction in Europe, though when we contemplate our losses we are overwhelmed by their extent. Not only millions of human beings were done to death, but great institutions which were also living organisms. Among the former, who knows how many Einsteins and Habers and Willstätters there may have been; they perished with the center of learning which would have helped to mold their gifts.

Our great men were always a product of symbiosis between the ancient, traditional Talmudic learning in which our ancestors were steeped in the Polish or Galician ghettos or even in Spain, and the modern Western universities with which their children came in contact. There is often as not a long list of Talmudic scholars and Rabbis in the pedigrees of our modern scientists. In many cases they themselves have come from Talmudic schools, breaking away in their twenties and struggling through to Paris or Zurich or Princeton. It is this extraordinary phenomenon—a great tradition of learning fructified by modern methods—which has given us both first-class scientists and competent men in every branch of academic activity, out of all relation to our numbers.

Now these great places of Jewish learning in Vilna, Warsaw, Kovno, Breslau, Vienna, Pressburg, have been wiped off the face of the earth; the great Jewish archives have been plundered or destroyed, and we have to reconstruct them fragmentarily page by page. We have suffered not only physically; we have been murdered intellectually, and the world scarcely realizes the extent of our affliction. It sounds like a cruel irony when British or American statesmen reproach the remnants of Jewry when they wish to leave the graves in Germany and Austria and Holland and move to Palestine, where they hope to build a new life under more stable conditions. For whatever the aberrations of a few at the top, that is the longing of the great majority of the survivors.

Among the most gifted of the younger scientists who were expelled from their posts with the advent of Hitler was Dr. David Bergmann. He had been the soul of the first university chemical laboratory in Berlin, had had many collaborators, and promised to become one of Germany's leading scientists. I had never met him personally, but I knew of his work. One morning in the spring of 1933 I received a telegram from a friend of mine still working at the Dahlem Institute, telling me that Bergmann had been thrown out. Almost by return of post, and without having any real budget for it, I invited Bergmann and his wife, who was also a chemist, to come over to London and join me. It will always be a deep source of satisfaction to me that I did not hesitate, or wait to obtain a budget, but just took the plunge and brought over this man, who was destined to play such an important part in my life as one of my nearest and most devoted friends, and in the scientific and technical development of Palestine. I did not learn till later that Bergmann was a Zionist, and that he was the son of a Rabbi, that he had received a sound Jewish education, was a Hebrew scholar and a great intellect, and that he lived and worked for Palestine and for Palestine only.

It did not take him long to establish himself on my premises in Holborn. I took another floor in the somewhat ancient house and rigged up a sort of laboratory for him, and there he proceeded to work—for something like eighteen hours a day. He entered with the utmost enthusiasm into my plans for the Sieff Institute. I remember a conversation I had in Paris not long after, with Willstätter and Haber, with Bergmann present. He developed before them his plans for work in the institute which was then nearing completion. The two eminent scientists listened very attentively, and then Willstätter asked me ironically: "How many floors has the Daniel Sieff Institute?" To which I replied, "As far as I know it will have two floors." "Well," said Willstätter, "you had better build a skyscraper if you wish to carry out the program Bergmann has outlined to us."

I happened to be in Palestine when the first stream of German immigrants came in. Here they were, these German Jews, used to a regular and sheltered life, mostly in solid businesses or professional pursuits, altogether unfamiliar with social earthquakes of this kind, which were more or less commonplaces to East European Jewry. They lacked, therefore, the flexibility and adaptability of Russian and Polish Jews; they were more rigid in their customs and habits; they took their tragedy—which in 1932-1933 still resembled the old Russian expulsions, and had not yet reached the bestiality of the extermination chambers— more desperately to heart.

I saw them also in Germany as the shadows were closing on them, and remember with particular vividness an evening late in December 1932, when I went from Willstätter's house to that of my old friend Eli Strauss. Strauss was a Zionist more or less of my generation, the head of the Munich Jewish community, a distinguished and upright man. He was very sick, suffering from cancer of the throat, without, of course, knowing it. He insisted on getting up, receiving me more or less in state, and offering me a meal. All my attempts to dissuade him from undergoing this strain were futile. Not only did we sit out this meal, during which I watched him with great anxiety trying to swallow his

food, but in spite of the pain he insisted on talking about the threat
hanging over German Jewry and the world at large.

After dinner there arrived a few leading members of the community,
and I have seldom lived through such a sad evening. Our host was
obviously a dying man, and his condition seemed symbolic of German
Jewry generally and of the Munich community in particular. They besieged me with questions. What did I think of the situation? Was it
going to be really as bad as they were inclined to think at the moment?
Would England try to stretch out a protecting hand over the persecuted?
I had no comfort for them. Already the signs of what was later to be
called appeasement were in the air. It was heartrending to see these men
—all of whom had built up fine lives, who had taken part in German
public affairs, and contributed to the greatness of their country—feeling
that the storm was about to break upon them, and at a loss where to
turn for comfort and succor. When I parted from these people, I knew
I was seeing Eli Strauss for the last time, and that I would never again
see a Jewish community in Munich. The tears stood in their eyes as they
watched me leave, and all I was able to utter at that moment was, "May
God protect you."

These were the people who began to stream into Palestine in 1933
and 1934. I knew them, and I had a profound respect for the role which
all of them had played in the life of their country, and some of them had
played in the Zionist movement. But I was somewhat estranged from
them by their social rigidity, so different from the life and surroundings
in which I had grown up. I came into a Seder ceremony in Haifa, attended by newly arrived German immigrants. They sang the *Hagaddah*,
but though the tune was rather a gay one, it sounded like a dirge, and
I could see, written large on the faces of these people, the memory of
their homes. These were people, who only a little while before had felt
secure; they had represented a great moral, social and intellectual force.
Now they were uprooted, brought into a country with which few of them
had had any physical connection, compelled to build up a new life—some
of them at an advanced age—in a climate unsuitable for many of them,
in a place lacking the amenities to which they were accustomed. Watching these people one asked oneself: Will they succeed? Will they be able
to push new roots into the hard soil of Palestine? Or will they end their
lives here in a sort of exile, forever bewailing the past and unable to
reconcile themselves to the present?

Remembering that scene, which is ever present in my mind, I think
with pride and deep satisfaction of the transformation through which
the German Jews have passed in Palestine, and of the distinguished
contribution which they have made to the orderliness, discipline, efficiency, and general quality of our work. They exercised a great educa-

tional influence on the East European Jews who still form a majority, and who were inclined to look down upon the newcomers, though prepared to give them all the assistance in their power. I could not help thinking of the streams of Russian Jews who used to pass through the German ports of Hamburg and Lübeck on their way to America, in my student days toward the close of the last century; I remembered how they used to be kindly—and patronizingly—received by the committees of German Jewry, guided from the frontier to the ports and given a send-off on the Hamburg-Amerika line. I used to come very often to the central station in Berlin, to see the emigrants and exchange a few words with them in their own language. I did not think then that a similar fate would befall the solid and powerful German Jewry, that they in their turn would be driven from their homes. There was, however, one profound difference between those East European emigrants and these of the nineteen thirties: the latter were coming home! True, their home was still alien to them, but their children adapted themselves swiftly—and the parents followed suit not long after.

It was not easy at first. We faced difficulties of a new character, for this was not a *chalutz* immigration whose nature was familiar to us and to which we could apply known and tested methods. It was a middle-class immigration, not all young people and not all adaptable to hard physical work. We founded for them special types of suburban settlements, in which the family could devote itself to the lighter kind of agricultural work, while the head of the family was within easy distance of the city. Between the garden plot and the occupation, such as it was, of the head of the family, a livelihood could be eked out, and in time the system worked itself in and yielded good results.

There was a transitional period when we were disquieted by the great increase of the urban population, particularly in Haifa and Tel Aviv, due to the advent of the German immigrants. I had, as the reader now knows, always been fearful of an undue urbanization of the *Yishuv*. The tendency was always there; land settlement is by its nature slower and more difficult, and the acquisition of land in Palestine is fraught with its own problems. It was therefore natural that the drift to the towns should have been accentuated by the stream of German immigrants. We sought to arrest it by the halfway system I have described, and our success was due to the adaptability of the younger generation, which in this as in other respects led the way. The new types of settlement like Ramath Ha-Shavim, and Kiryat Bialik and Nahariah, created in those years, have taken firm root. They are till this day, as they were at the beginning, composed almost entirely of German Jews; they stand as model communities, reflecting great credit both on the founders and on the country.

Thus my four years out of office were filled with laboratory work in London and Rehovoth, fund raising, visits to America, South Africa and other countries, the founding and launching of the Sieff Institute in Rehovoth, the resettlement of German refugees, and other duties. They were full years, but not happy ones, for the world was darkening toward the eclipse of the Second World War.

CHAPTER 33

Return to Office

The International World Darkens—The Abyssinian War, a Prelude—Zionist Illusions—Pinchas Rutenberg and His Great Plan—Premature Emphasis on Private Initiative in Palestine —The Unwritten Covenant with the Workers—Chalutzim, Past and Present—The Moral Ballast of the Movement.

IN 1935 I returned to office as President of the World Zionist Organization and of the Jewish Agency. I did it reluctantly, and after long and earnest pleading on the part of my friends, particularly of the labor movement. I had got into the stride of my scientific work again, spending more and more time in the laboratory in the new Institute, among my colleagues. For several months in the latter part of 1934 and the beginning of 1935 my wife and I had lived in a little bungalow in Rehovoth, which we had rented from the poetess, Jessie Sampter. And we had begun to plan our own home, which was completed in 1937 and where we finally settled down. I used to go every morning to the laboratories of the Sieff Institute, working myself and following the work of my colleagues. Every week I attended the meeting of the Zionist Executive in Jerusalem. I went about the country a good bit, but in general I tried to lead a regular life, or at least one not as fragmentated as I had led in years past. I believe that my activities were not without value for the National Home.

Yet this was not the fundamental reason for my reluctance. It was rather that I did not see a genuine change of heart in the movement, or, let me say, of the majority which had ejected me in 1931. They were asking for me because a certain number of Zionists were now of the opinion that they had nobody who could do much better! Sokolow, though respected by the British as a man of learning and dignity, had not got very far with them. Curiously enough, those of the general Zionists who had been my strongest opponents in 1931, namely, the Americans, were now among the most vigorous proponents of my return. I could not help thinking that very soon after taking office I would be faced with the same old troubles. I would again be made the scapegoat for the sins of the British Government. Indeed, I anticipated a harder time than before 1931, for circumstances were becoming more and more unfavorable. After a long threatening, the Abyssinian war finally broke out in the summer of 1935. I said to the Congress: "The Mediterranean is becoming stormy, and we occupy on its shores one of the key positions." I regarded the Abyssinian war and the Spanish Civil War as the curtain raisers of a much greater struggle. Both Mussolini and Hitler were arming at a great pace, while the democracies showed both weakness and lack of foresight. It was not to be expected that our path would be made easier.

The reactionary spirit which was rapidly spreading over the whole world was affecting the Zionist movement too, and this had been evident even in 1931. The change was unhappily fostered by the illusory promises of quick results which were held out by certain prominent people in the movement—promises which played upon the natural impatience of our workers to get on with the job, and led to counsels of despair. It was made to appear that the gap between the desirable and the possible was very easy to bridge, a doctrine which I have always opposed. The encouragement of this error went back to the time of the so-called Brandeis struggle, and it always had, in the strangest way, the support, or promised support, of men who were not Zionists at all. And always, perhaps not so strangely, it was associated with an attitude of hostility to our most characteristic creation in Palestine, the communal colonies, the cooperatives, and the labor movement generally.

The history of the later years of Pinchas Rutenberg provides an apt illustration.

Here was a man whose role in Palestinian life as a great builder was outstanding, whose devotion and *savoir faire* were beyond question. Had he confined his activities to his engineering work, he would have achieved even more in his own field. Unfortunately, like a great many people in Palestine, he had political ambitions, and he did not realize that he was by nature and temperament utterly unfit to stand at the head of a complex political organization. He combined, in political matters, a childish naïveté with a colossal self-confidence, and he always dreamed of raising vast sums of money—say of the order of fifty million dollars, which was in fact a vast sum in Zionist work twelve or fifteen years ago—so as to build up a huge land reserve and proceed with colonization on a massive scale.

He did not realize that the privately owned land organization which he projected would have to sell its land to the highest bidder and that, if the enterprise were at all attractive financially, large tracts would pass into the hands of speculators. I was astonished and shocked when I received his first annual report of the activities of the Palestine Electric Corporation, of which he was the manager. It was divided into two parts. The first was devoted to the proper business of the corporation. The second contained an attack on the national funds of the Zionist Organization, and the outline of a plan whereby the building of the

Jewish National Home was to be taken over by the Board of Directors of
the Palestine Electric Corporation!

A long and unhappy controversy ensued, and again I found myself
fighting against men—Rutenberg was one of them—for whom I had both
respect and admiration, but whose views on the development of Palestine
did violence to my conception of the organic character of Zionism. Whatever form the controversy took, I was always in opposition to the "quick
and easy" way. Today this aspect of the controversy has lost some of its
edge; there are at present several investment companies in Palestine which
work successfully. They are, I repeat, due to the groundwork done by
the National Funds, and done under conditions rendered unnecessarily
difficult by the very advocates of private initiative. It was not easy, in
America, to explain the basic problem to donors who would have preferred to give their money to those who promised them returns, rather
than to a "philanthropic" organization of which it was freely said that
it was incapable of handling finances. Those that spread such rumors,
perhaps quite honestly, did not seem to understand that they were undermining their own position. It was my task during my many journeys in
America, during my pilgrimages from city to city—some were quite small
ones—to counteract these nefarious influences, and to build up, painfully
and systematically, good will for a Palestine which was not showing
financial returns at the time, but which was increasing its absorptive
capacity for those who wished to go and settle there. It was a remarkable
fact, which testified to a sound instinct and real patriotism, that just the
poor elements responded to such treatment and gave liberally of their
substance. It was the richer people who were keen on investment.

Here was the fundamental difference between the two views of Zionism,
the views put forward long ago by Greenberg and Marmorek and Nordau,
and later by Jabotinsky and the Revisionists, and those held by our group.
That impatience, that lack of faith, was constantly pulling the movement
toward the abyss; and between the abyss and the acual work in Palestine
stood the phalanx of the workers, to whom—though I never identified
myself with them—I considered myself attached. Gradually an unwritten
covenant was created between the small group of my friends in the so-
called general Zionist movement and the great mass of workers in the
settlements and factories of Palestine which formed the core of the
Zionist movement. This was the guarantee of our political sanity, of
our sense of realism and of our freedom alike from Revisionist delusions
and methods of violence.

There was something more than a personal bond between me and the
labor leaders and the rank and file, the men of Nahalal, Ain Harod and
the Emek generally. There was a partnership in effort and in suffering,
and but for them I do not think I could have endured the nervous and
physical grind of my fund-collecting tours of America and other countries.

I always bore in mind that the money would go toward redeeming the Emek, the Jordan Valley and other waste places: and sometimes, when I remembered the workers as I had last seen them, in Nahalal, their eyes glittering with the hunger of weeks and months, greeting me cheerfully and hopefully—I felt I had a part, however small, in their suffering and their achievement.

Much has been written about the efforts of our pioneers, and unfortunately much has been forgotten; and there were many good Zionists who, in the years I am now writing of, were under the impression that the old pioneering days were over in Palestine, and that the great days of the *chalutzim* were forever a thing of the past. Not only was this untrue of 1935; it is not true in 1947.

One has only to go down these days to the Dead Sea, where the young people who have come out of the Diaspora are leeching the salty earth of Sodom and Gomorrah—earth which for thousands of years has borne nothing but Dead Sea fruit—and with patient effort are bringing it to life again, in order to know that the struggle still goes on. Or one may visit the groups of young men and women who have settled in the Negev desert, in the dangerous outpost positions between Gaza and the Egyptian frontier, rebuilding a part of Palestine on which, with the exception of a few thin strips which the Bedouins have sown with scanty barley, not a blade of grass has grown for thousands of years. I have watched the work for the last three years, and I always approach these settlements with a feeling of awe; and every time I go to bed I cannot help reflecting on those small groups of young men and women—most of them members of the Youth Aliyah, saved from Germany only a few years ago—in the middle of the desert, quite alone, working energetically, gaily, without making a single complaint. For all I know they come from families as good as and better than mine, and grew up in circumstances very different from those they are placed in now. But they have gone through a hardening process, in which they witnessed the destruction of their near and dear ones. I remember the inscription on one of the "illegal" ships which sailed once into the harbor of Haifa—a streamer prepared for the benefit of the British soldiers and sailors: *Don't shoot, we are not frightened: we made our acquaintance with death long ago.*

Our workers are the moral ballast of the movement today, just as they were in the early days of the Zionist movement, and as they were in the years of which I am writing. It is only of late that a negative relation has sprung up between a few of the urban labor leaders and my group. And again, significantly enough, inevitably, I might say, it is a struggle between those who proclaim that they know how to bring a million and two million Jews into Palestine in three or four years, and those who know the possibilities and accept them.

CHAPTER 34

Mediterranean Intrigue

*The French Attitude toward Palestine—M. de Jouvenel, High
Commissioner of Syria—M. Herriot's Astonishing Speech—
Italy and Palestine—Conversations with Mussolini—Count
Theodoli, Italian Representative on the Permanent Mandates
Commission—Turkey and Palestine—Visit to Turkey, 1938.*

AMONG the tasks which fell on the shoulders of the President of the
Zionist Organization was the maintenance of contacts with the various
governments of the Powers which were represented on the League of
Nations. Foremost among these were the French, who, besides being
England's immediate neighbors across the Channel, were also her Man-
datory neighbor in Syria on the northern border of Palestine; and the
Italians.

I was therefore frequently in Paris and in Rome—and each city presented its own problem to us.

In Paris I met, I believe, every Premier between the two wars, from
Poincaré to Reynaud. Léon Blum had a long record of co-operation with
us. In the days when Nahum Sokolow was conducting our negotiations
on the Continent he was always kept informed semiofficially of the
French situation by M. Blum. In later years M. Blum came to take a
real interest in the movement, working closely with M. Marc Jarblum,
one of the leaders of the French Zionist Organization. M. Aristide
Briand was also quite sympathetic, although a little vague as to what
was going on. Briand used to say: "Palestine must be a wonderful
country, and a very impressive one," and praise the oranges which he
used to receive from us every Christmas as the best he had ever eaten.
But his sentiments went no deeper than the skin of the oranges. He was
a warmhearted man of strong liberal sympathies, and was attracted by
the idea of the Jewish renaissance, but he knew little about the moral
force of the Zionist movement, and made no effort to find out more.

By far the largest majority of the officials of the Quai d'Orsay were
either indifferent or hostile; occasionally they were jealous of our progress. I have remarked already that the French followed the Arab lead in
regarding Palestine merely as the southern part of Syria, and when
Palestine was given a separate Mandate they felt they had a grievance.

The French, moreover, had always considered themselves *the* representatives of Europe in the eastern Mediterranean, and the protectors of the Christians in those parts. English was practically unknown until after Allenby's time. It is too often forgotten in England that it was the Balfour Declaration which brought her to Palestine, and gave her the *raison d'être* for being there. The French were inclined to look at the revival of Jewish Palestine through Catholic eyes, and as an encroachment on the French tradition.

An exception was M. de Saint Quentin, whose connection with the Levant went back to the First World War, when he was liaison officer between the French Army and Allenby. He had encouraged me at the time of my visit to Feisal; and later he encouraged me to make several visits to Syria, and to meet the French High Commissioners.

Among these the most interesting, in my opinion, was M. de Jouvenel, who was opposite number to Field-Marshal Lord Plumer. M. de Jouvenel had been the editor of *le Matin*, one of the most influential French newspapers; he was hostile to the Zionist idea and anything connected with it, and we were never able to get a favorable line in his paper. When I first met him he was not slow, either, in giving expression to his views.

This happened in Beyrouth, where I was presented to him by some French friends. He made use of the occasion to unburden himself, and I let him go on; then I said: "Your Excellency really cannot speak of Zionism and Palestine, never having studied the one or seen the other. The latter is right on your Syrian frontier, and if you were to visit it for only a couple of days, you might change your views."

He agreed, and came over shortly afterward to stay with the High Commissioner of Palestine, where I met him again. A very queer contrast he made, by the way, with Lord Plumer: the one a sophisticated and gallant Frenchman, the other a staid and serious English aristocrat of the Victorian era. He toured the country, and then I met him again a third time, and the change which had come over his views reminded me a little of the transformation which the first visit to Palestine had wrought in Felix Warburg. M. de Jouvenel not only retracted his previous criticisms; he even reproached the Zionists for never having made any attempt to come and work in Syria!

I was very much startled by his suggestion, and answered that we had plenty to do in Palestine, where we were working under the terms of a Mandate, without coming to Syria, where we had no standing and would be regarded by the Arabs as intruders—the vanguard perhaps of Jewish expansion over the entire Middle East. But de Jouvenel insisted that the Jews were the only people who could develop Syria.

"Of course," he added, "I would not want you to work in southern Syria, because immediately after you'd come to Tyre and Saïda you would want the frontier rectified. But I have one great project, and that is the development of the region of the Euphrates. It is of course many hundreds of miles away from Palestine," and he produced a map on the spot, and showed me where the Euphrates crosses great stretches of desert country with a very thin population, mostly Bedouin. "Thousands of square miles," he said, enthusiastically, "could be irrigated here and nourish a great population."

He went on to mention that French aviators who had flown over the Euphrates basin had found traces of the ancient canals which had brought water thence to the oasis of Palmyra, where a considerable civilization had flourished in ancient times. "What has been done in ancient times," he said, "can certainly be done in modern," and he grew eloquent on the possibilities. But the only reply it provoked from me was: "You know, M. de Jouvenel, we have our own water problem in Palestine, but we shall have to be satisfied with the modest Jordan. Wonderful as the picture is, we can't be tempted by it." He even pleaded on historic grounds. "Dr. Weizmann, it is written in the Book of Nehemiah that Tadmor, which as you know is Palmyra, was built by the Jews."

He raised the subject again when we met later in Paris, and even persuaded Léon Blum of the soundness of the idea. But it had no practical value for us.

A very queer incident sticks in my mind in connection with my visits to France and my efforts to influence public opinion in our favor. This took place in 1933, when with Hitler's ascent the tide of German refugees was beginning to move toward Palestine.

I received one day a telegram from Mlle. Louise Weiss, a French journalist of distinction, who had wide contacts in political circles, inviting me to deliver an address on Zionism and Palestine in the lecture theater of the Sorbonne. She assured me that the meeting would be held under the most distinguished auspices and would attract an important audience. I hesitated for one reason only. I felt that it would be impossible for me to avoid speaking on the events in Germany; my feelings might perhaps run away with me, and we had too many hostages in Hitler's hands. I would never forgive myself if I made their position even harder than it was. On the other hand this was a unique opportunity to state our case to an influential part of the French public. I weighed the pros and cons, sought the advice of a few friends, and finally accepted.

The meeting was all that Mlle. Weiss had promised. The lecture hall was packed. The chairman was M. Martin, an ex-Minister of Finance, and I was informed that there was present *tout Paris*. I recognized in the audience some members of the British Embassy, friends from the Quai d'Orsay, representatives of the Rothschild family, the son of Captain Dreyfus, the Chief Rabbi of Paris, and others.

I tried to speak calmly of conditions in Germany and of the responsibility which rested upon the civilized world toward the victims of

German policy. I spoke of the refuge which some of them were finding in Palestine—it was more than a refuge: for the children it was, after a few months, a homecoming. I had seen the German children mixing with the Palestinian and becoming, in a short time, indistinguishable from them. I then dealt with the country itself, which, in spite of its smallness, seemed to be able to expand its capacity as the need presented itself.

The audience followed my statement with intense interest, and when I had ended I was somewhat astonished to hear the chairman say that I ought to repeat the same lecture in the same place the following day. There were, he was certain, numbers of people who would like to hear it again, and a chance should also be given to those who had been unable to obtain admittance the first evening. He stated further that he was quite certain that M. Herriot would be glad to act as chairman for the second evening. I could not but accept.

I spoke again, the next day, before a packed audience, but my chairman was not M. Herriot. He failed to appear, so we went ahead without an official chairman, Mlle. Weiss opening the meeting. I was in the middle of my address when M. Herriot suddenly irrupted into the hall. Without paying the slightest attention to me—perhaps he did not even notice me, for I had stopped speaking when he entered—he rushed on to the platform and in a stentorian voice delivered himself of a twenty-minute address on matters which had nothing to do with Zionism, Palestine or the Jews: it was all about the greatness of French civilization, done in magnificent style, but consisting of generalities. He finished as abruptly as he had burst in. The audience was utterly nonplussed by this extraordinary intermezzo, but Mlle. Weiss calmly took the chair again, and asked me to resume.

I never met M. Herriot again, and I am quite certain that he had not the faintest notion what the meeting was all about.

Of the attitude of the Italian Government to the Zionist movement I have already spoken in the chapter describing the struggle round the ratification of the Mandate. Italy had been, prior to the advent of fascism, entirely free from anti-Semitism, but a change began to appear shortly after the accession of Mussolini. He himself violently denied any anti-Semitic tendencies, but they were fostered by underlings like Staracci and Federzoni, and the whole Fascist press was flavored with anti-Semitism. From time to time articles appeared attacking Zionism and the participation of Italian Jews in the movement. The Zionists, and the Jews generally, though they did not give loud expression to their views on the subject, were known to be anti-Fascist. Enzo Sereni, a member of a very distinguished family—later one of the founders of the co-operative colony Givat Brenner—was marked by the Italian police. A brother of his, a known Communist, was arrested and condemned to the

Lipari Islands. He could have obtained his release by recanting. His father, who was the King's physician, pleaded with him to do so. He refused. Later he escaped from the Lipari Islands and made his way to Moscow. Other Jews were caught smuggling anti-Fascist literature from France into Italy, and the position of the community became a difficult one.

All these circumstances made my visits to Rome matters of some importance to the Italian Jews. They felt that my talks with the head of the government, my explanations of the aims of the Zionist movement, would help ease the situation for them.

I had three conversations with Mussolini, spaced over a number of years. My first took place shortly after the First World War, and he received me in his famous office—a long room, dimly lighted and almost empty of furniture. He sat at a small desk at the furthest corner from the door, so that the visitor had to walk quite a distance to meet him. Before the table stood a hard chair, for the visitor. It was all somewhat theatrical, and in no way contributed—was perhaps not intended to contribute—to putting the visitor at his ease.

However, he greeted me affably enough, shook hands with me, and after the usual exchange of politenesses led off with the remark, in French: "You know, Dr. Weizmann, not all Jews are Zionists." To which I replied, "Of course, I know it only too well, and not all Italians are Fascisti." He smiled wryly, and did not take it too badly. At any rate, the conversation became very normal and there was no attempt to browbeat or intimidate me. I told him about our plans and intentions, and he was interested in finding out whether much of our immigration went through Italian ports. I explained that Trieste was very important for us and that we had extremely friendly relations with the Lloyd Triestino. We were also using Genoa, Venice, and Naples; and we were anxious to cultivate the good will of the Italian people.

Mussolini then spoke of England and insinuated that we Zionists were merely a pawn in Great Britain's power game. I said that I had never seen any particularly sinister intentions behind Britain's Zionist policy; so far England was the only great country that had shown readiness to help us begin actual operations in Palestine. What ulterior motives there may have been in the minds of certain British statesmen I could not know; but as long as these operations were possible, and we could carry on without too many difficulties, we should maintain our relations with England, which I considered essential. He said, suddenly: "You know, we could build your state *en toute pièce*." To which I replied: "I remember that the Romans destroyed it *en toute pièce*."

He was not particularly pleased with this answer. He probably had expected me to say what I thought the Italian Government could do for us, but I was not going to walk into that trap. He went on to ask whether the Italian language was being taught or spoken in our schools, and I had to answer in the negative. However, I added, there would certainly be a chair of Italian language and literature at the Hebrew university. The Jews had always admired the Italian spirit of freedom and tolerance, and as the Premier knew, many Jews had distinguished themselves in the service of Italy. There might be some disagreement in certain sections of young Jewry on the subject of fascism, but this should not be construed as unfriendliness toward Italy. We greatly admired the Italian civilization.

I felt I was skating on thin ice and wanted to end the conversation as soon as I had spoken my piece on Jews and fascism and Italy, but he kept me for some time, asking me about our various undertakings in Palestine, which were then in the embryonic stage. He was obviously keen that the port of Haifa, which was already being talked about, should be built by Italian firms. He hinted at Jews who were leaders in this field, and I knew that he meant the firm of Almaja. I said I would be glad to know more about them.

I carried away the impression that Mussolini was not hostile to the Zionist idea, or to our work in Palestine; his suspicion and hostility were directed at the British, who in his opinion were using the Jews in the eastern Mediterranean in order to cut across the Italian control of Mare Nostrum.

I became acquainted with the Almajas, a very distinguished old family which still maintained the Jewish tradition, and they mentioned their interest in the port of Haifa. I had to answer truthfully that we would not have much to say in this matter, and that there were great British firms of ship and port builders, like Armstrong Whitworth. It might be well for the Almajas to get in touch with them.

As fascism became more strongly established in Italy it fell more deeply under the influence of German anti-Semitism, and the attacks in the Fascist press increased in number and violence. Mussolini was still hesitating between linking up with the Western Powers and throwing in his lot with Germany. His price—from whichever side he might obtain it—was expansion in Africa, and gains in Europe—Savoy, Nice, Corsica. There was hesitation and uncertainty of direction in the Fascist camp. The Germans, as always, were extremely active in Italy. It was not that they considered Italy a particularly valuable ally; they were more concerned with a springboard for action in the Mediterranean, directed against Britain.

We were an insignificant factor in this struggle of the Great Powers; still, there we were, growing, pushing our roots into an important part of the Mediterranean shore, and the Italians did not like it. Their attitude found more than journalistic expression in the Permanent Mandates Commission, where the Italian representative, Count Theodoli, could always be relied on to veto any constructive suggestion in our behalf.

What Count Theodoli's personal convictions on the subject of Zionism were, I do not know; but he did have a personal relation to it. He was connected with a great Arab family in Beyrouth, the Sursuks, who were the absentee landlords from whom we had bought large stretches of land in the Valley of Jezreel. Neither Theodoli nor his relatives the Sursuks could get over the fact that they had sold the land so cheaply— actually they got a very high price for areas which our work made valuable later—and they always threw the blame on Victor Sursuk, a member of the family who kept a great establishment in Alexandria, and whom they accused of Zionist leanings. They should have held on to the land, and they would have got for it five times as much as they did. In vain did I explain to Theodoli and his Arab relatives that what they had sold us was a deadly marsh, and they better than anyone else should have known how the Arab villages in that district had disappeared, and how we had had to sink hundreds of thousands of pounds into drainage and improvement and roads. If the land was so valuable now, it had become so through our work and effort, our sacrifices in blood and money. This, incidentally, is a phenomenon we are constantly running up against in Palestine. Visitors who know nothing about the country and its history are always making the unfounded charge that the Jews have taken the best land. Actually we took the worst, and made it the best by our efforts. It seems as if God has covered the soil of Palestine with rocks and marshes and sand, so that its real beauty can only be brought out by those who love it and will devote their lives to healing its wounds.

On the Permanent Mandates Commission Count Theodoli, following instructions, posed as the great defender of Arab rights and of the Catholic Church against the imaginary encroachments of the Jews. The Italians were worried by the excessive liberalism of the new Jewish institutions, and helped spread the legend of the flagrant atheism of the Jewish settlements in the Holy Land. This was a time when the Fascists were entering into close relations with the Vatican, and making what political capital they could of the combination.

I paid a second visit to Italy to see Mussolini and to tour the Italian-Jewish communities. The Rome-Berlin Axis had not yet been forged, the issue of Italy's alliance was still in doubt, and I hoped to make some improvement in our relations with the Italians. I believe my second talk with Mussolini was not without value. He said he had been delighted to learn that the Zionists in Jerusalem were on excellent terms with the local Italians; also that our colonies were making good progress. After this second interview a better tone toward us could be observed in the Italian press; the substance of the interview got out, and its friendly character contributed a great deal toward improving the position of the

Jewish community. I have a particularly vivid recollection of the second interview with Mussolini because it took place on the eve of *Yom Kippur*.

My third and last interview with Mussolini still fell within the period of Italian indecision; it was the longest of the interviews and the most substantial in content. Count Theodoli arranged it, and on this occasion he showed himself full of good will and friendliness—a Saul changed into a Paul. Mussolini too was extremely affable, and talked freely of a Rome-Paris-London combination, which, he said, was the logical one for Italy. He spoke also of the chemical industry, and of the Italian need of pharmaceuticals, which we could produce in Palestine. He regretted that his gestures toward London and Paris had not met with the proper response.

I repeated the substance of this conversation to my British friends in London, but it had no consequences. Shortly before the outbreak of the war Halifax and Chamberlain visited Mussolini and tried to win him over but by then it was too late. He was hopelessly in the clutch of the Germans, whom he strongly disliked, always speaking with contempt of their manners and their overbearing character. The contempt was, of course, quite mutual. I do not know whether detaching Rome from Berlin would have prevented the outbreak of the war, but it certainly might have made a great difference to the war in the Mediterranean, might have saved many lives and shortened the agony by many months.

It was not without a certain discomfort that I used to make my views known to British officials. The British Jews were in an awkward predicament. Their hostility to Germany, their manifest unhappiness at seeing British statesmen on friendly terms with our bitterest persecutors, could give the impression that they wanted the British to fight our war for us; the fact that what they sought was consonant with England's interests was thereby obscured.

There was another instance of this kind which occurred much later, in fact only a year before the outbreak of the Second World War. Relations between the Jews and Arabs in Palestine were very strained—this was the time of the Arab terror—and I was advised by many friends to see whether I could not persuade the Turkish Government to use its good offices as intermediary between us and the Arabs.

It struck me as a sound idea. It should be borne in mind that although Kemal Attaturk had secularized the Government, Turkey was still viewed by the Arab world as a major Moslem community. Its progressive record, its position as a bridge between Europe and Asia, its standing with the Western world, all helped to enhance its prestige in the eyes of the Arabs. There was no doubt that the good will of the Turks could go a long way in improving relations between us and the Arabs, more so as the Turks had begun to take an interest in our work. We had put up a pavilion at a Turkish Exhibition in Smyrna, with samples of Palestinian industrial and agricultural products, and the usual statistical tables on education, hygiene, and so on. These had made a profound impression on visitors, and Kemal Attaturk had sent a number of Government representatives to Palestine to see whether our methods could not be applied to the revival of Turkey. We knew, of course, that the Turks would be very careful not to offend the susceptibilities of the Arabs; also that there was much bitterness in Turkey over the fact that the liberated Arabs had taken possession of vast tracts of the former Turkish Empire and were doing nothing to develop them. It would therefore not be plain sailing to get the Turks to act as intermediaries for us; but it was certainly worth trying.

There was another purpose in my visit to Turkey in 1938. One already felt the approach of the war. Germany was doing everything in her power to attach Turkey to the Axis, and anything that might be done to counteract this influence was of value. Although my main interest was Zionist, I kept the British Government informed of my conversations with Turkish officials and of the views I gained in regard to general matters.

My wife and I arrived in Istanbul on November 27, 1938. Istanbul made on us the impression of a city almost devoid of life and movement— a vast agglomeration of houses and abandoned palaces, exquisitely beautiful in certain parts, but in a dying condition. The shops of Istanbul were full of German rubbish, evidence of the inroads which German trade had made on the Turkish market.

Ankara made a very different impression. Situated in the interior of Asia Minor, amid picturesque surroundings, in the heart of the agricultural country, it was new, healthy and alive, corresponding to the new spirit of the Turkish people. Very impressive, too, were the "Gates of Tamerlane," a great fissure in the rocks dominating Ankara, through which the Tartars are said to have irrupted into Asia Minor on their way to Europe.

We spent a few days in the two main cities and I had numerous conversations with Turkish officials, chief among them Jellal Bayard, the Prime Minister, and Ismet Inonu, then Finance Minister. I found, as I had expected, a considerable interest in Palestine, but what permanent results the conversations might have had for us it would be difficult to say. The war intervened shortly after. But the secondary aspect of my visit may still be of interest.

The Turkish officials approached me from a single point of view: they wanted to know whether the Jews could help them to obtain a gold loan. Of course I could not hold out any promises. I had, before leaving London, consulted several banker friends (this after a couple of visits to the Turkish Embassy) and all I could suggest was that the Turkish Government invite out a committee qualified to discuss such matters. The proposal, practical as it seemed to me, did not appeal to the Turkish authorities, who were probably under the naïve impression that I was in control of vast fortunes, and was merely putting them off.

I discussed the matter with the British Ambassador, Sir Percy Lorraine, who told me that what the Turks needed was about half a million gold pounds per annum to see them through their immediate difficulties. Astonished at the smallness of the sum, I ventured to suggest that the British might, usefully and without much risk, negotiate such a loan for the Turks, and that it might go a long way to neutralize German influence. My suggestion found no echo, and again I had the feeling that I was suspected of looking at matters entirely from the Jewish point of view; I was not being as careful as British officialdom in taking the feelings of the Germans into account! I do not assert that one could have bought a Turkish alliance with the sum proposed; but I imagine that a gesture of good will on the part of Great Britain would have been of value. In any case, Turkish neutrality during the war cost the Allies a great deal more than the half-million pounds per annum asked.

It was during this visit that I came in contact with the German Jewish scientists who had accepted positions at the universities of Istanbul and Ankara. They were an unhappy lot. They did not complain of any derogatory treatment, but most of them were faced again by the problem they thought they had solved five years before: refuge. Their contracts were expiring, and there was no prospect of renewal.

CHAPTER 35

The Permanent Mandates Commission

Function of the Commission—Professor William Rappard of Switzerland—M. Orts of Belgium—Lord Lugard of England —Attitude of the Colonial Office.

Among the many activities which took me periodically out of England was the maintenance of contacts with the Permanent Mandates Commission of the League of Nations. Although we had an office in Geneva to take care of matters in a routine way, there were the special occasions when the members of the Permanent Mandates Commission came together to receive reports and pass on them. Except for Professor Rappard none of them lived in Switzerland. They therefore had to be kept informed by special and individual contacts between sessions.

Whether the views and criticisms of the Mandates Commission carried much weight with the Mandatory Power is doubtful; but the cumulative effect of those annual reports was not without importance, both for the record and for its effect on public opinion. It was our business to present our case in the best possible way, to bring out the facts in exact and proper form, and to see to it that the reports should not be limited merely to criticism of administrative details, but should give a general picture of our work and the growth of the National Home in the face of the difficulties we encountered.

We were not entitled to appear at the sessions of the Mandates Commission, nor did I consider it dignified or proper to come to Geneva during such sessions and lobby in the antechambers. The members of the commission were very much overworked at those periods, and had as much as they could do to study the reports. To approach them then would have been an imposition, the more so as the Arabs and other interested parties would have followed suit, and an impossible situation would have ensued. It was therefore necessary to see the various members of the Mandates Commission in their respective countries.

On the whole this very distinguished body, which had a unique task to perform, was impartial, honest, and industrious in its attempts to get at the truth. Occasionally it was overimpressed by the might of the Mandatory Power, but on the whole we were given a good chance to present our case, and in the course of the years some of the members became thoroughly acquainted with the details of our work in Palestine and with the various aspects of our movement. I am anxious to make it clear that I have never found any bias in any of the members, excepting Count Theodoli of Italy. We had some well-wishers in the commission, but their friendliness did not blind them in the performance of their duties or incline them to view the facts otherwise than with absolute objectivity.

Foremost among the members of the commission was Professor William Rappard, of the University of Geneva. He was well acquainted with the Anglo-Saxon mentality, had lived for many years in America and had been, I believe, one of Woodrow Wilson's favorite secretaries. He was a man of the greatest intellectual capacity, with a deep understanding of the Jewish problem in all its bearings and as deep a sympathy with our hopes and endeavors.

Professor Rappard was a helpful guide to us, and to me in particular, in the inner workings of the League, an intricate labyrinth leading to many dark domains in European and world politics. It is a source of pleasure, and of not a little pride, to recall that our acquaintance, which was purely formal and official at first, crystallized into a lifelong friendship. Whenever M. Rappard came over to England, which happened once or twice every year, we always met if I happened to be in the country, as we did if I happened to be passing through Switzerland when he was there. It was always a delight to converse with this sage and experienced man, in whom I found a peculiar and impressive blend of the intellectuality of the scholar and statesman with the simplicity and solidity of the Swiss peasant.

Another member of the commission who was a commanding personality was the Belgian M. Orts, a man of great administrative experience, who had occupied a high position in the Congo. Interestingly enough, this experience had taught him that there is a world of difference between the black Congo and white Palestine, and he understood the incongruity of British attempts to apply the methods of the first to the problems of the second—attempts which, among a sensitive and sophisticated population, often turned the machinery of administration into a sort of Procrustean bed. M. Orts fought against that, sometimes quite effectively. In him too we found a sympathetic and critical appreciation of our efforts, and a deep understanding of the bearing of the Jewish problem on the National Home. He saw the latter not simply as a place of refuge for immigrants, but as a center of civilization built by a modern people drawing on an ancient tradition in a land hallowed by memories and associations. I used to visit M. Orts once or twice a year in Brussels and spend a long evening with him in his study, sometimes explaining our position to him, sometimes sitting at his feet and learning from his wide experience as a great administrator, statesman, and man of the world.

A third leading member of the Mandates Commission was Lord Lugard, the British representative; again a personality of great power, commanding the respect and affection of those whose privilege it was to come in touch with him. One of the most remarkable features in my relations with Lord Lugard was his complete impartiality in dealing with a matter closely affecting the interests of Great Britain. He had been a lifelong servant of British imperial interests, and, like M. Orts, the administrator of a large African dependency. He had been one of the first to try to associate the native population with the administration, and he had made an enviable name for himself throughout the black continent. He was humane in his outlook, sympathizing with the submerged and dispossessed, but at the same time strong in his views and severe in his criticisms. In conversation he always made on me the impression of a great judge called upon to try a complicated case. This manner of his did not disturb me at all; his severe exterior was belied by a pair of kindly and understanding eyes. He felt deeply with the Jewish plight, and I always knew that he would put the Jewish case in the best possible light, though he would not say a word about it to me.

It became almost a tradition for me to pay him regular visits at his modest place in Little Parkhurst, near Dorking, in Surrey. Curiously enough, his residence was very close to that of Claude Montefiore, one of the spiritual leaders of English Jewry, but (as the reader may remember from earlier chapters) an avowed and active anti-Zionist. These two men were apparently on terms of close friendship; I never met Montefiore there, but from some hints dropped by Lord Lugard I gathered that they had discussed the Jewish National Home more than once.

It was always an intellectual and spiritual occasion to spend a few hours with Lord Lugard, though it was not without its drawbacks. He was advanced in years and hard of hearing, and I had to make a considerable physical effort to make him understand what I was saying. Now and then I used to meet him in town, at his request, once or twice in the offices of Barclays Bank, of which he was a director.

These three persons formed the core of the Mandates Commission, and I could easily imagine a clash between them and the rather dry functionaries who came before them to justify the actions of the Colonial Office. These used to complain about the necessity of having to account to a lot of foreigners for the administration of Palestine, asking somewhat ironically what a foreigner could understand of British methods and British mentality. They usually forgot that among the members of the Mandates Commission there was Lord Lugard, an Englishman, and a magnificent administrator, who understood their methods only too thoroughly, and did not by any means always approve of them. For that matter, the ways of the Colonial Office were not beyond the comprehension of men like Rappard and Orts, either.

CHAPTER 36

Riot and the Peel Commission

Appeasement of the Arabs—The Legislative Council—An Undemocratic Proposal—Riots in Palestine, April, 1936—The Mufti to the Fore—The Administration Fumbles—Appointment of the Peel Commission—I Give Evidence before It—Partition Comes up—The Twentieth Zionist Congress—Violent Controversy—The Jewish Position Misrepresented.

THE beginnings of the strain which developed between us and Sir Arthur Wauchope were to be found in his advocacy of a legislative council, to which he was committed by the Government, but which he himself also favored. This difficulty, by itself, might have been overcome, for Sir Arthur's sympathies with the National Home were, as I have said, profound and informed.

From the time of his arrival in 1931 Sir Arthur had entered into the problems of the country with great enthusiasm and had realized from the outset that the mainspring of our progress was immigration. By 1935 the annual immigration figure passed the sixty thousand mark, and we thought that if this would only continue for another few years we would be past the difficulties which had given us most trouble. Fate decreed otherwise. We can see now that this period was an oasis in the desert of time.

The Abyssinian war came in 1935, and with it the accentuation of England's policy of appeasement toward the aggressive powers and their possible satellites. Among the latter the Foreign Office placed the Arabs— and here began the deterioration both of our position and of our relations with Sir Arthur Wauchope.

Appeasement of the Arabs did not at first take the form of limitation of Jewish immigration; that, in 1934, 1935, and part of 1936 was more or less regulated by the absorptive capacity of the country. It took, instead, a form which, if allowed to develop, would have led to the complete arrest both of Jewish immigration and of Jewish progress generally: namely, British advocacy of a legislative council with Arabs in the majority.

The idea of a legislative council had been mooted as far back as 1922, in the Churchill White Paper. It was raised again in the Passfield White Paper of 1931. It was contained in the instructions with which Ramsay MacDonald had sent Sir Arthur Wauchope to Palestine, and Sir Arthur had always been favorably inclined to the idea. But he did not begin to press it upon us until he himself was under strong pressure from the Colonial Office. The proposal submitted to us was for a council consisting of fourteen Arabs (nine elected, five appointed), seven Jews (three elected, four appointed), two members of the commercial community of unspecified race (appointed) and five British officials.

Discussions regarding a legislative council had, then, been going on for years. During my out-of-office period Sir Arthur had frequently consulted me on the subject, and I had pointed out that to talk of elected Arabs representing their people was to contradict the democratic principle which it was supposed to further. A legislative council in Palestine would be merely a modernized cloak for the old feudal system, that is, a continuation in power of the family cliques which had held the country in their thrall for centuries and ground down the faces of the poor.

I pointed out what was equally obvious, that official election to power would enable the Husseinis, the Mufti and their group to terrorize the villages even more effectively than before. Sir Arthur may or may not have agreed with me; he pressed his line with increasing insistence from the winter of 1935 on.

It was true that the proposed council would be so constructed that the number of Arabs would be balanced by the combination of Jews, British officials and unspecified members; and it was also true that the granting of certificates of immigration would be reserved to the High Commissioner. But as to the first point, we had had experience enough with the British officials in Palestine to know that we could not rely on them to defend the principles of the Mandate; as to the second, we foresaw that once the council was set up, the next step would be to give the Arabs increasing powers over the reserved subjects, and we would find ourselves confronted by the danger of the premature crystallization of the Jewish National Home. We would not agree to the council; we fought it in Palestine and in London.

Again I must, in fairness, stress the good relationship which had existed between us and Wauchope until that time. His attitude had been positive and helpful ever since his arrival in the country. When I saw a pro-Zionist administrator coming out to Palestine I was full of apprehension, and I usually gave him six to ten months in which to forget his Zionist tendencies and revert to the regulation type of administrator such as may be found on the Gold Coast or in Tanganyika or some other British dependency. We became natives in his eyes, and he resented the difficulties we created for him; we, on the other hand, resented the application of Gold Coast administrative measures to a highly developed, highly differentiated, critical and skeptical society like the *Yishuv* in Palestine. It says a great deal for the intellectual acumen and stamina of Sir Arthur Wauchope that he kept his original ideals for four years, and yielded only under the influence of events which were casting their shadows on the life of the whole world.

Among the various counterproposals to the form of legislative council urged by the Government, was one on which Jews and Arabs would be equal in number, with balance of power held by British officials. This seemed to me to present a possible solution. I knew the dangers inherent in it, but I felt that we might find some compensation in the public opinion of the world; for the position in which we placed ourselves by our refusal to consider the legislative council was, as I have explained, an unfortunate one. The public heard the words "legislative council for Palestine"; it heard of Zionist opposition; the obvious conclusion was that the Zionists were undemocratic, or antidemocratic! I had a second point in mind: on a council with equal Jewish and Arab representation there would be regular contacts between the two peoples; perhaps by patience and by fair dealing we might diminish the fears which kept the two peoples asunder. Fears are unconquerable by ordinary logic; but they sometimes yield to daily contact.

The council, as we know, was never set up in any form; but the fact that I was prepared to consider it if there was equality of representation was made the occasion for some of the bitterest attacks to which I have ever been subjected. I was called not merely an appeaser, but a British agent—and this accusation was periodically revived whenever I clashed with the extremists of the movement. It is no doubt still current. I can only quote, in this connection, the words of Nietzsche: *"Dem Reinem ist alles rein, dem Schweine ist alles Schwein."*

With the deterioration of the international situation, the rise of Hitler Germany, the Italo-Abyssinian war, the preliminaries to the Civil War in Spain, the lack of policy on the part of the democracies, new and disturbing elements were injected into the picture. France's indecisiveness toward Hitler, who was moving toward the Rhine, England's indecisiveness toward Mussolini, who was sending his warships through the Suez Canal, tended to give the Arabs the impression that with the democracies force alone won concessions. In April 1936 rioting broke out in Palestine, and a new and unhappy chapter opened in Zionist history.

The outbreaks were sporadic at first. In the general spirit of the period, the Government did not act decisively. For a long time no serious effort was made to cope with the rioting so that the Arabs gained the impression that they had in fact chosen the means and the moment well. A month elapsed, and the Arab leaders, encouraged by developments, formed the

Arab Higher Committee, headed by the Grand Mufti, and called a general strike.

The connection between the Arab Higher Committee and the rioting was clear enough. Fawzi Kawakji, the Syrian guerrilla fighter who came into Palestine to organize the bandits, was an old friend of the Mufti's. The waylaying and murdering of Jewish travelers, the attacks on Jewish settlements, the burning of Jewish fields, the uprooting of Jewish trees, spread over the entire country. The Palestine administration, undoubtedly acting on instructions from London, encouraged the intervention of the Arab states, and in August 1936 invited the Foreign Minister of Iraq to negotiate with the Arab Higher Committee, thereby giving a sort of official status to the employers of Kawakji. It was all in the true spirit of "appeasement."

That military action was feeble, and administrative action unwise, was the opinion of a British staff officer then serving in Palestine under General Dill. In his account of the early months of the riots, "British Rule and Rebellion," H. J. Simpson writes: "The delay in obtaining reinforcements, the restrictions placed on the actions of the troops from the outset, and the latitude to the other side to obstruct their movement became of secondary importance in view of the freedom of movement allowed to rebel leaders." And again: "The connection between the Arab leaders in Palestine and the armed bands raised in Palestine, as well as those brought in from abroad, seems to be established. The civil authorities persisted in maintaining that there was no connection and persisted in trying to squeeze a public pronouncement against the use of armed force out of the Mufti . . . they refused to act vigorously against the Arab leaders. Why that theory was fixed in their minds remains a mystery."

It was not much of a mystery to those who looked at Palestine in a larger setting, and saw in it as it were the mirror of events in Spain, at the other end of the Mediterranean, where England and France "persisted in maintaining that there was no connection" between the rebels and the Axis powers. Similarly, England was refusing to admit, at least publicly, that Axis encouragement and Axis money were playing a part in the Palestine riots.

Once the situation had been permitted to get out of hand, once the bandits had organized in the hills, the military had a real problem on its hands. An army is always at a disadvantage against guerrilla fighters, especially in a country with the geographic features of Palestine. Fawzi was a skillful fighter, and he managed his small forces well. In particular he trained them to disband, melt into the villages, and reassemble. The British troops, with their heavy equipment, could not cope with the light-armed, fast-moving Arabs. Nor was the attitude of the Palestine administration particularly helpful, as we have seen. The officer in command, General Dill, was a brilliant military leader, as was proved later in the war; but he rather resented, I believe, the awkward situation in which he was placed.

In May 1936, the British Government decided to appoint a royal commission to "investigate the causes of unrest and alleged grievances of Arabs or of Jews." This was the now famous "Peel Commission," so called from its chairman, Earl Peel—by far the most distinguished and ablest of the investigatory bodies ever sent out to Palestine. Its members were men with excellent training and in some cases of wide experience. There were among them an ex-administrator of a province in India, a professor of colonial history at Oxford, an ex-Ambassador, a judge of the High Court, and a lawyer of eminence. The chairman was of ministerial rank. Many of us felt that this was not only an extremely competent body, but that it would prove to be both thorough and impartial. The findings of such a commission, we believed, would go a long way toward solving our problems.

For my own part, I must state that when the commission arrived in Palestine—this was not until November 1936—and the time for the hearings approached, I became deeply convinced that a new and possibly decisive phase in our movement might now be beginning. Knowing something of the records of the members of the commission, I had complete confidence in their fairness and their intellectual honesty. Nevertheless it was with considerable trepidation that I went up to Jerusalem on November 25 to deliver my evidence. I remember that, as I walked between two rows of spectators to the door of the building where the sessions were being held, there were audible whispers on either side of me *"Ha-shem yatzliach darkecho"* (God prosper you on your mission), and I felt that I not only carried the burden of these well-wishers, and of countless others in other lands, but that I would be speaking for generations long since dead, for those who lay buried in the ancient and thickly populated cemeteries on Mount Scopus, and those whose last resting places were scattered all over the world. And I knew that any misstep of mine, any error, however involuntary, would be not mine alone, but would redound to the discredit of my people. I was aware, as on few occasions before or since, of a crushing sense of responsibility.

I must confess, further, that the few friendly words addressed to me in the way of introduction by the chairman, as he asked me to sit down, meant a great deal to me, and perhaps carried more encouragement than was intended. In them one felt the innate courtesy of a gentleman, whose patience and kindliness at that time were the more remarkable as he was in great physical pain. Lord Peel was suffering from cancer, and died of it shortly after the publication of his report.

I began my address in slow, measured sentences. I had no prepared text, for I could not on such an occasion have read out a written document. I did, however, have comprehensive notes, which I had worked out with my colleagues, and I kept close to these. Not knowing how patient my auditors would be, I probably attempted to compress too much, but after speaking for perhaps half an hour, I noticed to my deep joy that they were following me with interest. They had moved forward, so that their chairs almost formed a semicircle round me, and I did not have to strain my voice. I went on practically without interruption for about an hour and a half, when I asked for a drink and a short break, as I was feeling a little faint. The chairman offered me something stronger, which I refused. I was now at my ease, and resumed my address, which took up another forty minutes or so.

I believe that the reader who has followed the narrative so far will already have some notion of the contents of my address, into which I sought to put both the permanent principles of the Zionist movement and the immediate urgency of the Jewish problem. I spoke of the six million Jews (a bitter and unconscious prophecy of the number exterminated not long after by Hitler) "pent up in places where they are not wanted, and for whom the world is divided into places where they cannot live and places which they may not enter." For them "a certificate for Palestine is the highest boon. One in twenty, one in thirty may get it, and for them it is redemption." Seeking to explain how they had reached this condition, I told of the deterioration of Jewish life in Central and Eastern Europe under the impact of new forces. But I sought to go deeper, into more enduring causes. "When one speaks of the Jewish people one speaks of a people which is a minority everywhere, a majority nowhere, which is to some extent identified with the races among which it lives, but is still not quite identical. It is a disembodied ghost of a race, and it inspires suspicion, and suspicion breeds hatred. There should be one place in the world, in God's wide world, where we could live and express ourselves in accordance with our character, and make our contribution to civilization in our own way, and through our own channels."

I spoke next of the Balfour Declaration, of which "it has sometimes been glibly said, 'Here is a document, somewhat vague in its nature, issued in time of war. It was a wartime expedient.'" I disproved, I believe, that the Balfour Declaration had been issued hastily and frivolously; and I cited the words of Lord Robert Cecil as to what the Balfour Declaration had been intended to convey: "Arabia for the Arabs, Judaea for the Jews, Armenia for the Armenians." I spoke finally of what we had achieved in Palestine, which, at the time of the Peel Commission, contained four hundred thousand Jews as against the fifty-five thousand of the time of the Balfour Declaration; pointing, of course, to the general benefits which had accrued to the country from our work.

So much for the opening address; I had an opportunity, on ensuing days, to go into the details of our difficulties, during a long and thorough cross-examination. I was greatly impressed by the seriousness, patience, and relevance of the proceedings. I left Jerusalem and returned to Rehovoth, to resume my laboratory work, but was recalled to Jerusalem on several occasions to appear before the commission.

The subject of the partition of Palestine was first broached to me by the commission at a session which was held *in camera* on January 8, 1937. No colleague was with me. I was asked how the idea struck me, and naturally answered that I could not tell on the spur of the moment, nor would I give my own impressions except after consultation with my colleagues. Actually I felt that the suggestion held out great possibilities and hopes. Something new had been born into the Zionist movement, something which had to be handled with great care and tenderness, which should not be permitted to become a matter for crude slogans and angry controversy. I remember saying not long afterward to a colleague: "A Jewish State, the idea of Jewish independence in Palestine, even if only in part of Palestine, is such a lofty thing that it ought to be treated like the Ineffable Name, which is never pronounced in vain. By talking about it too much, by dragging it down to the level of the banal, you desecrate that which should be approached only with reverence."

The idea of partition was, as I have said, first imparted to me *in camera*. A few days later I replied that this was an impossible position for me. I was the President of a democratic organization, and I could not give the commission my views on such an important subject without having consulted my colleagues.

It was obvious from the beginning that the territory to be "offered" us would be a small one. Part of it would be the Negev, or southern desert. A possible alternative would be a shift to the north, leaving out the Negev. I will not go into further details here.

Apart from the practical details of a partition plan, there was the fundamental question of partition as such. It had, besides its political and economic problems, its religious aspect. I took the matter up with a number of men for whose religious convictions I had the deepest respect, but men not involved in any way in the politics of the movement, and I did not find too much resistance. I put it to them thus: "I know that God promised Palestine to the children of Israel, but I do not know what boundaries He set. I believe that they were wider than the ones now proposed, and may have included Trans-Jordan. Still, we have foregone the eastern part and are now asked to forego some of the western part. If God will keep His promise to His people in His own time, our business as poor humans, who live in a difficult age, is to save as much as we can of the remnants of Israel. By adopting this project we can save more of them than by continuing the Mandatory policy."

It was my own deep conviction that God had always chosen small countries through which to convey His messages to humanity. It was from Judaea and from Greece, not from Carthage or Babylonia that the great ideas which form the most precious possessions of mankind emerged. I believed that a small Jewish State, well organized, living in peace with its neighbors, a State on which would be lavished the love and devotion of the Jewish communities throughout the world —such a State would be a great credit to us and an equally great contribution to civilization.

There were—and are—immediate political considerations which inclined me toward the idea of partition. I saw in the establishment of a Jewish State a real possibility of coming to terms with the Arabs. As long as the Mandatory policy prevails, the Arabs are afraid that we shall absorb the whole of Palestine. Say what we will about the preservation of their rights, they are dominated by fear and will not listen to reason. A Jewish State with definite boundaries internationally guaranteed would be something final; the transgressing of these boundaries would be an act of war which the Jews would not commit, not merely because of its moral implications, but because it would arouse the whole world against them. Instead of being a minority in Palestine, we would be a majority in our own State, and be able to deal on terms of equality with our Arab neighbors in Palestine, Egypt and Iraq. As to our immediate neighbors, the Palestinians, we would have a great many interests in common—customs, harbors, railways, irrigation and development projects; such a community of interests, if properly handled, becomes the basis of peaceful and fruitful co-operation.

My hope that the question of partition would be dealt with on the high level to which it belonged was disappointed. It became the focus of one of the most violent controversies that has ever divided the Zionist movement. The Twentieth Zionist Congress, held in Basle in August 1937, in the gathering shadows of the Nazi domination of Europe, broke into the *Ja-sager* and the *Nein-sager*, the proponents and the opponents of partition; not, I am compelled to say, on the merits of the question, but very often on the basis of prejudgments. I pleaded in vain that in the opinion of our most capable experts a Jewish State in part of Palestine would be able to absorb one hundred thousand immigrants a year, and sustain a Jewish population of two and a half to three millions. The divisions of opinion followed familiar lines, and I found myself again opposed by the combination of an American group, the *Mizrachi*, and that section of the Revisionists which had not seceded from the Zionist Organization.

But even the opposition could not wholly ignore the threat which now hung over the Jews of Europe, and the prospects of substantial rescue which a Jewish State held out made impossible outright rejection of partition. The following resolutions, among others, were accepted:

> The Congress declares that the scheme of partition put forward by the Royal Commission is unacceptable.
> The Congress empowers the Executive to enter into negotiations with a view to ascertaining the precise terms of His Majesty's Government for the proposed establishment of a Jewish State.
> In such negotiations the Executive shall not commit either itself or the Zionist Organization, but in the event of the emergence of a definite scheme for the establishment of a Jewish State, such scheme shall be brought before a newly elected Congress for decision.

In this roundabout way the Congress indicated that it was ready to talk partition, and the issue seemed chiefly to be between those who had the courage to say so frankly, and those who wanted to retain a reputation for uncompromising maximalism.

But the battle was fought in vain, at least for the time being. The partition plan put forward by the British Government on the basis of the Peel Report was not followed up seriously. The rumor was started, and gained wide currency, that the Jews were against partition. This was simply not true. Considering the vital departure from the original Zionist program which partition represented, considering also the internal political by-play of the various parties, the two to one vote of the Congress for the above-mentioned resolutions was very significant. I explained all this to Ormsby-Gore and to members of the Mandates Commission shortly after the Congress. That I had correctly interpreted the Jewish attitude toward partition has been made very clear to the world since that time.

Toward Nullification

BRITAIN'S official offer of a partition plan was contained in a White Paper issued early in July 1937. The offer was accompanied by a series of interim administrative measures—"while the form of a scheme of partition is being worked out"—which struck heavily at the Jewish National Home. These measures were put into effect before Jewish opinion on partition had been tested. They were the first steps toward the nullification of the Balfour Declaration: actual nullification came with the White Paper of 1939. It was the classic technique of the step-by-step sellout of small nations which the great democracies practiced in the appeasement period.

The Government White Paper of 1937 was based on the Peel Report. The latter was an extraordinary document. On the one hand it testified to the achievements of the Jews in Palestine, on the other hand it recommended measures which seemed to us to be in complete contradiction with that testimony. The report put an end to the persistent falsehood that Jewish land purchases and land development had led to the displacement of Arabs; then it recommended severe restrictions on Jewish purchases of land. It asserted that Jewish immigration had brought benefits to the Arab people; then it recommended the severe curtailment of Jewish immigration. And it did this last in a form which was all the more shocking because it practically conceded the point made by the Arab terrorists, and undermined the very foundations of the Mandate.

By the terms of the Mandate, and by the agreement between the Jewish Agency and Great Britain, Jewish immigration into Palestine was to be controlled by the economic absorptive capacity of the country. This was the safeguard against undue harm to the population of the country. The Jews were in Palestine "as of right and not on sufferance," and they came there as the opportunities were created for their employment. It was an arrangement which had worked according to the Peel Commission; Jews had come into Palestine in large numbers—over forty thousand in 1934, over sixty thousand in 1935—and the Arabs had benefited economically by their coming. Now the Peel Report recommended that in granting immigration permits to the Zionists, "political and psychological factors must be taken into consideration." In other words, our entry into Palestine was made conditional on the mood of the Arabs. It was not put so frankly, of course. That last brutal clarification was reserved for the White Paper of 1939. But that was what it amounted to. Arab terrorism had won its first major victory. The Mandate was pronounced unworkable.

The Peel Report and the White Paper were issued simultaneously; and I felt it to be a very bad augury that I could not, almost up to the last minute, obtain an advance copy of the report. I called up Ormsby-Gore, then the Colonial Minister, and angry words passed between us. A day or two later I wrote him at length. The letter follows in its entirety. I make no apology for reproducing it, and one or two others belonging to that time. There has been so much talk about my inability or refusal to stand up to British officialdom, ("British agent," it will be recalled, are words that have been used about me) that I feel myself entitled to the publication of these letters. It might be added, in this connection, that it is easy to hurl denunciations at a government from the platform at a public meeting; it is another matter to carry the fight to the men with whom you are negotiating.

London
July 4, 1937

DEAR ORMSBY-GORE:

I have to thank you for your letter of July 1st. I am extremely sorry that you should have been distressed at my tone and manner over the telephone. It was certainly never my intention to say anything that might give you personal offense, and if I have done so, I sincerely regret it.

You think that I am under some grave misapprehension—namely, that the Cabinet will be taking far-reaching and final decisions of policy before the publication of the Report. This is not the main cause of my present anxieties. I quite understand that it would be impossible for the Cabinet, in so short a space of time, and occupied as it must be with many other very grave problems, to come to a quick and final decision on the Report. I also fully appreciate that time must elapse before the Report can be implemented, either wholly or in part. Still, your refusal to let me have a copy of it for a few days in advance of its publication has rendered more difficult for me an anyhow very difficult situation.

We are now on the eve of events which will shape the destiny of Palestine and of the Jewish people for years to come, and which, as you said, will also prove of vital importance for the British Empire. May I therefore tell you, with perfect frankness, how I see the present situation? I have no desire to indulge in mere retrospect, still less in useless recrimination: but possibly what I have to say may be of value for you in the times that lie ahead, when you will have to decide the fate of Palestine.

In the last twenty years, and especially in the last two years since my re-election to the Presidency of the Jewish Agency, I have had ample opportunities to observe the attitude of the Palestine Administration toward us and the Mandate; and the conviction has been forced upon me by my experience that the Mandate for Palestine has hardly had a real chance, and that now as in the past it is being, consciously or unconsciously, undermined by those called upon to carry it out. It was the leitmotif of my evidence before the Royal Commission that things should never have been allowed to come to this pass; and that the present situation has not been brought about by any inherent defect in the Mandate (though this may have its weaknesses like all works of man). I understand from you that the Royal Commission, for whose impartiality and judgment I have the highest respect, have condemned the Mandate. I am prepared to accept their judgment of the situation, but with one fundamental reservation; it is not the Mandate that should be condemned, but the people who administered it. Had it been the aim of the Palestine Administration to prove that the Mandate was unworkable, it could be congratulated on the choice of the methods adopted in the past two years. This is the crux of the matter. A situation had been artificially created in which nothing was left for the Royal Commission but to bring in this verdict against the Mandate; and thus their work was vitiated from the very outset. What could they think, coming fresh to Palestine and staying there for a few months, when they found that the country had been in a state of armed revolt for the better part of a year, successfully defying the armed forces of the British Empire? They were inevitably driven to the conclusion that there must be some deep underlying cause, a movement of exceptional magnitude and with wide ramifications outside of Palestine; and naturally the Administration had every interest in persuading them of the existence of such a cause, and in painting the situation in the darkest colors in order to justify its own record. What was that record? Complete inaction; paralysis of Government; surrender to crime; demoralization of the Civil Service—men willing and able to do their duty prevented by the faintheartedness of their superiors: denial of justice;

failure to protect the lives and property of law-abiding citizens, Jewish and Arab; in short, a condition of things unthinkable in any other part of the British Empire. These things fall, to a great extent, into your own term of office. In vain did we appeal to you to see authority re-established in Palestine. Almost a year ago, when Wauchope gratuitously brought the Arab Kings upon the Palestinian stage, I pointed out to you the very grave dangers of this measure. For a moment the Government bethought itself, stopped the intervention of Nuri Pasha (a "force" that faded out overnight), decided to try the strong hand in Palestine and sent out General Dill at the head of an army. But the High Commissioner soon succeeded in frustrating this attempt and turned it into an expensive farce—the military authorities will best be able to tell you this part of the story. Through no fault of theirs, order was not re-established in Palestine, and Wauchope's regime continues, inflicting untold damage on us, and earning no credit for the British Government. The Mufti is still at large, and pandered to by the Administration; under its very eyes he now travels about, organizing armed resistance to the forthcoming recommendations of the Royal Commission, and enlisting the help of destructive elements in the neighboring countries. The Arab Kings are being mobilized once more to impress His Majesty's Government, and especially the Foreign Office, with the bogey of Pan-Islam and the strength of the Arab national movement—a movement which is crude in its nature, which tries tó work up the hatred of the British and the Jews, looks to Mussolini and Hitler as its heroes, and is supported by Italian money—you know it all, and still you allow these things to go on.

I take it that you have read the report for 1936 submitted by the Palestine Administration to the League of Nations Council. That report contains a deliberate distortion of the truth. Having failed to discharge the most elementary duty of any civilized Government, namely to maintain order and protect the lives and property of law-abiding citizens, the Administration now tries to suggest that we have been guilty of provoking the riots. I enclose a copy of my letter to the High Commissioner, which he has refrained from answering in writing. The blaming of the victims is a procedure with which I am painfully acquainted after pogroms in Czarist Russia, but I never expected to see it adopted by a British Administration. Can you possibly uphold such a report in Geneva?

We shall shortly be asked to acquiesce in a revolutionary plan which would amount to the abolition of the Mandate and a partition of Palestine. Not having seen the report, I am naturally unable to discuss its proposals. But I see that the High Commissioner has been specially summoned from Palestine, I presume to advise the Government on the statement of policy which you are about to issue; and is returning to

Palestine to maintain "order" there if a revolt breaks out. Frankly, considering his record during the past fifteen months, I view the immediate and the more distant future with the gravest apprehension. I understand that, if the scheme of partition is adopted, a period of transition is to intervene before a Jewish State is established. This will be a most delicate and dangerous time. Even the best proposals made by the Royal Commission are liable to suffer the fate of the Mandate, and for the same reasons; and the result will be that after the Mandate has been discredited and scrapped, there will be nothing to take its place.

I am speaking to you frankly, and without any of the circumlocutions usually employed in discussing such matters. The time is too serious and too much is at stake. I see no future for any constructive policy unless there is a complete change of heart and a clean sweep in Palestine. Successive Colonial Secretaries have left us to struggle all these years with an Administration which has been inefficient, unimaginative, obstructive and unfriendly. There have been and undoubtedly are good men among them, but they have not been able to prevail against the dead weight of others of a very different stamp. In spite of these, we have succeeded, and the greater our success, the bitterer they became. The process has reached its culminating point in the last two years, and it was my fate to bear the brunt of it. This is the more tragic for me when I see you at the head of the Colonial Office, you who have helped us wholeheartedly in earlier days; and I trust that even now you have not become "impartial" in the sense of the Palestine Administration, who refuse to distinguish between right and wrong, and try, in fact, to obliterate the difference between them.

Just before the riots broke out I had an intimate talk with the High Commissioner. He asked me whether I thought troubles were to be expected. I replied that in Czarist Russia I knew that if the Government did not wish for troubles, they never happened. The Palestine Administration did not wish for riots, but has done very little to prevent them; has let things go from bad to worse; has allowed the situation to get out of hand, and the country to sink into anarchy. Perhaps at the beginning of the troubles some officers were not even altogether sorry to see such a reply given to the debates in Parliament which had destroyed their scheme for a Legislative Council, and which they wrongly assumed to have been brought on by us. In the last resort, some of these men, with no faith in the Jewish National Home, can hardly have regretted to see the policy of the Balfour Declaration and of the Mandate discredited and dishonored.

What hope is there, then, for the future, after twenty years of such an Administration? This is at the root of my very grave anxiety. The account given of the disturbances in the Annual Report of the Palestine Administration to the League is only the last link in a long chain of obstruction and injustice.

You close your letter by urging me not to burn my boats, nor to go off at the deep end. I have no boats to burn. You further ask me not to come up with a flourish of trumpets. Can you in the last twenty years point to a single occasion on which I have done so? I have borne most things in silence; I have defended the British Administration before my own people, from public platforms, at Congresses, in all parts of the world, often against my own better knowledge, and almost invariably to my own detriment. Why did I do so? Because to me close co-operation with Great Britain was the cornerstone of our policy in Palestine. But this co-operation remained unilateral—it was unrequited love.

When you speak of "consultation" you suggest that were you to consult me on policy with regard to Palestine, you would hardly know where you could stop! I claim that what Palestine is now is due primarily to the work of my people; I have had my share in that work, and I represent them. This was the foundation of my claim, and I leave it to history to decide whether the claim was excessive.

You ask me for some measure of trust; to no one would I be happier to give it, because I remember—and I shall never forget—your old friendship, and the work we did in common in the difficult days now far removed. But however I may feel toward you personally, how can I trust the system with which you have now unfortunately become identified? You want me slowly to "feel my way." But I am not an isolated individual, and I ought to be able from the very outset to give a lead to my people. I cannot do so if I receive the Report, which you describe as voluminous and complex, two days before publication, about the same time as it will, I imagine, be given to the Lobby correspondents of newspapers. On my part there will be no flourish of trumpets—that is anyhow not my style—but something which may, in the result, prove very much worse: enforced silence.

The letter to the High Commissioner, above referred to, was addressed to him in London, where he had arrived for consultation with the Colonial Office. The reader will find it self-explanatory; but he should also bear in mind the total background. During those years of Arab violence the Jews of Palestine adopted and resolutely followed, in the face of the utmost provocation, the policy of *Havlagah*, or of self-restraint, which I think may be properly described as one of the great moral political acts of modern times. The Haganah remained throughout a defense organization, and the *Yishuv* as a whole did not believe in, did not practice or encourage, counterattack or retaliation. Yet it is hard to describe the heartsickness and bitterness of the Jews as they watched the larger Hitler terror engulf their kin in Europe, while the gates of Palestine were being shut as a concession to the Arabs and the Palestine administration failed to proceed with the necessary vigor against the Arab terrorists.

London
30th June, 1937

DEAR SIR ARTHUR:

I have just read the remarkable and peculiar account of last year's disturbances given in the Government's Report to the Mandates Commission. The story of the events at the outset of the disturbances has been made to convey the impression that these were to a large extent provoked by a series of Jewish attacks on Arabs. Further, in the record of the casualties suffered between the 19th and the 22nd April, no indication is given of the fact that not one of the Arabs killed was killed by a Jew. The impression thus given of the outbreak of the disturbances is at variance with your own communiqué of the 19th April, and any unbiased person with a knowledge of the facts must see in this account a calculated distortion of the truth.

In the entire Report, there is not a single reference to, still less a word of praise for, the restraint which the Jews have shown during the long months of violence directed against them by the Arabs. You yourself have, on various occasions, both in public and in private, expressed your admiration for the behavior of our people. That there should not be a single reference to it in the Report is, I think, an indictment of the authorities themselves.

I am both astonished and pained that such an account should appear in an official record which must be assumed to have received your approval.

The posture of affairs in the summer of 1937 may be gathered from the two foregoing letters. In the months that followed things went from bad to worse. In Palestine there was a spurt of military activity which promised for a time to put an end to the riots—Orde Wingate was then in the country; but the improvement was more than offset by the apparent indifference which the British Government manifested toward its own partition plan. Here I was, exerting myself to break down the resistance to the plan in our ranks, while the Government seemed to grow increasingly cool toward it. On the last day of that year I wrote to Sir John Shuckburgh, Permanent Under Secretary for the Colonies:

. . . . Nearly six months have elapsed since the Report of the Royal Commission and the White Paper were published, yet nothing has been done to advance matters. This inactivity of the Government in the political sphere is largely neutralizing the good effect produced by the active measures adopted by it in regard to security. There is utter confusion as to the political intentions of His Majesty's Government, which is doing infinite harm to the economic life of the country, to the authority of the Government and to the prospects of an eventual settlement. . . . The atmosphere of doubt and suspense thus engendered provides an ideal ground for every schemer and intriguer, self-appointed or foreign-paid, to try his hand at advertising alternative "solutions." All these schemes have one and the same object: the liquidation of the National Home and the virtual handing over of the country to the clique of so-called Arab leaders who organized the disturbances of last year and from their hiding places are now running the terrorist campaign . . . The terms are always the same: liquidation of the Mandate and Jewish acceptance of minority status, the Jewish position to be protected by that invaluable instrument of "minority rights" of which we have had such instructive experience in Eastern Europe. Let there be no mistake about the action of the representative bodies of the Jewish people to any of these schemes. Jews are not going to Palestine to become in their ancient home "Arabs of the Mosaic Faith" or to exchange their German or Polish ghetto for an Arab one. Whoever knows what Arab Government looks like, what "minority status" signifies nowadays, and what a Jewish ghetto in an Arab state means—there are quite a number of precedents—will be able to form his own conclusions as to what would be in store for us if we accepted the position allotted to us in these "solutions." It is not for the purpose of subjecting the Jewish people, which still stands in the front rank of civilization, to the rule of a set of unscrupulous Levantine politicians that this supreme effort is being made in Palestine. All the labors and sacrifices here owe their inspiration to one thing alone: to the belief that this at least is going to mean freedom and the end of the ghetto. Could there be a more appalling fraud on the hopes of a martyred people than to reduce it to ghetto status in the very land where it was promised national freedom?

Those who advance these schemes know perfectly well that there is no prospect of their acceptance by the Jews. Their purpose is not to find a solution which would meet our ever more urgent need for a national home but, on the contrary, to strangle our effort of national reconstruction. The same forces which last year used every device of violence and blackmail to destroy the Mandate are busy, now that they believe that object to have been essentially achieved, in undermining partition, which, they perceive, might still offer a chance of realizing the Jewish National Home even though in a much reduced area.

So, month after month, the technique of keeping a promise to the ear and breaking it to the heart, was applied to us. The offer of partition was stultified, first by delay, second by the manner in which the British Government approached it practically. Another commission was appointed, the Woodhead Commission, to suggest actual plans. But the instructions given it—the terms of reference—were such as to foredoom any sort of plan. For what was bound to emerge was a Jewish territory so small that there would hardly be standing room for the Jews who wanted to come; development and growth would be out of the question. Plans would be offered only for the planned purpose of being rejected.

Meanwhile the ground was burning under our feet. We saw the Second World War advancing inexorably, and hope for our millions in Europe diminishing. And the frustration was all the more unbearable because we knew that in the coming struggle the Jewish National Home could play a very considerable role in that part of the world as the one reliable ally of the democracies. It was quite fantastic to note the ingenuity and inventiveness which England expended, to her own hurt, on the shelving of that ally. But was not this the essence of the appeasement panic? I have already mentioned the assiduous spreading of the report that the Jews were opposed to the idea of partition as such. To make assurance double sure, the partition plan was finally put forward in obviously impossible form. Then, on top of that, quite a discussion developed in England on the strategic unimportance of Palestine as compared with Cyprus. In the letter to Sir John Shuckburgh, above quoted, I said:

Allow me to say one word on the strategical question which is so much in the fore of the discussion at the present. It would be presumptuous for a mere layman like myself to express any opinion as to the relative strategical values of Haifa and Cyprus, but there are some crude facts which even a plain chemist can understand. The pipe line, the aerodromes and the Carmel cannot be removed to Cyprus, nor the railway to Egypt, or the connection with the Suez Canal and the corridor, to Baghdad. More I would not presume to say on this point.

To Ormsby-Gore I wrote a little later, in April 1938:

We could form a force of something like 40,000 men now and with increased immigration into the future State area such a force would rapidly grow. I do not wish to overstate my case in any way, but I would like you and your colleagues to know it. The position is analogous to that of 1914-1917, if anything much more serious for everybody concerned and for us in particular. This again is another very urgent reason for speedy action. I have had some conversation on this subject with General Georges of the French General Staff, and found him very understanding indeed.

The futility of these arguments, and of all the practical considerations behind them, is only too well known. The British Government had simply made up its mind to crystallize the Jewish National Home and if not for the stubborn resistance of the Jews, who refuse to be trifled with in this matter, they would have succeeded.

In Palestine the Arab terror continued, with ups and downs which reflected not so much the fortunes of war as the fluctuations in British determination. In the autumn of 1936 there was vigorous action against the Arab terrorists, with good results. Numbers of Jews were enrolled as *ghaffirim*, or supernumerary police, for the defense of the colonies. The country was comparatively quiet during the presence of the Peel Commission. In the summer of 1937 the unrest intensified. Between April 1936 and March 1937, ninety three Jews were killed and over four hundred wounded. Damage to Jewish property amounted to nearly half a million pounds; but this does not take into account the heavy losses due to the diversion of men from productive work to defense, the disruption of communications and the economic deterioration due both to terrorism and the uncertainty of the political future.

In September the military again acted with energy, and again there was a lull in the terrorism; in October it again flared up. In the early months of 1938 the guerrillas in the hills were particularly active. In 1938, sixty nine British were killed, ninety two Jews and four hundred and eighty six Arab civilians. Over one thousand rebels were killed in action. The disturbances did not die down until September 1939, when the war began.

During the entire period of the rioting the Jews of Palestine exhibited that moral discipline of *Havlagah*, or self-restraint, which, following the highest traditions of Zionism, won the admiration of liberal opinion all over the world. The consistency with which this policy was maintained was the more remarkable when we consider that violence paid political dividends to the Arabs, while Jewish *Havlagah* was expected to be its own reward. It did not even win official recognition. Sir Arthur Wauchope's report—the subject of my letter to him, on p. 394—illustrates the point. The Jews followed their tradition of moral discipline, the Palestine administration followed its tradition of bracketing Jews and Arabs "impartially" in the "disturbances." It looked very much like incitement of Jews to terrorism, and the human thing happened when a dissident Jewish minority broke ranks at last in the summer of 1938, taking its cue from the Arabs—and from the administration. But it was still a very small minority. The *Yishuv* as a whole, then as now, stood firm against Jewish terrorism.

The darkness of those years is relieved by the memory of the strange and brilliant figure mentioned a few pages back—Orde Wingate, who has sometimes been called "the Lawrence of Judaea." He won that title not only for his military exploits as the leader of the Jewish groups which were organized against the terrorist activities, but for his passionate sympathy—one might say his self-identification—with the highest ideals of Zionism.

Of his gifts as a soldier, especially as the organizer and leader of the famous Chindits in Burma, there are several brilliant descriptions in contemporaneous literature, and it is not for me to pass judgment on them. But I can testify that he was idolized by the men who fought under him, and that they were filled with admiration for his qualities of endurance, courage, and originality. There are hundreds who recall how, having to cope with the Arab guerrillas who descended on the Haifa-Mosul pipe line from time to time, destroyed a section of it, and retreated as fast as they had come, Wingate created a special motorcycle squad to patrol the whole length of the line, and by matching speed against speed, eliminated the threat. The Jews under his command were especially feared by the Arabs. Wingate used to tell me that when, at the head of a Jewish squad, he ambushed a group of raiders, he would hear a shout: "Run! These are not British soldiers! They are Jews!"

I met Wingate and his beautiful young wife, Lorna, at Government House in Jerusalem. I was immediately struck by his powerful personality and by his spiritual outlook not only on problems in Palestine, but on those of the world at large. He came often to my house in Rehovoth, traveling alone in his little car, armed to the teeth. From the beginning he showed himself a fanatical Zionist, and he had come to his views not under any personal influence or propaganda, but by the effect of Zionist literature on his deep and lifelong study of the Bible. In this his superiors—Wingate had the rank of captain in the Palestine intelligence service—were entirely out of sympathy with his views; he in turn chafed under the command of men whom he considered intellectually and morally below him.

His two great intellectual passions were military science and the Bible, and there was in him a fusion of the student and the man of action which reminded me of T. E. Lawrence. There were other reminders, in his personality: his intenseness, his whimsicality, and his originality. I thought of Lawrence more than once when Wingate sat opposite me, arguing fiercely, and boring me through with his eyes; and I did not learn until many months after we had met and become friends that he was in fact a distant blood relative of Lawrence's.

To complete his Zionist education Wingate used to repair for days at a stretch to some of the settlements—Ain Harod being his favorite—and there he would try to speak Hebrew with the settlers and familiarize himself with their outlook and their way of life, to which he was greatly drawn. He was often very impatient with me and with what he called my cunctatorial methods. He was as critical of the Government as of his superiors, and preached the doctrine that unless one forced it, the Government would never do anything for us; the Palestine administration, in his opinion, consisted almost without exception of enemies of the Zionist movement.

He said, more than once: "You must find your way to Downing Street, go up to the Prime Minister and tell him that everything is wrong, the Government is letting you down, is behaving treacherously. And having said that, don't wait for an answer, leave the room."

To which I usually replied, "I won't have to leave it, if I follow your advice. I shall be thrown out." Much as I admired and loved Wingate, I did not think that his diplomatic abilities in any way matched his military performance or his personal integrity. Shortly before his death he wrote me from the Far East, and in this, his last letter to me, he admitted that my policy was the right one, the only one that could be pursued with any hope of success. He apologized for having chivvied me so often on my methods; the apology was not necessary—I knew in what spirit his reproaches had been made. My wife and I both loved and revered him.

Perhaps his own life taught him toward the end. He was a man who did not suffer fools gladly, was trenchant in his criticism of our betters, and was always in hot water with his superiors. General Wavell writes of him, after praising his brilliant work in Abyssinia: "When it was all over he sent to my headquarters a memorandum that would almost have justified my placing him under arrest for insubordination." When Wingate was on leave in London, during the war, he would get hold of all sorts of people and preach Zionism to them. Amongst others he hit on Lord Beaverbrook, whose anti-Zionist views are well known. In the course of the argument which developed, Beaverbrook tried to rebut Wingate saying, "I think thus and thus," and Wingate interrupted with: "What you think doesn't matter a damn; what matters is what God thinks, and that you don't know." Beaverbrook wasn't accustomed to this kind of talk, and complained to the War Office that a young officer was going about town making propaganda for Jews, an occupation unsuitable to his rank and the King's uniform. Wingate received a black mark, and this added to the many difficulties he had to contend with despite his brilliant performance on the battlefield.

After the Abyssinian campaign Wingate, desperately sick with malaria, and almost constantly drugged with quinine, became so embroiled with his superior officers that he fell seriously ill, and was hospitalized in Cairo. On returning to London he was shoved into an obscure job training raw recruits in some small place near London, being adjudged too unbalanced to command men in a responsible capacity. Had this continued for a longer time, it would have meant his

moral and physical collapse. He turned to me for advice. T was ignorant
of military procedure, and though I was anxious to help him hardly
knew where to begin. Then it occurred to me that I might put his case
before Lord Horder, a leading London physician and a very enlight-
ened and sympathetic person. To him I recounted briefly the facts of
Wingate's career, and asked him to go before the Army Medical Council and testify, if he thought fit, to Wingate's reliability and sense of
responsibility. He did this, and before long Wingate received an appointment—again under Wavell—to India, where he organized his
famous Chindits for the Burma campaign behind the Japanese lines.
His achievement in this enterprise has become one of the war's legends.
He was killed in an airplane accident when he insisted on flying to an
outpost in the jungle against the advice of the pilot. His body was not
found until some three years later.

Wingate's death was an irreparable loss to the British Army, to the
Jewish cause, and to my wife and myself personally. While he was
commanding the Chindits in Burma, Churchill learned of his exploits
and recalled him to London to attend the Allied Conference in Quebec.
On his return to London he was promoted to the rank of major general,
and it was vouchsafed us to see him for a few days, happy to have
found recognition at last, and modestly resplendent in his new uniform.
He left soon after for his command in the Far East, and this was the
last his friends saw of him.

He had one consuming desire which was not fulfilled: he wanted to
lead a British Army into Berlin. When, after long negotiation and discussion, the Jewish Brigade was agreed upon and actually formed, I
applied for the services of Wingate, but this request was, for obvious
reasons—as I think—refused. The idea of a Jewish fighting force was
never popular with the pundits of the War Office; and to have had such
a unit headed by an arch-Zionist like Wingate was just too much for
the generals in Whitehall. The refusal was definite and complete.

CHAPTER 38

The White Paper

Partition Torpedoed—The Tripartite Conference, February-March, 1939—The Days of Berchtesgaden and Gotesberg—The Coffin Boats on the Mediterranean—The Patria*—Lord Halifax's Astounding Proposal—How the White Paper Was Prepared—The Betrayal of Czechoslovakia—Jan Masaryk's Tragic Visit—Negotiations in Egypt—Last Warning to Chamberlain—His Infatuation with Appeasement—The White Paper Debated in Parliament—The Jews Unanimously Reject the White Paper.*

AT THE time it issued the Peel Report, in 1937, the British Government began to set up the Woodhead Commission, which was to submit a partition plan. The commission did not proceed to Palestine until April 1938; and in October of that year it published a report stating that it had no practical partition plan to offer. The following month the Government rejected the idea of partition. It looked as though the commission had been appointed merely to pave the way for a predetermined course of action for which no commission was necessary.

The same may be said of the Tripartite Conference—British, Arabs, Jews—which the Government now proceeded (December 1938) to call. Just as the Government of that time could and would have done what it did about partition without the gesture of a new commission, so it could and would have done what it did about nullifying the Balfour Declaration without the gesture of the St. James Conference of February-March 1939. The reader must bear the period in mind: in October 1938 the Sudetenland had been handed over to Hitler as a result of the Munich Conference; in March 1939 Hitler annexed the rest of Czechoslovakia; and Mr. Chamberlain still believed, or pretended to believe, that by these concessions he was purchasing "peace in our time." What chance had the Jewish National Home with such a Government, and what likelihood was there that Commissions and Conferences would deflect it from its appeasement course?

Nevertheless the Jews and Arabs were duly invited—Jews representing all sections of opinion, and Arabs representing Palestine and its

401

neighbors, Egypt, Iraq, and so on—and the Conference was opened with much solemnity in St. James's Palace on February 7, 1939. The dignity of the occasion was somewhat marred by the fact that Mr. Chamberlain's address of welcome had to be given twice, once to the Jews and once to the Arabs, since the latter would not sit with the former, and even used different entrances to the palace so as to avoid embarrassing contacts.

The proceedings were usually conducted by Colonial Secretary Malcolm MacDonald, supported by a staff of higher ranking officials of the Foreign and Colonial offices; they were attended from time to time by Foreign Secretary Lord Halifax. Toward the end, for reasons which will appear, they lost any appearance of purpose or intelligibility which may originally have been imparted to them. I did not attend the closing session. But during the Conference I exerted myself—as indeed I have always done—to maintain contacts with the most influential figures in and about the Conference, and with leading personalities generally, among them Lord Halifax, Prime Minister Chamberlain, Colonial Secretary Malcolm MacDonald and Winston Churchill.

The atmosphere of utter futility which dominated the Conference was, of course, part of the general atmosphere of the time. Those were the days of the Berchtesgaden and Gotesburg "conferences." The atmosphere was not peculiar to England; the French were as assiduous in their attendance on Hitler. I remember Léon Blum telling me at that time: "There is a wild hunger for physical safety which paralyzes the power of thought. People are ready to buy the illusion of security at any price, hoping against hope that something will happen to save their countries from invasion." My conversations with Halifax, Chamberlain, Malcolm MacDonald were vitiated from the outset by this frightful mood of frustration and panic. They were determined to placate the Arabs just as they were placating Hitler. That, of course, did not prevent me from carrying on until the last moment—and after.

My personal relations with Lord Halifax were of the best. I had made his acquaintance through an old friend, the late Victor Cazalet, member of Parliament, one of the few members of the House who never failed to speak up in defense of Zionism, and who did whatever he could to keep our case before the public eye. He was, in fact, chairman of the Parliamentary Pro-Palestine Committee. Through Cazalet's willing offices—he was an intimate friend of Halifax—I was able to meet the latter more frequently and a little more informally than might otherwise have been the case. The character of some of these private meetings may be indicated by the two following instances.

Some time before the issuance of the White Paper, when immigration restrictions were already in force, the desperation of the Jews fleeing from the coming destruction began to rise to its climax; the efforts to reach the safety of Palestine led to the tragic phenomenon of the coffin boats, as they were called, crowded and unseaworthy vessels which roamed the Mediterranean in the hope of being able ultimately to discharge their unhappy cargoes of men, women and children in Palestine. Some sank in the Mediterranean and Black seas. Some reached Palestine either to be turned back or to have their passengers taken off and interned or transshipped to Mauritius.

One of the worst cases—that of the *Patria*—occurred during the war under the Colonial Secretaryship of Lord Lloyd; and on hearing of it I went to him, in despair rather than in hope, to try and persuade him to give permission for the passengers to be landed. I was met with the usual arguments about the law being the law, to which I retorted: "A law is something which must have a moral basis, so that there is an inner compelling force for every citizen to obey. But if the majority of citizens is convinced that the law is merely an infliction, it can only be enforced at the point of the bayonet against the consent of the community."

My arguments were wasted. Lord Lloyd could not agree with me. He said so, and added: "I must tell you that I've blocked all the approaches for you. I know you will go to Churchill and try to get him to overrule me. I have therefore warned the Prime Minister that I will not consent. So please don't try to get at him."

But it seemed that Lord Lloyd had not blocked the approach to the Foreign Office, so I went to see Lord Halifax. Here again I had to rehearse all the arguments about law and ethics and the immorality of the White Paper which was not really a law but a ukase such as might have been issued by a Russian Czar or any other autocrat engaged in the systematic persecution of the Jews. I saw that I was making no dent in Lord Halifax's determination. Finally I said: "Look here, Lord Halifax. I thought that the difference between the Jews and the Christians is that we Jews are supposed to adhere to the letter of the law, whereas you Christians are supposed to temper the letter of the law with a sense of mercy." The words stung him. He got up and said: "All right, Dr. Weizmann, you'd better not continue this conversation. You will hear from me." To my immense relief and joy I heard the next day that he had sent a telegram to Palestine to permit the passengers to land. I met Lord Lloyd soon after, and he said, quite unresentfully: "Well you got past me that time. I thought I'd blocked all the holes, but it seems I'd forgotten Halifax." I was convinced in my heart of hearts that Lloyd was not displeased to have the incident end thus.

An interview of quite another kind with Lord Halifax sticks in my mind. During the Saint James Conference he called me in and addressed me thus: "There are moments in the lives of men and of groups when expediency takes precedence over principle. I think that such a moment has arrived now in the life of your movement. Of course I don't know whether you can or will accept my advice, but it would be desirable that you make an announcement of the great principles of the Zionist movement to which you adhere, and at the same time renounce your rights under the Mandate and under the various instruments deriving from it."

At first I did not quite appreciate the full bearing of this proposal. I paused for a few moments, then asked: "Tell me, Lord Halifax, what good would it do you if I were to agree, which in fact I won't and can't? Suppose, for argument's sake, I were to make such an announcement; there could be only one effect, that I would disappear from the ranks of the Zionist leaders, to be replaced by men much more extreme and intransigeant than I am, men who have not been brought up in the tradition I have been privileged to live in for the last forty years. You would achieve nothing except to provoke the Zionist movement to yield to its most extremist elements."

I added: "So much for the movement. And what of myself?" I briefly recounted to him the history of Sabbathai Zevi, who, in the seventeenth century, had been a successful leader of the "Return," who had gathered round him a mass following from all over the world, and who stood at the gates of Constantinople, constituting some sort of menace to the Sultan. The Sultan felt helpless in the presence of this mystical and dangerous assembly, and sent for his Jewish physician, who advised him as follows: "Call in this Jewish leader, and tell him you are prepared to give him Palestine on condition that he embrace Islam." Sabbathai Zevi accepted the proposal and became a Moslem, with the result that his adherents, who counted in the hundreds of thousands, melted away; and of his movement nothing remains except a small group of Turkish Jews who call themselves Dumbies, the descendants of the few apostates who followed Sabbathai Zevi into Mohammedanism. I wound up: "You do not expect me, Lord Halifax, to end my career in the same disgraceful manner." With that we parted.

Lord Halifax was strangely ignorant of what was happening to the Jews of Germany. During the St. James Conference he came up to me and said: "I have just received a letter from a friend in Germany, who describes some terrible things perpetrated by the Nazis in a concentration camp the name of which is not familiar to me," and when he began to grope for the name I realized it was Dachau he was talking about. He said the stories were entirely unbelievable, and if the letter had not been written by a man in whom he had full confidence he would not attach the slightest credence to it. For five or six years now the world had known of the infamous Dachau concentration camp, in which thousands of people had been tortured and maimed and done to death, and the British Foreign Secretary had never heard of the place, and would not believe that such things could go on; only the fortuitous circumstance that he had received the letter from a man in whom he had "full confidence" had arrested his attention. It is difficult to say whether this profound ignorance was typical for the British ruling class, but judging from its behavior at that time it either did not know, or else it did not wish to know because the knowledge was inconvenient, disturbing, and dangerous. Those were Germany's "internal affairs," and they should not be permitted to interfere with friendly relations between two Great Powers.

It was astounding to meet this bland surprise and indifference in high places. When the great burning of the synagogues took place, after the assassination of Vom Rath in Paris, I said to Anthony Eden: "The fire from the synagogues may easily spread from there to Westminster Abbey and the other great English cathedrals. If a government is allowed to destroy a whole community which has committed no crime save that of being a minority and having its own religion, if such a government, in the heart of Europe, is not even rebuked, it means the beginning of anarchy and the destruction of the basis of civilization. The powers which stand looking on without taking any measures to prevent the crime will one day be visited by severe punishment."

I need scarcely add that my words fell on deaf ears. British society was falling all over itself to attend the elegant parties given by Ribbentrop in the German Embassy; it was a sign of social distinction to receive an invitation, and the Jewish blood which stained the hands of the hosts was ignored though it cried out to heaven. I believe that the Duke of Devonshire never accepted any of von Ribbentrop's invitations.

It should be remembered, however, that things were not much better in France, where the walls were being chalked with the slogan *Mieux vaut Hitler que Blum*, though there the relationship with Germany was less amiable than in the case of England. Well, they got their Hitler, and no doubt the taste of it will remain with the French people for a long time. But whether those who used the slogan so widely have been cured of their affection for Hitlerism is much to be doubted.

In those days before the war, our protests, when voiced, were regarded as provocations; our very refusal to subscribe to our own death sentence became a public nuisance, and was taken in bad part. Alternating threats and appeals were addressed to us to acquiesce in the surrender of Palestine. On one occasion Lord Halifax said to me: "You know that we British have always been the friends of the Jews—and the Jews have very few friends in the world today." I need hardly say that this sort of argument had on us the opposite effect of what was intended.

That the tide was running heavily against us was obvious from the beginning of the Conference, but exactly what the Government would do was not so clear at first. In the early days of the Conference we gave a party at our house for all the members as well as the representatives of the Jewish organizations. Lord Halifax, Malcolm MacDonald and all the high officials accepted. Later the atmosphere was not so cordial. The debates and conversations meandered along, and the Government was reluctant to formulate a program. It limited itself to generalities and bided its time. But the Government had made up its mind. It was only waiting for the most favorable moment for the announcement of its plan.

One day, when the Conference was fairly advanced, we received an invitation to a lunch to be given by His Majesty's Government, and we of course accepted. The lunch was to take place on a Monday. On the Saturday preceding this Monday I received a letter from the Colonial Office, addressed to me obviously by a clerical error—it was apparently meant only for members of the Arab delegation. There, in clear terms, was the outline of what was afterward to be the White Paper, submitted for Arab approval! An Arab State of Palestine in five years; a limited Jewish immigration during these five years, and none thereafter without Arab consent. I could scarcely believe my eyes. We had, indeed, begun to feel that the discussions had become meaningless for us; and after what had happened to Austria and Czechoslovakia nothing should have surprised us. But to see the actual terms, black on white, already prepared and communicated to the Arabs while "negotiations" were proceeding, was utterly baffling.

I happened to remember, when I had finished perusing the extraordinary document, that most of my Zionist friends were at a party being given by Harry Sacher in his home, which was only a few doors from mine. I went over, and we managed to get Lord Reading and Malcolm MacDonald to join us. A heated and extremely unpleasant discussion ensued. We told MacDonald freely what we thought of the document and asked him to cancel our invitations to the luncheon: We would not break bread with a Government which could betray us in this manner. MacDonald was very crestfallen and stammered some ineffective excuses, falling back always on the argument that the document did not represent the final view of His Majesty's Government, that it was only a basis for discussion, that everything could still be changed, that we should not take it so tragically—the usual twaddle. The meeting lasted a long time; its only value, I suppose, was that our delegation was forewarned and the British Government clearly informed of the mood and temper of the Jews. If it was waiting for us to facilitate its publication of the document it was waiting in vain.

After the outbreak of the war I was to learn how elaborately and how far in advance the Government had been preparing the White Paper, and how meaningless the St. James Conference had been. I was in Switzerland on a special mission, and called on the British Minister at Berne, who received me very cordially with the words, "Oh, you're the man I've been wanting to see for quite a time, to get the other side of the story." I asked him to explain and he went on: "I was in on the White Paper. So were most of the Ambassadors and Ministers. Their opinion of it was asked in advance. Well, you know that most Ambassadors and Ministers take on the color of the countries to which they are assigned, and the views we presented were all one sided. That is why I would like to hear your side of the story." My reply was obvious: "It is too late—and too early—for you to listen to the other side. Had you listened a year ago, the verdict might possibly have been different. Now we are in the midst of the war, and we are trying for the time being to forget the White Paper. Perhaps when the war is over you may still be inclined to listen to the other side."

The disclosure to us of the Government document which was to become the White Paper coincided roughly with Hitler's unopposed and unprotested invasion of Czechoslovakia and the occupation of Prague. I remember that day well, because Jan Masaryk came to dinner with us. Between Masaryk and us there was, until the end, a deep friendship, both on personal and general grounds. There has always been a great affinity between the Masaryks and Zionism—Jan's father, the founder and first President of the Czechoslovak Republic had been a strong supporter of the Balfour Declaration—and now, in the days of the White Paper, the representatives of the Czechoslovak Republic were beginning to be treated by the Great Powers as if they were Jews.

Neither the Jews nor the Czechs will forget the words of Chamberlain on the occasion of Hitler's occupation of the Czech capital. Why should England risk war for the sake of "a far-away country of which we know very little and whose language we don't understand?" Words which were swallowed down by a docile Parliament many members of which must have known very well that the Czech Republic was a great bastion of liberty and democracy, and that its spirit and its institutions had all the meaning in the world for the Western Powers. It was, apart from everything else, a colossal insult to a great people. And I remember reflecting that if this was the way the Czechs were spoken of, what could we Jews expect from a Government of that kind?

When Jan arrived at our house that evening he was almost unrecognizable. The gaiety and high spirits which we always associated with him were gone. His face was the color of parchment, and he looked like an aged and broken man. My wife, my children and I felt deeply for him—perhaps more than anyone else in London—and without saying too much we tried to make him comfortable. For a while he was silent, then he turned to us and, pointing to the little dog he had brought with him, said: "That's all I have left, and believe me, I am ashamed to look him in the eyes." Once he had broken the silence he went on talking, and what he told us was terrible to listen to. He had had a conversation that morning with the Prime Minister, and had taxed him with the deliberate betrayal of Czechoslovakia. "Mr. Chamberlain sat absolutely unmoved. When I had finished he said: 'Mr. Masaryk, you happen to believe in Dr. Benes, I happen to trust Herr Hitler.'" There was nothing left for Masaryk but to get up and leave the room.

A great democratic country, a magnificent army and a superb munition plant had been delivered to the future conqueror of Europe, and a people which had fought valiantly for its freedom was betrayed by the democracies. It was cold comfort to us to reflect that the misfortunes which had befallen Czechoslovakia were in a way more poignant than those we faced—at least for the moment. We could not tell what the future held in store for us; we only knew that we had little to expect in the way of sympathy or action from the Western democracies.

However dark the outlook, however immovable the forces arrayed against us, one had to carry on. We explored the possibility of some sort of understanding with the Arabs. One or two meetings—more or less unofficial—were arranged between us and some members of the Arab Delegation. They served no immediate purpose, but they did help to bring about a kind of relationship. Mr. Aly Maher, the Egyptian delegate was personally friendly. Some of the Iraqi people were inclined to discuss matters with us, and not merely to stare at us as the invaders and prospective destroyers of the Middle East. The most intransigeant among the non-Palestinian Arabs was the Iraqi Premier, Nuri Said Pasha. His attitude was stonily negative, but the probable explanation is illuminating. Iraq is immensely interested in finding an outlet to the Mediterranean; it would therefore look with favor on a greater Syria consisting of Iraq, Syria, Trans-Jordan and Palestine. Within the framework of such a union Iraq would probably concede the Jewish National Home, with certain limited possibilities of expansion and immigration. Opposition, therefore, to a Jewish National Home, had much more to do with particular Iraqi ambitions than with the rights and wrongs of the Jews and Arabs; but under the circumstances Nuri Said Pasha was adamant.

His colleagues, however, were not so firm in their opposition. Neither did I think the Saudi Arabia delegates entirely inaccessible to reason on our part. It seemed to me that however discouraging the prospect was, it ought to be pursued for whatever it was worth. We left London for Palestine on March 25, and stopped off in Egypt. There Aly Maher, who had arrived before me, arranged a meeting between me and a number of leading Egyptians, among them Mahommed Mahmoud, the Premier. We talked of co-operation between Egypt and the Jews of

Palestine, in the industrial and cultural field. The Egyptians were acquainted with and impressed by our progress, and suggested that perhaps in the future they might serve to bridge the gulf between us and the Arabs of Palestine. They assumed that the White Paper (it was of course not yet in existence as such) would be adopted by England, but its effects might be mitigated, perhaps even nullified, if the Jews of Palestine showed themselves ready to co-operate with Egypt.

There was a ray of encouragement in these talks, especially after the dismal atmosphere of the St. James Conference. I felt again, as I have so often before and since, that if the British Government had really applied itself with energy and good will to the establishment of good relations between the Jews and the Arabs, much could have been accomplished. But whenever we discussed the problem with the British they found its difficulties insuperable. This was not our impression at all. Of course one had to discount, in these unofficial conversations, both the usual Oriental politeness and the fact that private utterances are somewhat less cautious than official ones.

On my brief visit to Palestine in April 1939, I was able to confirm at first hand what I already knew from reports—that the Jews would never accept the death-sentence contained in the Government proposals. I wrote to many friends in England, Leopold Amery, Archibald Sinclair, Lord Lothian (newly appointed Ambassador to the United States), Sir Warren Fisher, Lord Halifax, among them, to apprise them of this fact. I cabled the Prime Minister:

Feel it my solemn duty to warn H.M.G. before irrevocable step publication their proposals is taken that this will defeat their object pacification country surrender to demands terrorists will not produce peace but compel Government use force against Jews intensify hatred between Jews and Arabs hand over peaceful Arab population to terrorists and drive Jews who have nothing to lose anywhere to counsels of despair in Palestine. . . . Beg you not underestimate gravity this warning.

It had been my original intention to stay in Palestine for several months—perhaps until the forthcoming Congress which was to be held in Geneva that August. I did not believe that anything more could be done in London at the moment, I was tired out by the physical and nervous strain of the past few weeks, and I felt that it would be a sort of rest to resume my work in Palestine. But my friends insisted that I return to London and make a last-minute effort to convince the Prime Minister in person of the frightful harm which the publication of the White Paper would do to us and to the prestige of England. I was convinced that it was useless, and I told my colleagues so. But still they insisted that the effort be sustained until the last moment.

It was not easy for me to leave my wife in Palestine that spring of
1939. She fortunately did have, for company, Lorna Wingate, staying
with us at the house. There was also, as visitor, a young boy of twenty-
two by the name of Michael Clark, a charming youngster who was a
schoolmate and great friend of my younger son, Michael. Michael Clark
had come to Palestine by motorcycle, making his way alone across
Europe and Turkey, over the Balkan and the Taurus mountains. With
these young people staying at the house in Rehovoth I should have felt
more or less easy in mind; but I could not get rid of a feeling of depression when I took my leave. As it turned out, my forebodings were
justified. Young Michael had the habit, in spite of the unrest in the
country, of traveling about alone on his motorcycle. My wife pleaded
with him repeatedly not to expose himself in this reckless fashion, but
he gave no heed to her expostulations. Then one day the poor boy was
shot from ambush by an Arab near the railway line where it passes
through Rehovoth. He was buried in the military cemetery at Ramleh.
I was already in England when this happened, and my wife was so
shaken by the dreadful incident that I cabled her to come to London by
plane. Meanwhile I had the melancholy task of breaking the news to
his mother. I met my wife in Paris, and found her shaken and depressed.
We had both been deeply attached to Michael.

In spite of the hopelessness of the prospect, I again made arrangements
to see Mr. Chamberlain, and again I traveled the *via dolorosa* to Downing Street. I pleaded once more with the Prime Minister to stay his
hand and not to publish the White Paper. I said: "That will happen to
us which has happened to Austria and Czechoslovakia. It will overwhelm a people which is not a state union, but which nevertheless is
playing a great role in the world, and will continue to play one." The
Prime Minister of England sat before me like a marble statue; his ex-
pressionless eyes were fixed on me, but he said never a word. He had
received me, I suppose, because he could not possibly refuse to see someone who, at my age, had made the exhausting flight from Palestine to
London just to have a few minutes with him. But I got no response.
He was bent on appeasement of the Arabs and nothing could change
his course. What he gained by it is now a matter of history: the Raschid
Ali revolt in Iraq, the Mufti's services to Hitler, the famous "neutrality" of Egypt, the ill-concealed hostility of practically every Arab
country.

Much has been written of Mr. Chamberlain's infatuation with his
idea of appeasement, and of his imperviousness to anything which might
modify it. I have only one more illustrative incident to add. Some time
before the St. James Conference I happened to receive through secret
channels an extraordinary German document which I was urgently requested to bring to the attention of the Prime Minister. It had been

prepared and forwarded, at the risk of his life, by Herr Goerdeler, the mayor of Leipzig, who shortly before the end of the war was implicated in the unsuccessful plot to assassinate Hitler, and executed. The document was a detailed exposé of conditions in Germany, and wound up with an appeal to Mr. Chamberlain not to be bluffed into further concessions when he went to meet Hitler in Godesburg or Munich.

I showed the document to a friend of mine in the cabinet, and asked him to get Mr. Chamberlain to read it. He failed. I then went to see Sir Warren Fisher, one of the heads of the Civil Service, a close friend of Mr. Chamberlain's, with a room adjacent to his in Downing Street. I showed him the document, and explained that undoubtedly Herr Gördler had risked his life several times over to accumulate the information it contained. Sir Warren Fisher opened his desk and showed me an exact copy of the document. "I've had this," he said, "for the last ten days, and I've tried and tried again to get Mr. Chamberlain to look at it. It's no use."

The St. James Conference came to its undignified end, the Government proceeded with its preparation of the White Paper, and the time approached for the debate in the House of Commons. We knew that the vote would go against us, such was the temper of the House, which had behind it the record of Vienna and Prague. Our appeals to public opinion were in vain. Shortly after my return from my brief visit to Palestine, I met Winston Churchill, and he told me he would take part in the debate, speaking of course against the proposed White Paper. He suggested that I have lunch with him on the day of the debate. I reported the appointment to my colleagues. They were full of ideas of what Churchill ought to say, and each one told me, "Don't forget this thought," and "Don't forget that thought." I listened respectfully, but was quite certain that a speaker of Mr. Churchill's caliber would have his speech completely mapped out, and that he would not wish to have anyone come along with suggestions an hour or so before it was delivered.

There were present at the lunch, besides Mr. Churchill and myself, Randolph Churchill and Lord Cherwell. I was not mistaken in my assumption. Mr. Churchill was thoroughly prepared. He produced a packet of small cards and read his speech out to us; then he asked me if I had any changes to suggest. I answered that the architecture of the speech was so perfect that there were only one or two small points I might want to alter—but they were so unimportant that I would not bother him with them. As everyone now knows, Mr. Churchill delivered against the White Paper one of the great speeches of his career. The whole debate, indeed, went against the Government. The most important figures in the House attacked the White Paper; and I remember particularly Mr. Herbert Morrison shaking a finger in the direction of Malcolm MacDonald, and reminding him of the days when he was a Socialist;

declaring, further, that if a Socialist Government should come into power, it would not consider itself bound by the terms of the White Paper. This last statement, delivered with much emphasis, was loudly applauded by the Labor benches.

The Government answer, delivered by Mr. MacDonald, was a clever piece of sophistry which could carry conviction only to those who were ignorant of the details of the problem. As for those with whom the question of conviction was secondary in that time of panic, nothing that was said mattered. But it is worth recording that even in that atmosphere the Government victory was extremely narrow. There were two hundred sixty-eight votes in favor, one hundred seventy-nine against, with one hundred ten abstaining. As a rule the Government obtained over four hundred votes for its measures. As I left the House with my friends I could not help overhearing the remarks of several Members, to the effect that the Jews had been given a very raw deal.

One consolation emerged for us in those days: the firmness and unanimity of the Jewish delegation. There were represented on it all the major Jewish communities of the world, and every variety of opinion from the stalwart and extremist Zionism of Menachem Ussishkin to the cautious and conciliatory philanthropic outlook of Lords Bearsted and Reading. At a meeting in the offices of the Zionist Organization the question was put to the formal vote whether the White Paper could be considered as forming a basis for discussion. The unanimous decision, without a single abstention, was in the negative.

CHAPTER 39

War

Mandates Commission Rejects White Paper—Twenty-First Zionist Congress—We Pledge Co-operation with England in War—Paradox of Our Position—Paris in the Second World War—Difference from 1914—The Young Men Who Denounced Chamberlain now Enlist.

AN ATMOSPHERE of unreality and irrelevance hung over the twenty-first Zionist Congress which sat in Geneva from August 16 to 'August 25, 1939. We met under the shadow of the White Paper, which threatened the destruction of the National Home, and under the shadow of a war which threatened the destruction of all human liberties, perhaps of humanity itself. The difference between the two threats was that the first was already in action, while the second only pended; so that most of our attention was given to the first, and we strove to assume, at least until the fateful August 22, when the treaty was signed between Germany and Russia, that the second might yet be averted, or might be delayed. But on that day, when Hitler was relieved of the nightmare of having to wage war on two fronts, even the most optimistic of us gave up hope. The Jewish calamity merged with, was engulfed by, the world calamity.

The Congress debates pursued their usual course. Every party had its say, every resolution was fought out in traditional fashion. The record was scrutinized and criticized, the administration attacked and defended. But in the lobbies of the Congress, and outside the walls of the Geneva Theater where it met, knots of delegates discussed the latest bulletins, and then escaped from the realities by taking refuge within. We went through all the gestures, but felt that nothing said or done at such a moment could have meaning for a long time to come.

Of course we rejected the White Paper unanimously. We declared it illegal; or, rather, we drew attention to the fact that the Mandates Commission, after examining the White Paper, and after having listened to Malcolm MacDonald's defense of it, had declared it illegal, stating explicitly: "The policy set out in the White Paper is not in accordance with the interpretation which, in agreement with the Mandatory Power and the Council, the Commission has placed upon the Palestine Mandate." We took note of the fact that hardly a statesman of standing in the House of Commons had failed to declare the White Paper a breach of faith; and we felt that not we, in opposing the White Paper, were the law-breakers, but the British Government in declaring it to be the law. Now, with war upon us, the decision of the Mandates Commission would not for a long time—if ever—come before the Council of the League. Our protest against the White Paper ran parallel with our solemn declaration that in the coming world struggle we stood committed more than any other people in the world to the defense of democracy and therefore to co-operation with England—author of the White Paper. Such was the paradox of our position, a paradox created not by us, but by England.

After August 22 the Congress hastened its pace, the discussions were curtailed, the resolutions adopted with greater speed. The Executive was re-elected, and on the evening of the twenty-fourth, a day before the closing, I took my leave of the Congress. It was a painful leave-taking in which personal and general forebodings were mingled, and hopes expressed that these forebodings might come to naught. I turned to the Polish delegates in particular, saying: "God grant that your fate be not that of the Jews in the neighboring land"—and all of us felt that this indeed was the only prayer we could offer up for them. Most of our Polish friends we never saw again. They perished, with over three million other Polish Jews, in the concentration camps and the gas chambers or in the last desperate uprising of the Warsaw ghetto.

We drove that night toward the Swiss frontier, my wife, Mrs. Blanche Dugdale and I, in one car, another car with our baggage following. Very vividly my wife and I recalled how, twenty-five years before, almost to the day, we had been making our way back to England from Switzerland on the outbreak of the First World War. But on that first occasion the war was already several weeks old, and it had come with incredible suddenness; now it was just looming over the horizon, and had been approaching for years. We found the frontier closed; to our expostulations that war had not yet been declared, that we were British citizens going home, that if we had taken the train instead of traveling by car we would certainly have got through, the gendarme kept repeating: *"On ne passe plus."* The illogicality and confusion of war was already upon us. After endless repetition of the arguments on our side, and of the formula on the other side, the gendarme sent for his superior officer; we went through the whole rigmarole again, and were finally permitted to pass into the neutral zone dividing the province of Savoie from Switzerland.

We spent the night in the charming little summer resort of Divonne les Bains, which was filled with excited French and British holiday makers all intent on getting out as fast as possible. Early in the morning we came to the frontier of the neutral zone—and once more the ritual began. There was no passing—until the officer in charge, seeing that we had an extra car for our baggage, asked us if we would not take his son along to Paris, where he had to report for mobilization. Of course we were happy to oblige. How other people got through, I do not know.

We traveled all day long, avoiding the central artery which was blocked by tens of thousands of vehicles. We reached Paris in the evening, and were joined at the hotel by our two sons, who had been in the south of France, and whom we had wired before leaving Geneva. It is strange to recall that in those closing days of August 1939, there were still people in high places who believed that war might yet be averted. M. Reynaud, whom I saw the morning after my arrival, and M. Palevski, his *chef de cabinet*, a man of great intelligence, did not think the political situation entirely hopeless. I did not share that view; but I decided nevertheless to risk another couple of days in Paris to see my friends and acquaintances, and to obtain some sort of picture of the public state of mind.

The mood was altogether unlike that which I had found in the war days twenty-five years before. Then, although the Germans had advanced deep into French territory, and were already at Amiens, Paris had been in an exalted and confident mood. There was in the air a religious fervor and an unshakable belief in ultimate victory, however distant it might be. The young men were gone from the city, which looked beautiful and sad; many women were already in mourning; but Paris was proud and confident. Now, although mobilization was in progress, one sensed neither enthusiasm nor depression; there was only a spiritless facing up to an unpleasant fact. There were complaints, of course: two such wars in one lifetime was too much. *"Il faut en finir"* was the cry. Other remarks were heard, *sotto voce:* "The war isn't necessary. . . . Means must be found of coming to terms with the enemy. . . . Chamberlain's method is the right one. . . . One has to persevere in it. . . . There are people enough in the country who know and understand the regime in Germany, and who can mediate for us. . . ." I must confess that though I heard these voices all around me, and very often in the most unexpected places, I did not appreciate to the full the danger which they represented. It seemed to me that Reynaud and his Government were determined to fight to the end; and undoubtedly they were; but they too do not seem to have appreciated the extent to which the Fascist evil had eaten into French life and led to the demoralization of the army.

I came back to England, and that happened in my home which happened in thousands of others—the young generation which had been so outraged by the policy of the Chamberlain Government forgot its grievances and came to the defense of the country as one man. It might have been amusing if it had not been so tragic. I remember how, soon after Munich, a group of young students, mostly from Oxford and Cambridge, friends of my sons, Benjy and Michael, were gathered in the house in Addison Crescent, and with what indignation they denounced Chamberlain, asserting that on no account would they enlist in the army if the disgraceful behavior of the government brought on a war by its encouragement of Hitler. All of them—young scientists, students of medicine and law—were agreed on that point. And all of them enlisted when the crisis came. Our younger son, Michael, enlisted in the RAF, and was as eager to get into action as he had been in his denunciation of the Government. Our older son, Benjy, joined an artillery battalion commanded by my friend Victor Cazalet, and stationed in the south of England.

CHAPTER 40

The First War Years

Gates of Palestine Closed—Our Offers of Help Brushed Aside —Friendly Talk with Churchill—First Wartime Visit to America—America's Touchy Neutrality—First Incredible Rumors of Planned Extermination of Jews—Talk with Roosevelt— Benjy and Michael in the Army—War Work Again—Rubber and High Octane Fuel—Vested Interests—I Propose a Jewish Palestinian Fighting Force to Churchill—A Story of Frustration—Second Wartime Visit to America—Mr. Sumner Welles —State Department and Palestine.

THE paradox which was revealed with the opening of the war deepened with the passing of the months. In the fight against the Nazi monster no one could have had a deeper stake, no one could have been more fanatically eager to contribute to the common cause, than the Jews. At the same time England, then the leader of the anti-Nazi coalition, was keeping the gates of Palestine closed against the unhappy thousands of men, women and children who were making the last desperate effort to reach the safety of the National Home. It had been our hope that when at last there was no longer the ignominious need to appease Nazis and Arab leaders, there would be a relaxation of the anti-immigration rulings for Palestine. Nothing of the sort happened. The coffin boats continued to wander over the Mediterranean, unable to discharge their human cargoes. The pressure within Europe intensified. And yet we were determined to place all our manpower, all our facilities in Palestine, at the disposal of England and her Allies. What else was there for us to do?

Perhaps the bitterest touch of irony in the situation was the failure of certain British circles to understand how inevitably, White Paper or no White Paper, we had to work for the victory of Britain and her Allies. Either that, or else those sections of the Government would rather forego the not inconsiderable assistance we could offer than let the Jews acquire "credits" for what they had done during the war! Often I was offended by unintelligent remarks I heard in British circles which apparently could not appreciate that a Hitler victory would mean the obliteration of the Jewish people, and that this consideration completely overrode, until Hitler's defeat, all other considerations.

I took the offer of help which the Congress in Geneva had sent to the British Government literally and personally. About a month after the declaration of war I went on a special mission to Switzerland, to try and find out what substance there was in the rumors that the Germans had prepared new methods of chemical warfare. I did not obtain much information, but I did gather the impression that the rumors of tremendous preparations for the destruction of whole cities by gas attacks were without foundation. I so reported to the Government. Incidentally, this was the occasion which brought me in contact with the British Minister at Berne who wanted "to hear the other side of the story."

A period of mingled suspense and indecision ensued—the period which was to become known as "the phony war." A number of people actually believed that there was going to be no real struggle. I remember vividly how Hore-Belisha, our War Minister, then on an official visit to the French Government, made the curious statement, widely reported in the press: *"Pour moi la guerre est finie"* (as far as I'm concerned, the war is over). I thought it not only an irresponsibly lighthearted statement, but one calculated to bring aid and comfort to those sections of French public opinion which did not want to see a showdown between Hitlerism and democracy. On the other hand it was, for Hore-Belisha himself, a prophetic statement. He ceased, soon after, to be War Minister, and has hardly been heard of since.

In that general atmosphere the impulse to do something constructive and helpful faced frustration everywhere. I began to think of a trip to America, the country which, I already felt, would be later the center of gravity and the center of decision in the world struggle. I had nothing too specific in mind. It was to be an exploratory trip, for the purpose of getting my bearings. I was, in a sense, merely laying the groundwork for later trips.

I had been seeing a good deal of the higher administrative officials since my return from Switzerland, among them Lord Halifax, the Duke of Devonshire and Sir Edmund Ironside, of the Imperial General Staff. We had already discussed the idea of a Jewish fighting force, though nothing definite was yet suggested. We had also talked of the possibilities in America. When I advised Mr. Churchill, who was back in the Admiralty—exactly where he had been when the First World War broke out—that I was thinking of going to America, he expressed the desire to see me, and on December 17, three days before my departure, I called on him at the Admiralty Office.

I found him not only cordial, but full of optimism about the war. Almost his first words after he had greeted me were: "Well, Dr. Weizmann, we've got them beat!"

I did not quite think so, and did not say so. I turned the subject, instead to our own problem, and thanked him for his unceasing interest in Zionist affairs. I said: "You have stood at the cradle of the enterprise. I hope you will see it through." Then I added that after the war we would want to build up a State of three or four million Jews in Palestine. His answer was: "Yes, indeed, I quite agree with that."

We talked of certain land legislation, very unfavorable to us, which was being proposed for Palestine, and of the port of Tel Aviv. Mr. Churchill asked for a memorandum on these subjects, which were to come up before the War Cabinet. He also asked that someone be assigned to keep in touch with him during my absence in America. Gradually one perceived that his optimism was not that of a man who underrated the perils confronting England; it was more a long-range confidence which went with coolness in planning and attention to details. It was particularly encouraging to find him, at such a time, mindful of us and our problems.

The trip to America—the first of a series my wife and I made during the war—gave me a glimpse of the disorganization and demoralization which were setting in in Europe. I planned to go by air via Paris and Lisbon—the latter city had already become the fire escape to the west— but in Lisbon the transatlantic flights were canceled, and we sat about for ten wretched days in an atmosphere of international intrigue, spying, rumors and secrecy. There was no one to speak to, and if there had been one did not dare to speak. It was an extremely ugly little world.

By the turn of the year some seventy or eighty air passengers for America had accumulated, and Imperial Airways made arrangements with the Italian steamship *Rex* to take us over. The trip was, if anything, more unpleasant than our stay in Lisbon. Italy was not yet at war, but we were treated practically as enemy nationals. The Italians were arrogant toward all the English passengers; they were confident of an early Axis victory and of England's downfall and ruin. The charges both for the trip and for services on board were exorbitant— and they refused to take English money! We would have had a doubly bad time of it if we had not met in Lisbon an old friend of ours, Mr. Siegfried Kamarsky, a Dutch banker and a good Zionist, for whom, queerly enough, I had been instrumental in obtaining a Canadian visa a few months earlier. He and his family traveled with us to America; they were among the very few Dutch Jews who managed to escape before Hitler invaded Holland.

We found America in that strange prewar mood which it is now so difficult to recall. Pearl Harbor was still two years off. America was, so to speak, violently neutral, and making an extraordinary effort to live in the ordinary way. One had to be extremely careful of one's utterances. As I said in one of my addresses: "I am not sure whether mentioning the Ten Commandments will not be considered a statement of policy, since one of them says: Thou shalt not kill." I was frustrated both in my Jewish and my general work.

On the Jewish side the position recalled prewar England, when mention of the Jewish tragedy was associated with warmongering. It had been bad enough in the days of the "cold pogrom," of concentration camps, economic strangulation, mass expulsions and humiliation. Now for the first time rumors began to reach us of plans so hideous as to be quite incredible—plans for the literal mass extermination of the Jews. I received a letter from an old Zionist friend, Richard Lichtheim, who lived in Geneva and had good sources of information in Germany, warning us that if Hitler overran Europe Zionism would lose all its meaning because no Jews would be left alive. It was like a nightmare which was all the more oppressive because one had to maintain silence: to speak of such things in public was "propaganda"!

On the general side there was the same frustration. One did not dare to say that England's cause was America's cause; one did not dare to speak of the inevitable. One did not dare to discuss even the most urgent practical problems facing England in the life and death struggle. There was, for instance, rubber, the supply of which from the Far East had been cut off. I had been interested in the chemistry of rubber substitutes since the time of the First World War. But I found it difficult to start any sort of practical discussion with American manufacturers. They were neutral. They were not ready for a great war effort until Pearl Harbor—and even for some time after.

I had a talk with President Roosevelt early in February 1940. He showed a lively interest in the latest developments in Palestine, and I tried to sound him out on the likelihood of American interest in a new departure in Palestine, away from the White Paper, when the war was over. He showed himself friendly, but the discussion remained theoretical. Before I left he told me with great gusto the story of Felix Frankfurter's visit some time before, to a Palestinian colony where a magnificent prize bull was on show. Frankfurter asked idly what they called the bull, and received the answer "Franklin D. Roosevelt!"

I spoke at Zionist meetings in New York, Baltimore, Chicago, Detroit and Cleveland, always with the utmost caution, seeking to call the attention of my fellow-Jews to the doom hanging over European Jewry and yet avoiding anything that might be interpreted as propaganda. I could only stress our positive achievements in Palestine, and express the hope that the end of the war would bring with it the annulment of the White Paper and a new era of progress, on a hitherto unprecedented scale, for the National Home.

All in all, this first American trip, which lasted three months, was not a satisfactory one. There was, however, one considerable gain to record. It was during this visit that I made the closer acquaintance of two of the younger New England Zionists, Dewey Stone and Harry Levine, of whose activities I had heard for some time, but with whom I had had few contacts. Early in 1940 they added, to their general Zionist work, a special and sustained interest in the Sieff Research Institute, and later they were to take a leading part in the development of the Weizmann Institute of Science. They made, and still make, a rather remarkable team, a sort of Damon and Pythias combination, in their devotion to these special projects. Their co-operation is all the more welcome in that it is guided by a large view and a wide understanding of the future needs of Palestine. With them worked older friends of the scientific development of Palestine, such as Lewis Ruskin, of Chicago, who has been extremely helpful since the time of the founding of the Sieff Institute, and who continued his support throughout the war years. Of Albert K. Epstein and Benjamin Harris, also Chicagoans, I have already spoken in connection with our Rehovoth scientific enterprises.

But, as I have said, the artificial atmosphere of America during that first period of the war, was an uncomfortable one, and it was a genuine relief to get back to the realities of England where, if the truth was harsh, it was at least being faced. The symbol of England's awakening to reality was Chamberlain's retirement and Churchill's assumption of office as Prime Minister. The illusions of "the phony war" were gone; Europe was being overrun by the Nazis, and England knew that, for a time at least, she would be standing alone.

Our two boys were in active service. Benjy, the older one, was with his antiaircraft artillery group on an aerodrome in Kent, in the path of the invasion. The battalion was often under fire for days at a stretch, and during such periods the men went without sleep or food or drink for thirty-six and forty-eight hours at a stretch. Many of them were so shattered by the bombardments that they ran away into the near-by woods, and had to be collected. After about half a year of service Benjy passed several months in the hospital, suffering from shell shock. Then he was invalided out of the service.

Benjy had married, in 1937, Maidie Pomerans, who comes of an excellent family of Russian Jewish origin living in Leicester, Midlands. Maidie studied medicine at London University, and it was in London that they met. Today she practices in the suburbs, running a number of children's clinics. She combines with her professional ability exceptional domestic skill, and maintains a modest but extremely attractive home. She is a charming hostess, reads widely on general subjects and keeps abreast of all developments in her own field. Young and lively, she is loved and respected by all who come in contact with her. Benjy and Maidie have one child, our grandson, David, a bright spark—almost too intelligent—who must constantly be kept back in order that he may not

develop into a so-called prodigy. He does admirably at school, and fortunately does as well at games as in his studies, so there is every chance
that he will not develop into the overgrown intellectual type with which
we meet so often in modern Jewish society.

I return to the story of the war years. Our younger son, Michael,
became an officer in the Air Force, and he devoted himself to his duties
heart and soul. He was a physicist by training; he had taken his tripos
in Cambridge, and engineering at the City and Guilds in London. He
was deeply interested in aeronautics and electronics, and in spite of repeated offers from leading physicists at the research stations of the Ministry of Aviation to come and work with them, he insisted on active
service. It was his view that one could do research properly only after
a long period of operational flying, and only those who had engaged in
actual warfare knew what combinations of scientific and practical knowledge would bring the best results.

His work consisted of patrol duty in two directions, one southward
across the Bay of Biscay, down to Gibraltar, the other westward almost
as far as Iceland. He was practically always on night service, and whenever we went to bed we thought of our son flying somewhere over the
ocean, dodging enemy planes, bringing in ships with food and ammunition from America to the western approaches of England, always alone,
always in danger.

He came on short leaves from time to time, and his visits were a great
joy and sadness. It seemed that no sooner did he arrive than the twenty-
four or forty-eight hours were over, and we had to part. I always used
to accompany him into the blackout, until he said good-by and disappeared into the unknown.

Meanwhile life in England moved into its wartime grimness. The air
attacks on London were intensified until they came with almost mathe-
matical regularity every night. Food became scarce, sleep almost impossible, and we reached a stage when we never went down to the shelter
in our hotel—the Dorchester—but remained fatalistically in our rooms.
Also it seemed to us that if it came to the worst we preferred to die in
our own bed rather than be cooped up in a cellar where, to the danger
of immediate death from explosion, was added the danger of suffocation.
In our rooms we at least had air and a certain amount of comfort.

Shortly after my return from America I was appointed honorary
chemical adviser to the Ministry of Supply, headed by Mr. Herbert
Morrison, and was given a little laboratory in 25 Grosvenor Crescent
Mews, where I set to work with a small group of chemists. The laboratory was not much more than a large matchbox with a great number of
glass windows, and I was always much more apprehensive of the shattering effect of a near-by explosion than of a direct hit. We were not
permitted to work in our laboratory until we had an air-raid shelter
available in the vicinity, and we found one in the back entrance to the

Alexandra Hotel in Knightsbridge, and thither we used to run when the alarm was sounded. But the attacks became so frequent that work proved to be impossible, so we arranged with the air-raid warden to give us a special whistle only when it looked as though the planes were coming overhead. Soon, however, he was whistling so often that we might just as well have listened to the siren; so we threw precaution to the winds and made up our minds to go on working through the air raids. Oddly enough, our particular shelter suffered a direct hit during one of the raids, and fourteen or fifteen people were killed; our lives were probably saved because we had gone on working. The only time when we were compelled to suspend work was when a delayed action bomb fell near the entrance to the laboratory, and the area was cordoned off until the bomb was removed.

The laboratory was conveniently situated across Hyde Park, a few minutes walk from the Dorchester Hotel. I found it a great comfort in this time of personal and general stress to have a serious occupation which absorbed a great deal of energy and attention, and gave one the feeling of making some sort of contribution to the national effort.

Early in the war, during my visit to Switzerland, already told of, I had stopped in Paris and talked with M. de Monzie, then French Minister of Armaments, of the possibility of making use of a certain process which we had worked out in Palestine at the Sieff Research Institute: the process is called aromatization, and is a sort of catalytic cracking of heavy oil leading to good yields of benzine, toluene, and so forth. My assistant, Dr. Bergmann, scientific director of the Research Institute, was invited to France by the Ministry of Armaments and set up a pilot plant for the aromatization of one kilogram of petroleum per hour. The work was then turned over to two French scientists who proved to be pro-German and antiwar. Dr. Bergmann returned to Palestine; not long after he and Dr. Benjamin Bloch, managing director of the Sieff Institute, came to London to discuss with me a program of pharmaceutical production in Palestine. When I was appointed chemical adviser to the Ministry of Supply I persuaded Dr. Bergmann to remain with me, and we worked on our problems together.

The outlines of our war work may be of some interest to the general reader. Apart from the aromatization process already mentioned, we investigated the fermentation of molasses by mass inoculation, the fermentation of wood and straw hydrolyzates, and the preparation of methyl-butinol and its transformation products, especially isoprene. This last was of interest in view of the approaching rubber crisis. We also worked on ketones and their use in high octane fuels. It was becoming obvious that aviation would develop, during the war, to hitherto undreamed of proportions, and there would be a shortage of high octane aviation fuel.

We soon discovered that our greatest difficulties would lie outside the laboratory. In our efforts to transfer results from the laboratory to mass production, we ran up against vested interests in the chemical field, which were strongly opposed to the entry of "outsiders," in spite of the national emergency. I had the support of a number of important people, among them Lord Mountbatten and Geoffrey Lloyd, but things moved very slowly. In the end it was decided that since the source of heavy oil was in any case America, our processes should be tried out there rather than in England. This was the reason for my long visit, from April 1942 to July 1943, to America.

Absorbed though I was in scientific work, I at no time could forget the danger which faced the National Home. That the war would spread to the Mediterranean was a foregone conclusion. In August 1940 I wrote to Mr. Churchill asking for an interview, and adding:

In a war with the magnitude of the present one, it is impossible to say what the strategic disposition of the British fleets and armies may be before victory is attained. Should it come to a temporary withdrawal from Palestine—a contingency which we hope will never arise—the Jews of Palestine would be exposed to wholesale massacre at the hands of the Arabs, encouraged and directed by the Nazis and the Fascists. This possibility reinforces the demand for our elementary human right to bear arms, which should not morally be denied to the loyal citizens of a country at war. Palestinian Jewry can furnish a force of 50,000 fighting men, all of them in the prime of their strength—no negligible force if properly trained, armed and led.

In September 1940, I again discussed the matter at some length at a lunch with Mr. Churchill at which there were also present, among others, Mr. Brenden Bracken and Mr. Bob Boothby, a close friend. Mr. Churchill was friendly about the idea, and was interested in the details, and we worked out there and then a five point program, the outline of which I had brought with me and which I was to submit immediately in a memorandum to Lieutenant General Sir John Dill, Chief of the Imperial General Staff.

The first point on the program called for "recruitment of the greatest possible number of Jews in Palestine for the fighting services, to be formed into Jewish battalions or larger formations." The third point (I shall return to the second) called for "officers cadres, sufficient for a Jewish division in the first instance, to be picked immediately from Jews in Palestine, and trained in Egypt." The fourth point dealt with a Jewish "desert unit," the fifth with the recruitment of foreign Jews in England.

The second point was ominous for us, if only as an indication of the difficulties we were to encounter in being permitted to serve. "The Colonial Office insists on an approximate parity in the number of Jews and of Arabs recruited for specific Jewish and Arab units in Palestine. As Jewish recruitment in Palestine is certain to yield much larger numbers than Arab, the excess of Jews is to be sent for training to Egypt or anywhere else in the Middle East." On this point Mr. Churchill yielded to the Foreign Office; on all others he was unreservedly co-operative. I was, on the whole, satisfied with the results; so were the others at the luncheon. Spirits were high, Mr. Churchill being in infectiously good humor. Toward the end of the lunch Mr. Boothby turned to me with a burst of laughter and said: "That's the way to handle the P.M., Dr. Weizmann, between cheese and coffee!" I answered that I would make a note of it for future reference.

The military authorities, unfortunately, were not so easy to handle. Mr. Churchill's consent to the above program was given in September 1940. Exactly four years were to pass before, in September 1944, the Jewish Brigade was officially formed! Its history does not form part of this record, and I will not go into further detail in regard to the negotiations. I believe enough has been said to provide some notion of the frustration we encountered here, as elsewhere, in our offers of co-operation.

In the spring of 1941 I broke off my work in London for a three month trip to America. I went at the request of the British Government, which was concerned at the extent of anti-British propaganda then rife in America, but I also gave a good deal of attention to Zionist questions. It was not easy for me to explain away to Jewish audiences the humiliating delays in the formation of a Jewish fighting force, the less so, in fact, as American Jewry, like English and Palestinian Jewry, was wholeheartedly with England. It was my impression that two-thirds of the sums collected in the Bundles for Britain campaign came from Jews!

Among the top political leaders in America I found real sympathy for our Zionist aspirations. I have mentioned my first interview with Mr. Roosevelt. I saw Mr. Sumner Welles several times during my American visits. He was well informed and well disposed toward us. The trouble always began when it came to the experts in the State Department. The head of the Eastern Division was an avowed anti-Zionist and an outspoken pro-Arab, and this naturally affected the attitude of his subordinates and associates. There was a definite cleavage between the White House and Mr. Sumner Welles on the one hand, and the rest of the State Department on the other, a situation not unlike the one we faced in England.

And, again as in England, I was to meet with a certain type of interested resistance to war work which had nothing to do with the Jewish question. This developed during my third visit, and I shall speak of it and of related matters, in the next chapter.

CHAPTER 41

America at War

EARLY in 1942 I received a call from Mr. Winant, the American Ambassador to Great Britain. When we met, he informed me that President Roosevelt had expressed the wish to have me come over to the United States in order to work there on the problem of synthetic rubber. Mr. Winant advised me earnestly to devote myself as completely as possible to chemistry; he believed that I would thus serve best both the Allied Powers, and the Zionist cause. I promised Mr. Winant to follow his advice to the best of my ability. Actually, I divided my time almost equally between science and Zionism.

My wife and I had arranged to fly to New York on February 13, and on February 12 we were in Bristol, where we spent the night. Early the next morning we were already in the car which was to to take us to the airfield when I was called to the telephone, and our friend Simon Marks, speaking from London, gave me the terrible news that our son Michael had been posted missing on the night of the eleventh. I came slowly down the stairs, completely shattered. My wife only asked: "Is he killed or missing?"

To proceed with our journey was utterly impossible. We turned back to London and I do not remember in all my life a bitterer or more tragic journey than ours that day from Bristol to London. Throughout all of it we did not say a word to each other. We were met at the station by our son Benjy, his wife, Maidie, and our lifetime friend, Lady Marks, and we proceeded silently to the hotel. There we learned something of the circumstances surrounding Michael's disappearance. He had come down off the coast of France, not far from St. Nazaire, on the night when the *Gneisenau* and the *Scharnhorst* made their dash through the English Channel. All available planes were engaged in the chase, and

Michael's signals to the station, repeated several times at intervals of twenty minutes, went unheeded. No plane could be spared to go to his rescue.

It was only when our friends were gone that the tears at last welled up in my wife's eyes, and it was a certain relief to see her shaken out of the stony silence of her grief. Then we talked, and we had the same thought, and the same hope. Perhaps Michael had come down safely after all; perhaps he was even a prisoner in the hands of the Germans, and we would not learn of it for a long time because he would not give his real name. Perhaps, then, some day we would hear from him again. It was a vain hope that pursued us for years, and it died completely only with the ending of the war.

The last time we spoke with Michael was on the night of February 10, 1942. He was usually quite cheerful when he phoned, but this time he sounded disconsolate, and I was rather startled by his tone. I tried to cheer him up, telling him that we would soon win the war, and got in reply a sad laugh. It still rings in my ears. It seems he had a premonition.

We left for America on March 11, and on the day of our departure I dropped in at 10 Downing Street to say good-by to Mr. John Martin, Mr. Churchill's private secretary, with whom we had been on friendly terms since he had been the able chief secretary of the Peel Commission. I had already taken farewell of him when he suddenly said: "The P.M. is in the other room. He has a few minutes' time, and I think I'll bring you in to him." And then a strange brief colloquy took place—or I should say monologue, for I hardly did more than say good-by to Mr. Churchill. He, however, packed a great deal into those few minutes which we passed together, standing on our feet.

He first wished me luck on my American trip, on which he was, of course, fully informed. "I am glad you are going," he said, "and I am sure you will find a great deal of work to do there." Then, without any questioning or prompting on my part, he went on: "I want you to know that I have a plan, which of course can only be carried into effect when the war is over. I would like to see Ibn Saud made lord of the Middle East—the boss of the bosses—provided he settles with you. It will be up to you to get the best possible conditions. Of course we shall help you. Keep this confidential, but you might talk it over with Roosevelt when you get to America. There's nothing he and I cannot do if we set our minds on it."

That was all. But it was so much that I was rather dazed by it; and the truth is that I would not have taken it all quite literally had it not been for a rather extraordinary circumstance which had puzzled me for some time and which only now became meaningful for me. A few months before I had met with St. John Philby, the famous traveler in Arabia and confidant of Ibn Saud. We had talked about Palestine and Arab relations, and he had made a statement which I had noted down, but which had seemed incomprehensible to me coming from him. He had said: "I believe that only two requirements, perhaps, are necessary to solve your problem: that Mr. Churchill and President Roosevelt should tell Ibn Saud that they wished to see your program carried through; that is number one; number two is that they should support his overlordship of the Arab countries and raise a loan for him to enable him to develop his territories." I now fitted together St. John Philby's "offer" and Mr. Churchill's "plan."

I had been asked by Mr. Churchill to keep the contents of the interview confidential. I have already said that I dislike these commitments to secrecy in matters which are of concern to the Zionist movement. Under the peculiar circumstances attending the talk with Mr. Churchill—we were on our way to the train which would take us to the airport—complete secrecy was quite impossible. I had with me at the time Mr. Joseph Linton, our political secretary and one of the most devoted and faithful servants of the movement. I told him, when I came out, what had happened, and said: "I shall be on the plane very soon. I'm going to make a brief note of this conversation, and you will put it in a sealed envelope and hand it to our friend, Mr. Sigmund Gestetner. He lives in the country, and his place is more or less free from bombing dangers. Should anything happen to me on this journey, or in America, you will open this envelope and disclose its contents to the Zionist Executive."

I did not discuss Mr. Churchill's plan with President Roosevelt on my arrival in America. Our interview was very brief, in fact little more than a friendly welcome. America had been in the war just about three months. At the moment Mr. Roosevelt saw in me only the scientific worker, and I remembered Mr. Winant's advice to me—to concentrate as much as I could on war work: I would serve the Zionist cause more effectively that way.

My first lead was a letter from Mr. Roosevelt to Mr. Vannevar Bush, then the head of war research. I am afraid that it did not do me much good, for I soon discovered that if I was going to do effective work, I would have to play the politician more than the scientist, a prospect which I found repugnant. The main question was not going to be one of process and production, but of overcoming the vested interests of great firms—particularly the oil firms. I occasionally met with extremely unpleasant treatment on the part of some of the representatives of these firms who were attached as experts to various Government departments.

My proposal, which I made officially to Mr. William Clayton, Under Secretary of State for Economics, was to ferment maize—of which millions of bushels were available in the United States and Canada—and convert them into butyl alcohol and acetone by my process, which was established and working on a large scale in various parts of America. The butyl alcohol could without difficulty be used for the making of butylene and the butylene easily converted into butadiene, the basis for rubber. I knew that large quantities of butadiene were already being made out of oil, but the trouble was, as far as I could gather, that the butadiene so produced was not pure, and the purification was slow and costly, whereas the butylene produced by my process was chemically pure, and would lend itself more easily for conversion into a purer form of butadiene. But I had come too late, or at any rate very late; the Government had already engaged the oil companies, and to initiate a process which had not the approval of the oil companies was almost too much of a task for any human being.

However, I did have as supporters of my process Mr. Henry A. Wallace, the Vice-President, and the National Farmers Union. One result was that I became, to my intense distaste, the center of an argument which took on a political character; it was the Farmers Union versus the oil companies. A more welcome result was the ultimate switching of a good deal of the production to alcohol and its derivatives. Some time later Mr. Wallace was kind enough to write of my war work in America in the following terms: "The world will never know what a significant contribution Weizmann made toward the success of the synthetic rubber program at a time when it was badly bogged down and going too slowly."

I have given above only one aspect of the war work in which I was engaged. It must be borne in mind that butylene is also needed for the production of high octane fuel. There was, moreover, another aspect of the rubber problem which was vitally affected, and that had to do with isoprene. Now whether one produces butadiene from oil or from alcohol there is no difference in the final character of the rubber, which when processed is hard, and is best used only for the outside part of the tire, rather than for the guts or soft inner tubing. I had answered this problem by another process—namely, the condensation of acetone and acetylene. I produced thereby an isoprene which is polymerized into isoprene rubber and gives a soft, malleable product which blends well with the butadiene rubber; so one could use pure butadiene rubber for the hard outer tube and a combination of the two rubbers for the soft inner tube.

Here too I must record a long history of delay and opposition. The Government appointed an important committee to go into the matter. Originally a member of the Supreme Court was to head the committee, and Mr. Justice Stone was proposed by the President. Through some administrative blunder Justice Stone refused the appointment, and Mr. Bernard Baruch took his place. Two important members of the committee were Professors Compton and Conant. Professor Conant was skeptical from the outset. He said that he too had been trying to synthesize isoprene from acetylene and acetone, and it seemed to him a tedious and expensive method. I answered, in some astonishment: "But you don't know what my process is!" I later submitted my findings in an elaborate report, but did not get much further. Colonel Bradley Dewey, assistant director of the Rubber Board, did express great interest in our process when Dr. Bergmann and I and some assistants produced several liters of synthetic isoprene; but when it came to mass production, he could not see his way to setting up a big plant, although Commercial Solvents, the firm which had been handling my processes for years, was prepared to go into it. It was the more puzzling as we had asked for no remuneration and formulated no demands.

To go ahead with our process we should have had to find a private firm, which would work without the assistance of the government. This would have been doubly difficult, because it was not easy to get licenses and permits for supplies and machinery. The struggle was long and tiring, but I would not give in. I achieved some partial success, as is evidenced by Mr. Wallace's letter: but the vested interests were too powerful to permit of a quick break-through. In the end I handed over my processes to a firm in Philadelphia, which began to apply it during the war, and continues to do so now.

The frustration which I felt during the early part of my third visit to America was intensified by the increasing sense of urgency connected with the war generally and with the Mediterranean war in particular. That summer Rommel was making tremendous strides toward Tobruk and Egypt and both the military communiqués and the newspaper reports were utterly depressing. One correspondent who had just flown in from Cairo and Palestine came specially to see me, and told me a shattering story. The Egyptians were preparing to receive the "conquerors" in great style. Mussolini was ready to fly over at a moment's notice, and a beautiful white charger was to carry him into Cairo, where, like Napoleon, he would address his armies at the foot of the pyramids. I saw in my mind's eye the mountebank posturing in imitation of his great hero, and the picture was a little revolting.

Equally serious, if without a touch of the grotesque, was the news the correspondent brought from Palestine. There, he said, the Arabs were already preparing for the division of the spoils. Some of them were going about the streets of Tel Aviv and the colonies marking up the houses they expected to take over: one Arab, it was reported, had been killed in a quarrel over the loot assigned to him. The correspondent further reported that General Wavell had called in some of the Jewish leaders and told them confidentially how deeply sorry he was that the

British Army could not do any more for the *Yishuv*: the troops were to be withdrawn toward India, the Jews would have to be left behind, and would be delivered up to the fury of the Germans, the Arabs, and the Italians. The correspondent had also heard that the Jewish leaders had held a meeting and made decisions of despair: they were to be divided into two age groups: the members of the older group would commit suicide; the younger ones would take to the hills to fight their last battle there and sell their lives as dearly as possible: thus the National Home would be liquidated.

There was enough to be heartsick about without taking all this literally, for what could be the fate of the Jews of Palestine, if Rommel broke through, after what was happening to the Jewish communities of conquered Europe? In those days, when it was touch and go with the African war, every effort was being made to induce America to send the maximum number of planes and tanks to that theater. I too added my plea, for what it was worth. Mr. Henry Morgenthau Jr. introduced me to General Marshall, and to the American Chief of Staff I explained what faced us if the needed munitions did not reach the British in time. General Marshall listened gravely and attentively, said very little, made notes of what I told him, and thanked me for the information. The story of how the supplies were rushed across the Atlantic and Africa, of how they arrived in the nick of time, of how the tide was turned at the last moment, has been told many times. But perhaps no one remembers those agonizing days more vividly than the Jews of Palestine, for whom that near-miraculous rescue of the Homeland from complete annihilation still has in it a Biblical echo, recalling the far-off story of the destruction of Sennacherib within sight of the gates of Jerusalem.

For the first few months of my visit I was almost completely absorbed by my chemical work and its attendant problems. When the summer had passed, and with it the immediate military danger to Palestine, and when I had a grip on my war assignment, I permitted myself some Zionist activity; not very much, to be sure, for I still bore in mind Mr. Winant's advice, but enough to maintain contact with external and internal developments.

As to the first, I have already mentioned that in my earlier interview with President Roosevelt we talked only of my scientific work. Later I began to sound out leading Americans on the kind of support we could expect for Zionist demands which we would formulate after the war. But our difficulties were not connected with the first rank statesmen. These had, for by far the greatest part, always understood our aspirations, and their statements in favor of the Jewish National Home really constitute a literature. It was always behind the scenes, and on the lower levels, that we encountered an obstinate, devious and secretive opposition which set at nought the public declarations of American statesmen. And in our efforts to counteract the influence of these behind-the-scenes forces, we were greatly handicapped because we had no foot-hold there. The Americans who worked in the Middle East were, with few exceptions, either connected with the oil companies or attached to the missions in Beyrouth and Cairo. For one reason or another, then, they were biased against us. They communicated their bias to American agents in their territory. Thus it came about that all the information supplied from the Middle East to the authorities in Washington worked against us.

Nor could we ever really find out what was happening behind the scenes. One story will illustrate the queer, obscure tangle of forces through which we had to find our way. I have told, in another part of this chapter, how Mr. St. John Philby, the confidential agent of Ibn Saud, brought us an "offer," which seemed to coincide with the "plan" which Mr. Churchill put so hastily before me a few hours before my departure for America. In America I met a Colonel Hoskins, of the Eastern Division of the State Department, whom I understood to be the President's personal representative in the Middle East. Colonel Hoskins was not friendly to our cause: on the other hand, he was not as hostile as his colleagues of the Eastern Division: in fact he was, by comparison, rather reasonable. In his opinion, something could be done in Palestine if the Jews would, as he called it, "moderate their demands." He spoke of bringing half a million Jews into Palestine in the course of the next twenty years, quite a "concession" for one who was opposed to Zionism.

Colonel Hoskins left for the Middle East, and when I saw him on his return his tone was very different. He said he had visited Ibn Saud, who had spoken of me in the angriest and most contemptuous manner, asserting that I had tried to bribe him with twenty million pounds to sell out Palestine to the Jews. I was quite staggered by this interpreta-tion put on a proposal which I had never made, but a form of which had in fact been made to me by Ibn Saud's representative—St. John Philby. Mr. Hoskins reported further that Ibn Saud would never again permit Mr. Philby to cross the frontiers of his kingdom. Some time later I told St. John Philby of Colonel Hoskins' report. Philby dis-missed it as "bloody nonsense." The truth was that the relations between Philby and Ibn Saud had never been better, and these relations, I might add, remain unchanged as I write this.

What was one, what is one, to make of all this? Did Ibn Saud deliber-ately misrepresent his position to Hoskins? Or had he said something which could be interpreted as a complete reversal of his previous position? And to whom else besides myself did Hoskins give this account of the conversation with Ibn Saud? And what effect did it have in the State Department? How was one to get at the truth—if there was a truth?

Nothing came of the "plan," as we know today: what prospect of realization it at one time had it is hard to say. Of further negotiations, and of other conversations with President Roosevelt and Mr. Churchill I shall speak in the next chapter.

CHAPTER 42

Peace and Disillusionment

High Hopes and Deep Disappointment—Roosevelt's Affirma-
tive Attitude on Palestine—British Labor Party's Repeated
Promises—Friendly Reassurances from Churchill—All Come
to Nothing—Moyne Assassination—My First Visit to Pales-
tine since 1939—Vast Changes—Frustrations—The Terror—
British Labor Comes to Power—Repudiates Its Palestine
Promises—Bevin's Attitude—Earl Harrison's Report and
President Truman's Recommendation—The Anglo-American
Commission—The First Postwar Zionist Congress.

DURING the latter years of the war two themes were dominant in
the minds of the Jewish people, one of despair and one of hope. The
tragedy of European Jewry was revealed to us slowly in all its incredible
starkness. It was not only a tragedy of physical suffering and destruction, so common throughout the world though nowhere so intensively
visited as upon the Jews. It was a tragedy of humiliation and betrayal.
Much of the calamity was unavoidable; but a great part of it could have
been mitigated, many thousands of lives could have been saved, both
in the period preceding the war, and during the war itself, had the
democratic countries and their governments been sufficiently concerned.
This is recalled not in a spirit of recrimination; the tragedy is too deep
for that. It is recalled in order that the Jewish position may be understood. As in all tragedies, the feeling that had people cared it might
have been different made the anguish less bearable.

The hope which was the counterpart of this despair and anguish was
born of the impending defeat of Nazi Germany and of the belief that
now, at last, with the coming of peace, the victorious democratic world
would bethink itself; less preoccupied with its fears and insecurities, it
would realize what had happened to the Jewish people, and give it its
chance, at last.

The period immediately following the war was, for the Jewish people
and the Zionist movement, one of intense disappointment. True, ours
was not the only disillusionment; but there were few demands as well

founded as ours, and fewer still which represented so bare a minimum of sheer need. All that we asked for was simply the opportunity to save, by our own efforts, the remnant of our people. This was the sum total of our hopes.

It cannot be made too clear that our hopes were not merely general, and based only on the prevailing mood of optimism. They were based equally on specific private and public assurances. Their disappointment was all the more shocking and unexpected because they had been deliberately nurtured by those who could have fulfilled them, promised to do so, and did not. On this the record is painfully clear.

I had taken with me to America, when I went there in 1942, the assurance of Mr. Churchill that he had a "plan" for us, that together with Mr. Roosevelt he could carry out the plan, and that the end of the war would see a change in the status of the Jewish National Home; The White Paper, which Mr. Churchill had so bitterly denounced in 1939, would go. Toward the end of my stay in America—a stay almost entirely devoted, as the reader may remember, to war work—I had a long interview with President Roosevelt, in the presence of Mr. Sumner Welles. The attitude of Mr. Roosevelt was completely affirmative.

He was of course aware of the Arab problem, and spoke in particular of Ibn Saud, whom he considered fanatical and difficult. I maintained the thesis that we could not rest our case on the consent of the Arabs; as long as their consent was asked they would naturally refuse it, but once they knew that Mr. Churchill and Mr. Roosevelt both supported the Jewish National Home, they would acquiesce. The moment they sensed a flaw in this support they would become negative, arrogant, and destructive. Mr. Roosevelt again assured me of his sympathies, and of his desire to settle the problem.

Throughout this interview I was supported by Mr. Welles, who had been somewhat cautious and reticent in our private conversations, but on this occasion was outspoken in his desire to concretize my proposals. Mr. Welles expressed the belief that America would be prepared to help financially in the setting up of the Jewish National Home. We did not go into details, but Mr. Welles had read my article in *Foreign Affairs*, in which I had outlined my views, and he was in agreement with them. Mr. Roosevelt, to whom I repeated the substance of Mr. Churchill's last statement to me, asked me to convey to the latter his positive reaction.

It must not be supposed that our negotiations were confined to groups, parties and individuals in power, and that the encouragement of our hopes flowed from these alone. Our appeal for justice was not a party matter, and we addressed ourselves to all men of good will. Since the Jewish Agency was a recognized public instrument in the administration of Palestine, we were naturally in more frequent contact with the British

Government; but my colleagues and I were constantly pressing our case in other circles. In 1943 and 1944 I discussed the question of the Jewish National Home with men like Archibald Sinclair, Creech-Jones, Ernest Bevin, Hugh Dalton. Mr. Berl Locker, one of the outstanding labor leaders of the Zionist movement, was active in British Labor circles. At the Conference of June 1943, the British Labor party reaffirmed its traditional support of the Jewish National Home. In the report of the Labor Party National Executive Committee, issued in April 1944, measures were recommended which in respect of the Arabs went beyond our own official program.

The report read in part: "There is surely neither hope nor meaning in a Jewish National Home unless we are prepared to let the Jews, if they wish, enter this tiny land in such numbers as to become a majority. There was a strong case for this before the war, and there is an irresistible case for it now, after the unspeakable atrocities of the cold-blooded, calculated German-Nazi plans to kill all the Jews of Europe.... Let the Arabs be encouraged to move out as the Jews move in. Let them be compensated handsomely for their land, and their settlement elsewhere be carefully organized and generously financed."

I remember that my labor Zionist friends were, like myself, greatly concerned about this proposal. We had never contemplated the removal of the Arabs, and the British laborites, in their pro-Zionist enthusiasm, went far beyond our intentions.

Again, I received friendly assurances from Mr. Churchill at a brief meeting in September 1943; and yet again, in greater detail, at Chequers, where I lunched with him and a small party, including his brother John Churchill, Mr. John Martin and Major Thompson, on November 4, 1944. Mr. Churchill was very specific in this last conversation.

He spoke of partition, and declared himself in favor of including the Negev in the Jewish territory. And while he made it clear that no active steps would be taken until the war with Germany was over, he was in close touch with America on the matter of the Jewish National Home. Hearing that I was going to Palestine shortly, he recommended that I stop off in Cairo, and see Lord Moyne who, he said, had changed and developed in the past two years. He asked me whether it was our intention to bring large numbers of Jews into Palestine. I replied that we had in mind something like one hundred thousand a year for about fifteen years. I spoke also of the large numbers of children who would have to be brought to Palestine; Mr. Churchill commented that it would be for the governments to worry about the children, and mentioned financial aid. I answered that if the political field were clear, the financial problem would become of secondary importance.

At one turn the conversation touched on oppositionist Jews, and Mr. Churchill mentioned Mr. Bernard Baruch, among others. I said there were still a few rich and powerful Jews who were against the idea of the Jewish National Home, but they did not know very much about the subject.

I asked myself at the time, as I have often done, why men who had given so little attention to an intricate problem like Zionism should take it upon themselves to speak disparagingly on the subject to men in high places, on whom so much depended. I had seen Mr. Baruch several times in America, in connection with my chemical work. Knowing his attitude, I had taken great care not to touch on the Jewish problem; nor had he shown any disposition to question me on it. Yet he had undertaken to state his negative views to Mr. Churchill. But I ought to add that later on, and especially during the period of the struggle for partition in the UN, Mr. Baruch changed a great deal; he was helpful to us in many respects, and used his influence freely in our favor.

When the lunch was over, Mr. Churchill took me into his study and repeated the points he had made in the general conversation. He seemed worried that America was more or less academic in its attitude on the question. He also added that he did not have a very high opinion of the role the Arabs had played in the war.

It was, on the whole, a long and most friendly conversation; it was also one of the rare occasions when Mr. Churchill did not do practically all of the talking. I left the meeting greatly encouraged, and shortly after gave a detailed report of it to my colleagues.

So much for the background of our hopes during the closing period of the war. I turn now, briefly, to part of the personal record.

I had not been in Palestine since the spring of 1939, in the hectic days preceding the issuance of the White Paper. During the early war years I had oscillated between England and America, occupied by Zionist and scientific duties. All this time my wife and I had hankered after the country, and after our home in Rehovoth, which we had managed to build after such long planning and which we had occupied so little. As my seventieth birthday approached, in the autumn of 1944, we made up our minds that we would spend it nowhere but in Palestine. The war was still on, but its outcome was clear. We felt we had earned a respite. America beckoned again; there were warm and pressing invitations to come there, and promises of great rewards in the shape of funds for the Jewish institutions. We did not accept. We needed a rest, and the place for it was our own home.

The journey began under an ominous cloud. On November 6 (1944), two days after my interview with Mr. Churchill, and five days before we set out, Lord Moyne was assassinated in Cairo. I wrote the next day to the Prime Minister:

I can hardly find words adequate to express the deep moral indignation and horror which I feel at the murder of Lord Moyne. I know that these feelings are shared by Jewry throughout the world. Whether or not the criminals prove to be Palestinian Jews, their act illumines the abyss to which terrorism leads. Political crimes of this kind are an especial abomination in that they make it possible to implicate whole communities in the guilt of a few. I can assure you that Palestine Jewry will, as its representative bodies have declared, go to the utmost limit of its power to cut out, root and branch, this evil from its midst.

There is not a single word in this letter which I have ever wanted to retract, even in the days of our bitterest disappointment. I shall have more to say of this utterly un-Jewish phenomenon. Here I only wish to observe that the harm done our cause by the assassination of Lord Moyne, and by the whole terror—this apart from the profound moral deterioration involved—was not in changing the intentions of the British Government, but rather in providing our enemies with a convenient excuse, and in helping to justify their course before the bar of public opinion.

The reception accorded me by the Jews of Palestine after my absence of more than five years was warm, generous, and spontaneous. It was a wonderful home-coming, all that the heart could wish; or rather, it would have been if there had not been certain phenomena which caused me grave concern. Since 1939 the Homeland had undergone great changes; and once at least, when Rommel stood at Alamein, it had passed through the valley of the shadow of death. There had been moments when a frightful premonition of ultimate disaster had haunted us, and we had had nightmares of the Germans and Italians marching into Palestine, and our cities and colonies, the tenderly nurtured achievements of two generations, given over to the same pillage and destruction as German and Polish Jewry. It had not happened, and the Homeland had come through, stronger than ever. The war years had knit the community into a powerful, self-conscious organism, and the great war effort, out of all proportion to the numerical strength of the *Yishuv*, had given the Jews of Palestine a heightened self-reliance, a justified sense of merit and achievement, a renewed claim on the democratic world, and a high degree of technical development. The productive capacity of the country had been given a powerful forward thrust. The National Home was in fact here—unrecognized, and by that lack of recognition frustrated in the fulfillment of its task. Here were over six hundred thousand Jews capable of a vast concerted action in behalf of the remnant of Jewry in Europe—to them no impersonal element but, in thousands of instances, composed of near and dear ones—capable of such action, frantically eager to undertake it, and forbidden to do so.

Side by side with these developments, in some ways linked with them, and in part arising from the bitter frustration of legitimate hopes, there were the negative features I have referred to: here and there a relaxation of the old, traditional Zionist purity of ethics, a touch of militarization, and a weakness for its trappings; here and there, something worse—the tragic, futile, un-Jewish resort to terrorism, a perversion of the purely defensive function of Haganah; and worst of all, in certain circles, a readiness to compound with the evil, to play politics with it, to condemn and not to condemn it, to treat it not as the thing it was, namely, an unmitigated curse to the National Home, but as a phenomenon which might have its advantages.

Sometimes it seemed as though the enemies of the Jewish Homeland without were determined to encourage only the destructive elements within. Long before the end of the war the last excuse for the White Paper—pacification of the Arabs, who incidentally were not pacified by it—had disappeared. By 1944, and even by 1943, the victory which the Arabs had done so little to help us obtain was in sight. The moral authority of the democracies was then supreme, and a declaration for the Jewish Homeland then would have had irresistible force. A new excuse replaced the old one: one had to wait for the end of the war. This was the pretext advanced me in private conversation by Mr. Churchill, and offered by him to the House of Commons on February 27, 1945, after the Yalta Conference. The European war ended in May, 1945; no action was taken.

In July of that year came the General Election in England, with a Labor triumph which astonished the whole world and delighted all liberal elements. If ever a political party had gone unequivocally on record with regard to a problem, it was the British Labor party with regard to the Jewish National Home; within three months of taking office, the British Labor Government repudiated the pledge so often and clearly—even vehemently—repeated to the Jewish people. Today it is clear from the course of events that the promises and protestations of friendship, the attacks on the White Paper in the House of Commons, by those who were to form future governments, the official resolutions of the British Labor party, lacked character and substance; they did not stand up to the pressure of those forces which, behind the scenes, have always worked against us.

It was on November 13, 1945, that the Labor Government officially repudiated the promises of the Labor party and offered us, instead of the abrogation of the White Paper, and relief for the Jews in the detention camps—a new Commission of Inquiry. The extraordinary spirit in which this declaration of policy was conceived may be understood from the opening. The British Government "would not accept the view that the Jews should be driven out of Europe or that they should not be permitted to live again in these countries without discrimination, contributing their ability and talent toward rebuilding the prosperity of Europe." The British Government, in other words, refused to accept the view that six million Jews had been done to death in Europe by various scientific mass methods, and that European anti-Semitism was as viciously alive as ever. The British Government wanted the Jews to stay on and contribute their talents (as I afterward told the United Nations Special Committee on Palestine) toward the rebuilding of Germany, so that the Germans might have another chance of destroying the last remnants of the Jewish people.

With such an exordium, the rest of the document can easily be guessed at. Instead of the mass movement of Jews into Palestine which the British Labor party had repeatedly promised, there was an offer of a trickle of fifteen hundred refugees a month; instead of the generous recognition of the original purposes of the Balfour Declaration, a reversion to the old, shifty double emphasis on the obligation toward the Arabs of Palestine as having equal weight with the promise of the Homeland to the Jews. The letdown was complete.

Mr. Bevin, who, as the new Foreign Secretary, issued the declaration of policy on behalf of the Labor Government, was apparently determined to make it clear that, at any rate as far as he was concerned, no doubts should be entertained anywhere as to his personal agreement with the worst implications of the declaration. At a press conference following the issue of the declaration he said, apparently apropos of our demand for the fulfillment of the Balfour Declaration and the promises of the Labor party: "If the Jews, with all their suffering, want to get too much at the head of the queue, you have the danger of another anti-Semitic reaction through it all."

I thought the remark gratuitously brutal, even coarse, but I cannot say that it surprised me. My personal contacts with Mr. Bevin have been unfortunate: that is, where Jewish matters have been concerned. His tone was hectoring. I first went to see him, in his capacity as Foreign Secretary, with regard to certificates for refugees. We had been offered a ludicrously small number—a remnant, it was stated, unused under the White Paper—which we could not offer the unhappy, clamoring inmates of the DP camps without a feeling of shame. We refused the certificates. Mr. Bevin's opening remarks to me were: "What do you mean by refusing certificates? Are you trying to force my hand? If you want a fight you can have it!" There was not the slightest effort to understand our point of view; there was only an overbearing, quarrelsome approach. An earlier contact with Mr. Bevin, when he had been Minister of Labor during the war, had been somewhat happier; but then Mr. Bevin had wanted my services.

Thus, in the two and a half years which followed my visit of 1944 to Palestine, no positive response came from British or world statesmanship to the pleas and protests of the great constructive majority of Jewish Palestine and the Diaspora. Every objective study of the immediate and long-range problem of European Jewry pointed to one solution: mass evacuation, as fast as economic absorption would permit, into Palestine. Every objective report on Palestine confirmed the claim of Palestinian Jewry, that it was capable of handling the problem. But nothing was done.

In the autumn of 1945 Mr. Earl Harrison, after personal investigation on the spot, reported to President Truman that there was no solution for the problem of the majority of European Jews other than Palestine; President Truman then suggested to Prime Minister Attlee that one hundred thousand Jews be admitted immediately to Palestine; and President Truman's suggestion was followed by Mr. Bevin's declaration above referred to. This was the origin of the Anglo-American Commission of 1946.

Profoundly disappointed though we were, for we had had our fill of inquiries and investigations, we co-operated loyally with the commission. Its personnel was of high caliber, and included a number of excellent men like Bartley Crum, of California, Frank Buxton, of Boston, Richard Crossman, of England, James G. Macdonald, of New York, and Judge Hutcheson of Texas.

With these and others I established friendly relations, and did what I could to place the facts before them. But though the commission held sessions in America and in Europe before it proceeded to Palestine, I would not appear before it except in the latter country. I considered that the proper setting, and I wanted the members of the commission to see the Homeland with their own eyes first. I pleaded then once more for the radical solution of the Jewish problem—the evacuation to Palestine of the remnant of European Jewry; and on the basis of our achievements, which they could survey for themselves, and of careful reports prepared by our experts, I submitted practical plans. The commission was favorably impressed; it issued positive though cautious recommendations, among them the admission of the one hundred thousand "displaced persons," as suggested by President Truman. It produced no effect, except to prove that the British Government had never intended to take affirmative action. The whole device had been nothing but a stall. The White Paper remained in force, our immigration was still limited to the tragically derisory figure of fifteen hundred a month.

The frustration of our creative impulses in Palestine, with all its demoralizing effects, had its repercussions on the Zionist movement everywhere. The ravages which the war had wrought on the Jewish people, and the political betrayal which had followed the war, were mirrored in our first postwar Zionist Conference, held in London in August 1945, at the time of the British General Election. It is true that the Labor Government had not yet reversed the decision of the Labor Party; but the Government of Mr. Churchill, in which places

of leadership were held by men who had denounced the White Paper
in 1939, had already failed us; and the effect, added to the calamities
of the war, was to depress the tone of the movement, and to encourage
counsels of despair. Even more marked, of course, was the effect by
the end of 1946, when the first postwar Zionist Congress was held in
Geneva. Since this second gathering was the larger, the more official,
and the more elaborately prepared, it will suffice to deal with that alone.

It was a dreadful experience to stand before that assembly and to run
one's eye along row after row of delegates, finding among them hardly
one of the friendly faces which had adorned past Congresses. Polish
Jewry was missing; Central and Southeast European Jewry was missing; German Jewry was missing. The two main groups represented were
the Palestinians and the Americans; between them sat the representatives
of the fragments of European Jewry, together with some small delegations from England, the Dominions, and South America.

The American group, led by Dr. Abba Hillel Silver, was from the
outset the strongest, not so much because of enlarged numbers, or by
virtue of the inherent strength of the delegates, but because of the weakness of the rest. The twenty-second Congress therefore had a special
character, differing in at least one respect from previous Congresses:
The absence—among very many delegates—of faith, or even hope, in
the British Government, and a tendency to rely on methods never known
or encouraged among Zionists before the war.

These methods were referred to by different names: "resistance,"
"defense," "activism." But whatever shades of meaning may have been
expressed by these terms—and the distinctions were by no means clear
—one feature was common to all of them: the conviction of the need for
fighting against British authority in Palestine—or anywhere else, for
that matter. My stand on these matters was well known; I made it
clear once more at the Congress. I stated my belief that our justified
protest against our frustrations, against the injustices we had suffered,
could have been made with dignity and force, yet without truckling to
the demoralizing forces in the movement. I became, therefore, as in the
past, the scapegoat for the sins of the British Government; and knowing
that their "assault" on the British Government was ineffective, the
"activists," or whatever they would call themselves, turned their shafts
on me. About half of the American delegation, led by Rabbi Silver, and
part of the Palestinian, led by Mr. Ben Gurion, had made up their minds
that I was to go. On the surface it was not a personal matter; the debate
hinged on whether we should or should not send delegates to the Conferences on Palestine, which were to be resumed in London toward the
end of January 1947, at the instance of the British Government. By a
tiny majority, it was decided not to send delegates—and this was taken

as the moral equivalent of a vote of no confidence in me. What happened in the end was that my election as President having been made impossible—no President was elected—the delegates went to London by a back door.

I left the Congress depressed, far more by the spirit in which it had been conducted than by the rebuff I had received. Perhaps it was in the nature of things that the Congress should be what it was; for not only were the old giants of the movement gone—Shmarya Levin and Ussishkin and Bialik, among others—but the in-between generation had been simply wiped out; the great fountains of European Jewry had been dried up. We seemed to be standing at the nadir of our fortunes.

In the early spring of 1947 we returned to Palestine and settled again in our home in Rehovoth. Here I busied myself with scientific work, with the building of the new scientific institute which was founded for my seventieth birthday—as described in the next chapter—and with the dictation of most of these memoirs. The United Nations Special Committee on Palestine, and the deliberations of the United Nations on the Palestine problem at Lake Success, were still to come.

CHAPTER 43

Science and Zionism

Oil and World Politics—The Need to Break Oil's Monopo-
listic Position—Possibilities of Fermentation Industries—
Other Enterprises—Palestine's Possible Role—Work Done at
Rehovoth—The Daniel Sieff Research Institute—Scientific
Pioneering in Palestine—Special Problems—Our Role in the
War—The Weizmann Institute of Science.

THE reader of these memoirs has long been aware in what an organic
fashion my Zionist and scientific interests have been interwoven from
my earliest years. This is not, I believe, a purely personal phenomenon.
It is, rather, the reflection of an objective historic condition. The question of oil, for instance, which hovers over the Zionist problem, as it
does, indeed, over the entire world problem, is a scientific one. It is part
of the general question of raw materials, which has been a preoccupation
with me for decades, both as a scientist and a Zionist; and it had always
been my view that Palestine could be made a center of the new scientific
development which would get the world past the conflict arising from
the monopolistic position of oil. Not that our scientific work would be
dedicated solely to that purpose; but it would certainly be one of its
main enterprises.

During my last and longest war visit to America the struggle between
oil and other interests had again been made abundantly manifest. The
same problem, in other forms, confronted England. I referred, in the
last chapter, to a friendly meeting with Mr. Ernest Bevin—one in which
he sought my services. It occurred in the midst of the war, when the
British Government sent out to West Africa a small commission to
investigate the short- and long-range possibilities of new sources of raw
material, with fuel chiefly in view. Walter Elliot and Creech-Jones were
on the commission, and I had several subsequent meetings with them.

I suggested that they try to determine whether various types of
starches could not be grown easily in West Africa. It is known that
Central or tropical Africa produces a great many root starches, like
manioc and tapioca; also cane sugar. I was of the opinion that if one
could grow abundant supplies of these commodities, one could introduce

a fermentation industry into that part of the world, with a large yield of ordinary alcohol, both for power and for the production of butyl alcohol and acetone. These three materials, in large quantities and at a low price, could form the basis of two or three great industries, among them high octane fuel, and would make the British Empire independent of oil wells.

The commission went out for a survey, and so far nothing has come of it. I am still of the opinion that the plan is feasible. Its most attractive feature is, perhaps, that it is not tied to a geographic point, like an oil supply, but is applicable wherever the substances I have mentioned can be grown. It is, moreover, part of what I believe to be a necessary and probably inevitable shift in a great sector of modern industry. Butyl alcohol, acetone, and ethyl alcohol are the bases of many products besides fuel and plastics. The acetylene chemistry derivatives start with methyl butinol, which is itself prepared from acetylene and acetone. Methyl alcohol is made from carbon dioxide and hydrogen, which are yielded as by-products from the fermentation of butyl alcohol; the methyl alcohol can easily be reconverted into formaldehyde, one of the best disinfectants. It is, moreover, widely used in synthetic chemistry. Methyl-butinol, again, leads to the formation of certain amino alcohols, which are most valuable constituents of dyestuffs.

It is on these lines that my collaborators and I have been working for a number of years. The program is still in its initial stages, and to elaborate it would require quite a number of chemists and a certain amount of time; but enough has been done—in Philadelphia, London, and Rehovoth—to indicate the lines of research on which we should move at present.

Another piece of work which has been occupying our attention for the last few years leads to the production of cheap but digestible and valuable nutritive products. It may be briefly described as the attempt to upgrade materials which are used as cattle food, converting them into human food. The materials are peanuts or peanut cake—after the oil has been extracted—soya beans and similar substances. This product has been tested in many hospitals as nutrition for patients, and for people with ulcerated stomachs, and it has proved very beneficial. It is, moreover, cheaply produced, and is within reach of the poorest populations, such as the coolies of India or China. It is entirely of a vegetable nature, is highly nutritive, and without containing a particle of meat has a meaty taste. It should be of particular benefit to those eastern countries in which meat is either too expensive or is prohibited for religious reasons.

This enterprise was worked out in its technical aspect by a group of capable workers in America, and has already produced results. My colleagues and I have been occupied with the chemical side since 1935, aided at the beginning by Willstätter, who was a great authority on the chemistry of proteins.

A third branch of research has occupied my attention in recent years, and in this Dr. David Bergmann and one or two others have participated to a considerable degree. In its early stages it was carried out at the Sieff Institute, later it was transferred to London. It is a process for converting the crude residues obtained after the distillation of oil into aromatic substances like benzine, toluene, xylene, naphthalene and certain gaseous substances like butylene, isobutylene, and so on. Our purpose was to create reserves of toluene, for we remembered our sad experiences in the last war, when we ran out of toluene, the basis of TNT. The process proved, however, to have wider value. It was taken up by a private firm to which the Manchester Oil Refinery belongs; a company was formed with a capital of two million pounds, the government participating to the extent of 50 per cent in view of the national importance of the process.

The ideas set forth in brief outline in the foregoing pages were germinating in my mind for many years. I followed closely the literature on the subject, and discussed it with scientists, particularly with Haber and Willstätter, whenever I could. It was my idea, as I have said, that Palestine might be one place where work of that kind might be initiated. Although it is not a country rich in the necessary raw materials, it is sufficiently near to Africa to enable one to survey the field without too much difficulty. It also has the advantage of standing on the borderline of two great zones, the tropical and the temperate, so that the climatic conditions are especially favorable.

Within Palestine, Rehovoth seemed to me the right place for a beginning. It was the seat of the Agricultural Experimental Station; we would have on the premises the botanists and plant physiologists who were already well acquainted with the country. There remained the question of means—and of getting together a group of scientists.

With regard to the first, I approached my friends of the Sieff and Marks family, and asked them if they would not be prepared to build such an institute as I had in mind as a memorial to young Daniel Sieff, who died prematurely, and had been very much interested in scientific problems. They responded at once. With regard to the second, the reader will recall how, in the early Hitler years in Germany, large numbers of first-rate scientists were driven from the German universities. Some of them, like Dr. David Bergmann, his brother Felix, and other chemists of distinction, joined our group. With these, and with my old colleague Mr. Harold Davies, with whom I have now been working for over thirty-five years, we began the work. This has been an especially interesting, instructive and, I believe, valuable chapter in the history of the Jewish National Home.

The whole experiment of setting up a research institute in a country as scientifically backward as Palestine is beset with pitfalls. There is, first, the risk of falling into the somewhat neglectful habits of Oriental countries; a second danger is that of losing a sense of proportion because of the lack of standards of comparison. One is always the best chemist in Egypt or in Palestine when there are no others. Also, if one turns out a piece of work which in America or England would be considered modest enough, one is apt to overevaluate it simply because it has been turned out in difficult circumstances. The standard and quality of the work must be watched over most critically and carefully. Many of the publications issued by scientific institutions in backward countries are very much below the level required elsewhere, but the contributors to these publications are very proud of them simply because the local level is not high. I made up my mind that this sort of atmosphere should not prevail in the Sieff Institute, and that it should live up to the highest standards.

There were several ways of combatting the dangers I have indicated. First there was the proper selection of the staff, and the infusion into it of the right spirit—that of maintaining the highest quality. Every member was enjoined to take his time over his piece of work, and not merely have publication in view.

Second, it became our policy to keep the workers in the institute in touch with what was being done in Europe and America, not merely by providing a good library, where they could read of the researches of others in scientific journals, but by arranging personal contacts. We made it a rule to invite scientists from other institutes to come and lecture in Rehovoth, spending a few weeks in the laboratories, sharing their experiences with us, and criticizing the efforts of the young research workers. In the years preceding the war we had visits from Professors Henri of Paris, Errera of Brussels, Wurmser of Paris and others of their standing. Unfortunately the war interrupted this practice, which we are trying to renew at present, and already professors Louis Fieser of Harvard, and Dr. Ernst Chain of Oxford, Herman Mark of the Brooklyn Polytechnic Institute, among others, have visited the institute since the end of the war.

We also worked in the reverse direction, sending our workers abroad, to the universities. Out of eleven senior workers four have been out in Paris, Ottawa, New York, Chicago, and Berkeley. As one returns, another leaves, and so continuous contact is maintained with the great scientific world.

The building and organization of the Sieff Institute was, even for Palestine, a unique case of pioneering. Apart from the psychological difficulties of maintaining a high standard, there was the physical difficulty of scientific organization. When, during the war, we undertook to manufacture certain drugs which till then had been a monopoly of the

Germans, we lacked both apparatus and raw material. The former we had to improvise, the latter to manufacture for ourselves. We got a small quantity of raw material from the Middle East supply center at Cairo, but always with great difficulty. It is almost impossible to develop a pharmaceutical industry unless one has at hand all the necessary raw materials. Pharmaceutical products of a certain complexity are so to speak the crown of the industry, the last stage of several chemical processes. Each of these requires the greatest care, because of the high standards of purity necessary in the end product. We could always handle the last stages, but without a great organic and inorganic chemical industry behind us, the early stages presented enormous difficulty. Thus, for instance, there was—and still is—a lack of sulphuric acid, without which almost nothing can be done. There is no local production of benzine or aniline or similar products. All these had to be obtained at very high prices—when they were obtainable—from sources which were not always ready to encourage the creation of a chemical industry in Palestine.

There were problems of another kind. When the institute was built, on the premises of the experimental station, it looked at first as if we were going to sink in a sea of sand. The buildings of the station were quite neat, as far as their external appearance was concerned, but there was not a tree or a blade of grass to adorn the vast courtyard in which the two institutions were housed, and I had before my eyes the green lawns of English and American universities and scientific academies, and thought that we would be showing a lamentable lack of aesthetic feeling if we merely planked down the buildings and did nothing with the surroundings.

I therefore set about building roads to connect one part of the institution with another, to plant trees and lay out lawns, and in general to indicate through externals that this was an agricultural station. Colors, flowers and creepers began to appear very soon, for we have plenty of water, and the soil is light and easily responds to good treatment. After two or three years of care, the whole was transformed into a garden which delights the eye, and every visitor and worker feels the effect.

There are certain human trifles which are of great importance. The people who came to visit us, brought here by their chauffeurs, did not show what I considered the proper respect for a public building. They had to be taught not to litter the place with cigarette and cigar ends, pieces of paper and other refuse. At first the injunctions against this practice met with a skeptical shrug of the shoulders, especially on the part of the critical chauffeurs. There were many ironical remarks at my insistence on tidiness; but soon it became known that such people would not be allowed to enter the premises; by now every chauffeur in Palestine knows that the Sieff Institute is one place in Palestine where one does not throw cigarette ends on the floor, but in the receptacles provided for that purpose.

A particular feature in the life of the Institute was the erection of a little club. We are outside the settlement of Rehovoth, and it would take time for the workers to go home for their midday meals; in the heat of the summer it would also mean quite an effort. We organized the club for the purpose of supplying cheap and wholesome meals. It is also a place where the workers can rest, read newspapers, hold meetings and arrange lectures and musical evenings. When I mentioned the idea of the club to Professor Willstätter, he said: "I hope you will set it up. Believe me, it is more important than one or two more laboratories."

The Sieff Institute has gradually won a good name for itself, both in the scientific and Jewish world, during the thirteen years of its existence. I believe we have done good practical work. The pharmaceutical company which we created during the war has turned over its experience and good will to a serious concern which will continue the manufacture and distribution of its products. In this way an industry requiring much skill and care has been created, and will carry on, I hope, with increasing effectiveness. Other problems which we have tackled have also led to practical results. I feel that on the whole the standard of our publications is high, and our papers have always been accepted in the best journals of England and America. The name of Rehovoth is familiar to every research chemist in these countries, and we receive quite a few applications from scientists who wish to come and work with us.

The Sieff Institute has proved to be only a beginning. On the occasion of my seventieth birthday a group of my American friends conceived a more ambitious project—a scientific center which would embrace not only organic chemistry, but physical chemistry and other branches on a much larger and more important scale. Those who had been active for the Sieff Institute in years past, Dewey Stone and Harry Levine of New England, Albert K. Epstein, Benjamin Harris and Lewis Ruskin of Chicago, were joined by new forces, like Edmund I. Kaufmann of Washington, who became President of the American Committee, and Sam Zacks, President of the Zionist Organization of Canada. Under the energetic guidance of my friend Meyer W. Weisgal, this larger project moved forward very rapidly, so that on the third of June, 1946, the cornerstone of the main building of the new institute could be laid. There were present at the ceremony, among others, Professors Fieser of Harvard, David Rittenberg and Chaim Pekeris of Columbia University, Herman Mark, Kurt G. Stern and Peter Hohenstein, of the Brooklyn Polytechnic Institute, and Dr. Yehudah Quastel, F.R.S., of University College, Cardiff. Several of these eminent scientists have agreed to accept permanent posts at the Institute, which is to bear the name of the Weizmann Institute of Science, as soon as research can be begun.

There was not a little in that ceremony of the summer of 1946 to remind us of that earlier ceremony, in the summer of 1918, when the cornerstone of the Hebrew University was laid. True, we were no longer in the midst of a general war, and the Jewish National Home to which we were dedicating the new enterprise was substantially in existence. But it was a time of stress and difficulty, when men's minds were little occupied with this type of activity. It was the time of the "terror," a time of bitter political disappointment and of impending struggle. Like the laying of the cornerstone of the University on Mount Scopus, this was an act of faith: and it has been a continuous act of faith to carry the work forward.

By the summer of 1947 the central building was completed, and it is now—in the fall of 1947—being supplied with first-class modern equipment. I think this will be not only an institution of great practical usefulness, but also a source of pride and satisfaction to all of us.

It is gratifying, too, that the new Institute has not remained the "hobby" of a small coterie. In various parts of the world increasing numbers of farsighted individuals are evincing a sustained and creative interest in the enterprise. In Palestine, burdened as it is with enormous and pressing material problems, substantial contributions have been made to the Institute. In England, the Marks-Sieff family, the original sponsors of the Sieff Institute, now seconded by my friend, Sigmund Gestetner, are the center of an active group. In the United States the friends of the Institute are too numerous to list here; but I cannot refrain from mentioning the Philadelphia group, headed by Fredric R. Mann, Walter Annenberg, Simon Neuman, and Judge Louis I. Levinthal, as well as a few individuals scattered throughout the country, like Harold Goldenberg, of Minneapolis, Paul Uhlmann, of Kansas City, William S. Paley, Abraham Feinberg and Rudolf Sonneborn, of New York, Charles Rosenbloom, of Pittsburgh, and my old friend, Samuel Zemurray, of New Orleans.

I have spoken, in an early chapter, of the frightful spiritual and intellectual losses we have suffered in the last war. The creation of scientific institutions in Palestine is essential if we are to insure the intellectual survival of the Jewish people. It may take us as much as fifty years to regain our strength in this field, and the only hope is that the men of high qualification who come to us will influence the young generation of Palestine in the direction of skill, discipline, order, and high quality performance.

These men will no doubt bring with them their own scientific problems. Many of them are engaged in modern physical, chemical, electronic and isotope researches, and no doubt will continue this work in the new institute, which will be equipped accordingly. But it will be the business of those charged with the guidance of the institute not merely to imitate work which is going on in other places, perhaps with superior effectiveness, but to concentrate on problems which are peculiarly Middle Eastern or Palestinian, like genetics, the introduction of new varieties of plants and fibers, and the exploitation of certain resources in the country which at present may not represent any considerable values but which if properly worked can become of great interest. These are matters which will have to be carefully examined when the scientists are assembled, and when they have discussed and distributed their tasks. It is a fascinating problem to the tackling of which I look forward with great eagerness, even though, personally, I can only listen and chime in occasionally, for owing both to my age and eyesight disability I cannot take part in the actual performance.

We must leave it to time to determine the actual lines of development. All that one can do at present is make the preparations as adequate as one can. The initiative of the scientists will make maximum use of the conditions which they will find in the new country, and I have no doubt that their devotion and skill will lead them into the solving of many problems connected with the future growth of the Homeland.

The Decision

THE final phase in the struggle for the establishment of the Jewish State may be said to have begun with Britain's decision in the spring of 1947 to refer the whole problem of Palestine to the United Nations. By that time the Anglo-American Commission, and the London Conference of January 1947, had been revealed as delaying devices. The same spirit motivated, I believe, the resort to the UN. It was not in Mr. Bevin's plans that the UN should express itself in favor of the creation of a Jewish State, which it did, by more than the requisite two-thirds majority, in its historic decision of November 29, 1947.

The first action of the UN was the creation of the United Nations Special Committee on Palestine, the UNSCOP, which proceeded to that country in the summer of 1947 to study the problem on the spot. Its recommendation of partition, the subsequent deliberations of the United Nations Ad Hoc Committee on Palestine at Lake Success, in October and November, and the decision of the Assembly, are recent history. A brief account of my part in these events will bring my life record to a close.

I appeared before the UNSCOP in Jerusalem at the request of the Vaad Leumi, or Jewish National Council, and before the Ad Hoc Committee at Lake Success at the request of the Jewish Agency. The official spokesmen of the latter body were Dr. Abba Hillel Silver and Mr. Moshe Shertok. I was no longer President of the Zionist Organization and Jewish Agency. I felt, nevertheless, that I spoke the mind of the overwhelming majority of Jews everywhere, and that I could, without immodesty, after more than half a century of activity, claim to speak for the spirit of the Zionist movement. The account which follows is not in strict chronological order; its chief purpose is to summarize the substance of my views on the Zionist situation as a whole.

It was, as I said before the Ad Hoc Committee at Lake Success, a moving experience for me to appear before the United Nations at this turning point in Jewish history, and I added: "My mind goes back something like twenty-five years to the time when, in the Council Chamber of the League of Nations, a somewhat similar discussion took place, and as a result of it there was the emergence of our program for the reconstitution of the Jewish National Home in Palestine." But my mind went back much further. I sought to restate, before the two committees, the fundamentals of the movement, its ethical and national meaning, and its historical character, as well as its position in regard to immediate problems. I went back not only a quarter of a century, but half a century and more. I presented to the best of my ability, a total picture of the meaning of Zionism.

Much of what I had to say to the committees the reader will have gathered from my life story. If I advert briefly to some points which are already familiar to the reader, it is because even the most immediate of our problems must be viewed against that background.

The environment I was born into, and grew up in as a child, the upbringing which I received, made Jewishness—the Jewish nation, nationalism, as others term it—an organic part of my being. I was never anything but Jewish, I could not conceive that a Jew could be anything else. It was very strange for me to hear Mr. Jamal Husseini, speaking for the Arab side at Lake Success, declare that Jews were not Jews at all; they were Khazars, or Tartars, or God knows what. I answered, simply: "I feel like a Jew and I have suffered like a Jew."

"To feel like a Jew" meant for me, as for all of those who have had that upbringing, to be a Zionist, and to express in the Zionist movement the ethical as well as the national spirit of our Jewishness. All this was already implicit in the early *Chibath Zion* movement, when the Russian Jewish masses were stirring under the promptings of Pinsker and Achad Ha-am. The coming of Herzl was an event of enormous importance, but not an unnatural one. It was no revolution; it was a fulfillment. But, as I have said, his creation of the Zionist Organization meant much more for us than his writing of the *Judenstaat*. It was not necessary to supply us with theories of Zionism; we had always had them. What we needed was a means and a way.

And that was what the Zionist Organization became for us. We watched it growing in strength from Congress to Congress. Sometimes we were compelled to fight certain destructive and reactionary forces which intruded into it. It seemed to me that these forces were seeking to increase the membership of the Zionist Organization at any cost, and were ready, for the sake of temporary assistance, to barter away the purity of its basic principles. The pressure of need has always spurred certain elements among the Jews to accept what I have so frequently called the fallacy of the short cut; and sometimes the results have been deeply disturbing. What was the terror in Palestine but the old evil in new and horrible guise? I said before the UNSCOP in Jerusalem: "The White Paper released certain phenomena in Jewish life which are un-Jewish, which are contrary to Jewish ethics, Jewish tradition. 'Thou shalt not kill' has been ingrained in us since Mount Sinai. It was inconceivable ten years ago that the Jews should break this commandment. Unfortunately they are breaking it today, and nobody deplores it more than the vast majority of the Jews. I hang my head in shame when I have to speak of this fact before you."

In this case, as in all others, a deviation from fundamental principle is not only a denial of ethics; it is self-defeating in its purpose. I have never believed that the Messiah would come to the sound of high explosives. The dissident groups which sprang up in Palestine, and which terrorized the government and to some extent the Jews, and kept up an unbearable tension in the country, represented to my notion a grave danger for the whole future of the Jewish State in Palestine.

I permit myself a digression at this point. What I said before the UNSCOP and the Ad Hoc Committee about the organic character of Zionism, and my detestation of the terror, was necessarily a brief summary of my views on those subjects. I believe that they should be treated at somewhat greater length here. There is a tendency to say that it was the activities of the Irgun which largely succeeded in drawing the attention of the world to the Palestine problem and in bringing it before the international forum of the United Nations. How the world was affected by the terror in Palestine it is difficult to gauge. We received more publicity than Herostratus, and I do not think that it is desirable to attract attention in that form.

I have said that the terrorist groups in Palestine represented a grave danger to the whole future of the Jewish State. Actually their behavior has been next door to anarchy. The analogy which is usually drawn between these groups and what happened in Ireland or South Africa presents only a half-truth. It leaves out of account that one fundamental fact with which the Jews have to reckon primarily: namely, that they have many hostages all over the world. And although Palestine is the primary consideration, it must not, it has no right to, endanger the situation of Jews outside of Palestine. Apart from which it must be remembered that after all the building of Palestine will depend to a large extent on the good will of Jews outside.

To return now to my addresses before the United Nations Committees. I dwelt at some length on our relations to the Arabs. I reiterated my belief—which I still hold strongly in spite of all that has happened—

that co-operation with the Arabs would come about only if we enjoyed a status equal to theirs. This, the reader may remember, was one of the important reasons which moved me to accept partition when the Peel Report first mooted the idea a decade ago. I continued to advocate it when "prudent" Zionists either treated the suggestion with great caution, or gained an easy popularity by attacking it. I pleaded for partition at the meetings of the UNSCOP in Jerusalem when no one could foresee that this would be its recommendation by an overwhelming majority. It seemed to me then—a great many others see it now—that the creation of a Jewish State, even within diminished boundaries, was the only way out of the impasse, particularly in our relations with our Arab neighbors.

It is also the only way to begin restoring those relations between ourselves and Great Britain which have deteriorated so sadly since the time of the Balfour Declaration. Even in the tense days of the summer and autumn of 1947 I was compelled by the feeling of historic justice to declare, both before the UNSCOP and the Ad Hoc Committee, that the Jewish people would be eternally grateful to Great Britain for the inauguration of that policy which the Balfour Declaration embodied. We must not, I insisted, permit ourselves to be blinded to the fact that the Mandate was inspired by high purposes, worthy of all the exertions and sacrifice which the Jewish people could bring to its implementation.

I said it at a time when the British Government, and its representatives in Palestine, were doing their best to turn the decision of the UNSCOP and the Ad Hoc Committee against us; at a time, I might say, when they were resurrecting arguments which had long since been disproved. I was, for instance, particularly struck by the complaint of the Palestine administration, in a document prepared for the United Nations Special Committee, that our achievements had "set up disparities" between us and the Arabs. Once upon a time we were accused of harming the Arabs by displacing them from the land, or by creating unemployment in their midst. This form of the accusation had been thrown out of court by the Peel Commission; the Palestine administration now revived it in another form. We were not harming the Arabs directly; it might even be conceded that we were bringing them benefits; but there were "disparities."

I contended, I think rightly, that these disparities were much smaller than those which exist between the backward population and the so-called master race in many civilized and powerful countries. One might very well ask these rich and powerful countries what they have done for their backward populations. In my opinion it falls far behind the benefits which the Arabs have derived from the Jewish population of Palestine. If more should have been done for the Arabs—and it should—that was the primary business of the Government, and not of the Jews.

But the so-called question of these "disparities" opened up a much wider field of discussion. The stability of the Near East has long occupied the attention of statesmen; there is a general fear that a political or social collapse in the Arab subcontinent will have grave consequences outside of that area. But the most notorious social feature of the Arab subcontinent is the shocking gap between the small layer of the over-rich and the vast base of the submerged and miserable population. Nor is anything of consequence being done, by those who profess to fear the consequences of this evil, to diminish its dangers. Where are the vast royalties from the oil fields going? What fraction of these sums which are being handed over to Arab potentates is applied to bettering the condition of the masses of the population? Only a minimal proportion is actually being used for the founding of schools, or the improvement of hygienic conditions.

One was sometimes driven to the painful conclusion that there was an unwritten covenant between certain elements among the European and Anglo-Saxon powers, and the middle eastern Arabs, which ran on something like the following lines: "We are adherents of noninter-vention. Whatever happens in the interior of your country is your busi-ness. You can go on dealing with your populations as you think fit. We want peace in order to tap the oil resources and keep the lines of com-munication open." But once again so-called "realism" defeats itself. These elements are the very ones who fear unrest in the Near East. They refuse to understand that this idyllic state of affairs cannot last very long under any circumstances; and therefore they dread the ex-ample and influence of the Jewish Homeland. Instead of applauding this example and influence, which has already in Palestine produced a con-siderable improvement in the condition of adjacent Arab communities, they wish to see it removed; they consider the Jews dangerous not because they exploit the fellaheen, but because they do not exploit them. They have not learned, perhaps in their anxiety for immediate profit they are unable to learn, that stability is not to be obtained by the dominion of the few over the many, but by the more even spread of wealth through all the levels of the population.

This, in brief, was the substance of some of the arguments which I submitted to the UNSCOP and the Ad Hoc Committee. But there was much to be done in the way of explanation and exposition apart from my public appearances. Both in Palestine and America I placed myself at the disposal of members of the committees, or of United Nations delegates, who were anxious for more detailed information. My activities were, so to speak, on the sidelines, rather than in bearing the brunt of the public political discussions. In Palestine my house was open at all times to members of the committee. In America I was in frequent attend-ance at the sessions. If things were going slowly during the rather feverish days preceding November 29, 1947, if unexpected difficulties arose, I was asked to come down to see some group of delegates—the French, the Bolivian, the American and so on.

The official pleading of our cause before the United Nations was conducted with great skill and energy by Mr. Moshe Shertok, the head of the Political Department of the Jewish Agency for Palestine, and Dr. Abba Hillel Silver, the head of the American Section of the Jewish Agency, but many American Jews who until recently were remote from the Zionist movement took a keen interest in the United Nations discussion and helped us in the work. There was a welcome and striking change in the attitude of the American Jewish Committee, under the leadership of Judge Joseph M. Proskauer. Mr. Bernard Baruch and Mr. Herbert Bayard Swope, particularly the latter, who visited me frequently, were helpful among the various delegations. Among the younger men there were George Backer and Edward M. Warburg, of whom the latter had inherited from his father a deep interest in Jewish affairs, and has come very close to the Zionist ideology. Of particular assistance was Mr. Henry Morgenthau Jr., with whom I had been privileged to come in contact some years before, when he was a member of the Roosevelt administration. This contact continued after he left the Cabinet and was strengthened when he became chairman of the United Jewish Appeal—a responsibility which he took very seriously, like everything else to which he devotes his attention. All these names, and many others which could be added, especially my good friend, Edward Jacobson, of Kansas City, make up an astonishing demonstration of the unity of American Jewry with regard to the Jewish National Home; it is in reality a fulfillment of what I had striven for in my old plans for the Jewish Agency.

There were many tense moments preceding the final decision on November 29, and these had to do not only with the probable votes of the delegates. There was, for instance, the actual territorial division. When this was discussed some of the American delegates felt that the Jews were getting too large a slice of Palestine, and that the Arabs might legitimately raise objections. It was proposed to cut out from the proposed Jewish State a considerable part of the Negev, taking Akaba away from us. Ever since the time of the Balfour Declaration I had attached great value to Akaba and the region about it. I had circumnavigated the gulf of Akaba as far back as 1918, when I went to see the Emir Feisal, and I had a notion of the character of the country. At present it looks a forbidding desert, and the scene of desolation masks the importance of the region. But with a little imagination it becomes quite clear that Akaba is the gate to the Indian Ocean, and constitutes a much shorter route from Palestine to the Far East than via Port Said and the Suez Canal.

I was somewhat alarmed when I learned, in the second week of November, that the American delegation, in its desire to find a compromise which would be more acceptable to the Arabs, advocated the excision of the southern part of the Negev, including Akaba. After consultation with members of the Jewish Agency Executive, I decided to go to Washington to see President Truman and to put the whole case before him.

On the morning of Wednesday, November 19, I was received by the President with the utmost cordiality. I spoke first of the Negev as a whole, which I believe is destined to become an important part of the Jewish State. The northern part, running from Gaza to Asluj or Beersheba, is beautiful country. It needs water, of course, which can either be brought from the North, as projected in the Lowdermilk scheme, or provided locally by desalting the brackish water which is found in abundance in these parts. We are, in fact, busily engaged in our Rehovoth Institute in experiments on the second alternative, and have succeeded in producing drinking water at an economic price; the question of larger quantities for irrigation still needs study. The settlements which are already receiving water from a pipe line are showing remarkable results. Mr. Henry A. Wallace, who had recently returned from a visit to the Negev, was struck by a great plantation of carrots, which had been preceded on the same soil by a good crop of potatoes, while near by there was a plantation of bananas. All this seems fantastic when one takes into account that there has not been a blade of grass in this part of the world for thousands of years. But it is, as I told the President, in line with what the Jews have done in many other parts of Palestine.

I then spoke of Akaba. I pleaded that if there was to be a division of the Negev, it ought to be vertical and not horizontal; this would be eminently fair, giving both sides part of the fertile soil and part of the desert. But for us it was imperative that in this division Akaba should go to the Jewish State. Akaba is at present a useless bay; it needs to be dredged, deepened and made into a waterway capable of accommodating ships of sizable dimensions. If Akaba were taken away from us, it would always remain a desert, or at any rate for a very long time to come. As part of the Jewish State it will very quickly become an object of development, and would make a real contribution to trade and commerce by opening up a new route. One can foresee the day when a canal will be cut from some part of the eastern Mediterranean coast to Akaba. It is not an easy undertaking, but it has already been adumbrated by American and Swedish engineers. This would become a parallel highway to the Suez Canal, and could shorten the route from Europe to India by a day or more.

I pleaded further with the President that if the Egyptians choose to be hostile to the Jewish State, which I hope will not be the case, they can close navigation to us through the Suez Canal when this becomes their property, as it will in a few years. The Iraqis, too, can make it difficult for us to pass through the Persian Gulf. Thus we might be cut off entirely from the Orient. We could meet such an eventuality by building our own canal from Haifa or Tel Aviv to Akaba. The project has a great many attractive possibilities; and the mere fact that such a thing could be done would probably serve as a deterrent against closing the road to India for the Jews. I was extremely happy to find that the President read the map very quickly and very clearly. He promised me that he would communicate at once with the American delegation at Lake Success.

At about three o'clock in the afternoon of the same day, Ambassador Herschel Johnson, head of the American delegation, called in Mr. Shertok of the Jewish Agency in order to advise him of the decision on the Negev, which by all indications excluded Akaba from the Jewish State. Shortly after Mr. Shertok entered, but before the subject was broached, the American delegates were called to the telephone. At the other end of the wire was the President of the United States, telling them that he considered the proposal to keep Akaba within the Jewish State a reasonable one, and that they should go forward with it. When Mr. Johnson and General Hilldring emerged from the telephone booth after a half-hour conversation, they returned to Mr. Shertok, who was waiting for them, tense with anxiety. All they had for him was the casual remark: "Oh, Mr. Shertok, we really haven't anything important to tell you." Obviously the President had been as good as his word, and a few short hours after I had seen him had given the necessary instructions to the American delegation.

This decision opened the way to the vote of the General Assembly on November 29, when, by a majority of thirty-three to thirteen, the United Nations declared: "The Mandate for Palestine shall terminate as soon as possible, but in any case not later than August first, 1948. . . . Independent Arab and Jewish States, and the specific international regime for the City of Jerusalem . . . shall come into existence in Palestine two months after the evacuation of the armed forces of the Mandatory Power has been completed, but in any case no later than October first, 1948."

CHAPTER 45

The Challenge

*The Problems of the Jewish State—Immigration—Defense—
American Help in Finance and Human Resources—Constitu-
tion of the New State—Justice—The Arab Minority—One
Law for All—A Unified School System—Industry and Tech-
nology—Quality Goods—Rural Foundations—Religion and the
State—Relations with Arabs and Neighboring States—The
Bridge between East and West—Building a High Civiliza-
tion.*

I WRITE this on the day following the historic decision of the United
Nations.

As the year 1947 draws to a close, the Jewish people, and particularly
the Zionists, face a very great challenge. Before another year is over
we must found a Jewish State; we must prepare a constitution, set up a
government, organize our defenses and begin to reconstruct the present
National Home so as to make it capable of absorbing, according to the
plan, some six to eight thousand immigrants a month.

This last item alone is a tremendous task. Seventy to a hundred thousand immigrants a year represents an increase of over 12 per cent in a
community of six hundred and fifty thousand. But the numbers express
only a part of the problem. In past years immigration included a large
class of people who, if not rich, certainly could not be classified as paupers.
The majority of them had some worldly possessions; they were in good
health, some had a little capital, others brought their machinery with
them, nearly all of them had a trade. The financing of this immigration
was a difficult but not unduly heavy task. The immigrant who comes in
today is completely destitute. He has been robbed of everything. In many
cases he is morally and physically sick and must undergo a long process
of rehabilitation and adjustment before he can become productive. This
task alone will tax to a very high degree the financial powers of Jewry;
and as European Jewry is today small in numbers, and, apart from a
few Western communities, quite impoverished, the burden of this operation will fall on the American Jewish community.

To the foregoing must be added the requirements for defense, which, as I hear now, are mounting to something like twenty-five million dollars a year, but will probably increase. We must also undertake a number of necessary technical improvements, like the renovation of means of communication, roads, rolling stock, and harbors. A large number of new buildings will be required. All this will put before us the necessity of raising a loan and of introducing taxes as quickly as possible. In short, we face the difficult and complex problem of the financing of the new State.

Nor is it by any means solely a question of finance. It is proper to ask whether we have all the men needed for our task. Without wishing to reflect on the men who have carried the burden hitherto, I believe we would do well not only to seek financial assistance from the American Jews, but to draw on the human resources of this country. There are many young people sympathetic to the movement who have had vast experience in running important state services, and who are willing to help. There are numbers of such persons in England. It will be a very severe test for the Zionists; they must show that they can divest themselves of their legitimate desires to become high public servants and to occupy positions which they may have deserved because of their activities. They must recognize that it is in the interest of the State to bring new forces and new points of view to bear on the whole situation.

A great deal will also depend on the constitution. It would be regrettable if the constitution of the new republic were to be fashioned in the image of that of the Zionist Organization. The latter is based on the principle of proportionate representation, which necessarily leads to the existence of a great many parties. We must try to avoid a repetition of the elections to the Vaad Leumi—the representative body of Palestinian Jewry hitherto. I think it would be sounder to have a constitution like the American, or almost no constitution, like the British, at any rate for the beginning, and to feel our way for the first few years before laying down hard and fast rules.

But all these matters, whether in the realm of finance or of constitutional arrangements, really deal with the externals of the situation. As the State is merely a means to an end it is necessary to envisage the end; or, to change the figure, the State is merely a vessel into which the contents still have to be poured, and it is necessary to know what the contents are likely to be.

Now the first element in such contents, and in my opinion the very lifeblood of a stable society, is justice; and not merely as an abstract principle, but as carried out in the law courts and by the judiciary. It must be quick, it must not be expensive—so that everyone has access to it—and it must be equal for everyone. There must not be one law for the Jew and another for the Arabs. We must stand firm by the ancient principle enunciated in our Torah: "One law and one manner shall be for you and for the stranger that sojourneth with you." In saying this, I do not assume that there are tendencies toward inequality or discrimination. It is merely a timely warning which is particularly necessary because we shall have a very large Arab minority. I am certain that the world will judge the Jewish State by what it will do with the Arabs, just as the Jewish people at large will be judged by what we do or fail to do in this State where we have been given such a wonderful opportunity after thousands of years of wandering and suffering.

It is such an extraordinary phenomenon that it will no doubt be the sensation of the century, and both our friends and our enemies—the latter more than the former—will be watching us carefully. Palestine has always been a powerful sounding board; it will become much more so when the Jewish State has been formed. Our security will to a great extent depend not only on the armies and navies which we can create, but on the internal moral stability of the country, which will in turn influence its external political stability.

But justice, though the first, is only one of the elements in the contents of the State. We shall be faced with an important reform in the whole system of education, and particularly in our elementary and secondary schools. We have at present a system based on class divisions. I think it is essential to see that we have a unified school system for which the State as a whole is responsible, and not some political party which tries to shape the mind of the child almost from the cradle. Party control of education makes for inefficiency and produces a bias in the mind and soul of the child from the very start. It will weaken, and not strengthen the State. Instead of partisanship there must be citizenship, which of course transcends party interests.

Our technical and higher education has to be brought up to date and expanded with the new needs of the State. We shall need railway engineers, harbor engineers and shipbuilders. We shall now have the opportunity of introducing new industries; to this end we must enlarge greatly the available technical skill, increasing it in quantity and improving it in quality and efficiency. This again is a matter of schooling, beginning sometimes with the early years of the child. So, for instance, there is in Switzerland a very long course—six or seven years—in the watchmaking school, which turns out skilled workmen and foremen. This is why Swiss watchmaking has taken such a high place in world industry. The same principle is applicable to all other industrial enterprises.

Palestine will have to produce quality goods; only in this way can it compete with larger and more powerful countries which swamp the market with mass-produced goods. Now the production of quality goods is not merely a matter of skill. It is also based on an honest relationship to the task in hand, on a desire to do justice to the product, to allow only the best to come out of the workshop, and to avoid shoddiness. It is in this way that a name and reputation are acquired, which is a very substantial part of the economic battle.

Into the same category fall honesty and frank relationships with the world outside; in the long run these are also profitable. One may be tempted to get rich quickly by producing shabby stuff which may find an initial sale, particularly in backward countries; but this sort of production corrupts the producer, who in the end becomes unable to improve himself, and remains on a low level in the industrial world. Therefore integrity in commercial and industrial relations, efficiency, and the desire to produce the best and the most beautiful, are the essential props on which a great industry can be built even in a small country. Again and again I should like to quote the example of Switzerland. The nature of the industry differs from country to country, depending on climate, geographic position, availability of this or that raw material; but the principles behind the fashioning of the product out of the raw material are the same. One may, indeed, speak of moral industrial development.

Happily we have made an excellent beginning in our agricultural colonization. I believe we have, through our system of land nationalization and co-operatives, avoided many mistakes from which old and powerful states suffer in their economy today. We have no "poor whites," and we also have no feudal landlords. We have a healthy, intelligent, educated small holder, who cultivates his land intensively, in a scientific way, is able to extract sustenance in a dignified fashion from a comparatively small plot, have a house and hearth, and even economize a little for a rainy day. So much has been written and said about this side of our life, that I need not expatiate on it here. I would only like to add that if I had to begin my life over again, and educate my children again, I would perhaps emulate the example of our peasants in Nahalal or Daganiah.

There is now an opportunity to acquire more land, create more and more of these settlements, and establish again a sort of balance between the town and the village. Civilization is based more on the village and on God's earth than on the town, however attractive certain features of our town life may be. It is in the quiet nooks and corners of the village that the language, the poetry and literature of a country are enriched. The stability of the country does not depend so much on the towns as on the rural population. The more numerous and the more settled the latter, the wider and more solid is the basis of the State. We do not need, in our case, to fear the conservatism or backwardness of the Jewish peasant, or the emergence of a kulak type. This cannot happen any more under our system. One would like to see an offset against the rapid growth of towns like Tel Aviv and Haifa. One should strive toward decentralization of the urban population, and not toward the creation of monster cities as we see them in Europe or America. These monster cities are of necessity composed of slums and something like luxurious dwellings, not to say palaces. We have still time to avoid these extremes in our city and village planning. A village in Palestine can have all the advantages of the town because of its nearness to the latter, and all the amenities of a village life, distances being very small.

Many questions will emerge in the formative stages of the State with regard to religion. There are powerful religious communities in Palestine which now, under a democratic regime, will rightly demand to assert themselves. I think it is our duty to make it clear to them from the very beginning that whereas the State will treat with the highest respect the true religious feelings of the community, it cannot put the clock back by making religion the cardinal principle in the conduct of the state. Religion should be relegated to the synagogue and the homes of those families that want it; it should occupy a special position in the schools; but it shall not control the ministries of State.

I have never feared really religious people. The genuine type has never been politically aggressive; on the contrary, he seeks no power, he is modest and retiring—and modesty was the great feature in the lives of our saintly Rabbis and sages in olden times. It is the new, secularized type of Rabbi, resembling somewhat a member of a clerical party in Germany, France or Belgium, who is the menace, and who will make a heavy bid for power by parading his religious convictions. It is useless to point out to such people that they transgress a fundamental principle which has been laid down by our sages: "Thou shalt not make of the Torah a crown to glory in, or a spade to dig with." There will be a great struggle. I foresee something which will perhaps be reminiscent of the *Kulturkampf* in Germany, but we must be firm if we are to survive; we must have a clear line of demarcation between legitimate religious aspirations and the duty of the State toward preserving such aspirations, on the one hand, and on the other hand the lust for power which is sometimes exhibited by pseudo-religious groups.

I have spoken of the problem of our internal relations with our Arab minority; we must also face the arduous task of achieving understanding and co-operation with the Arabs of the Middle East. The successful accomplishment of this task will depend on two important factors. First, the Arabs must be given the feeling that the decision of the United Nations is final, and that the Jews will not trespass on any territory outside the boundaries assigned to them. As to the latter, there does exist such a fear in the heart of many Arabs, and this fear must be eliminated in every way. Second—and this links up with our internal problem— they must see from the outset that their brethren within the Jewish State are treated exactly like the Jewish citizens. It will be necessary to create a special department dealing with the non-Jewish minority. The object of the department shall be to associate this minority with all the benefits and activities which will grow up in the Jewish State.

The situation requires tact, understanding, human sympathy, and a great deal of political wisdom; but I believe that if we follow the lines indicated, the much-desired co-operation will come about, even if slowly. But we must also turn our face to the Oriental countries beyond the Middle East. It was my good fortune during those fateful days of the United Nations sittings to come in close contacts with the Indian delegation, which contained a number of highly distinguished men and women. We had many talks with them, and it was they who took the initiative in proposing, first, that I should visit India; second, that we should send a group of Jewish scientists and engineers to India in order to propose new developments; third, the Indian students should come to the Jewish places of learning in Palestine. These men look upon Palestine as an outpost of Western civilization in relation to the Orient. Here is a mighty opportunity to build a bridge between the East and the West, which is one of the most attractive roles which the Jewish State in Palestine can play. It is a task which by itself is of a magnitude which calls for the efforts of many able men. Do our people, in their present mood of victory, realize all the implications of this new state of affairs, and have we the personnel capable of implementing the possibilities after they have been weighed correctly?

I have spoken of the East. There is also a Western region of Mediterranean countries with which good neighborly relations will have to be established: Greece, Italy, the Mediterranean islands, as far as Gibraltar. There is Turkey, which also looks upon Palestine as an outpost of European civilization. Our commercial and industrial development will depend to a great extent on our relations with these countries. Given the right relations, Palestine can become a modern Phoenecia, and her ships can trade as far as the coasts of America.

It is not the purpose of these closing pages to outline the full program of the Jewish State. An enormous amount will have to be left to trial and error, and we shall have to learn the hard way—by experience. These are merely indications and signposts pointing along the road which in my opinion must be followed if we are to reach our goal. This goal is the building of a high civilization based on the austere standards of Jewish ethics. From these standards we must not swerve, as some elements have done during the short period of the National Home, by bending the knee to strange gods. The Prophets have always chastized the Jewish people with the utmost severity for this tendency; and whenever it slipped back into paganism, whenever it reverted, it was punished by the stern God of Israel. Whether prophets will once more arise among the Jews in the near future it is difficult to say. But if they choose the way of honest and hard and clean living, on the land in settlements built on the old principles, and in cities cleansed of the dross which has been sometimes mistaken for civilization; if they center their activities on genuine values, whether in industry, agriculture, science, literature or art; then God will look down benignly on His children who after a long wandering have come home to serve Him with a psalm on their lips and a spade in their hands, reviving their old country and making it a center of human civilization.

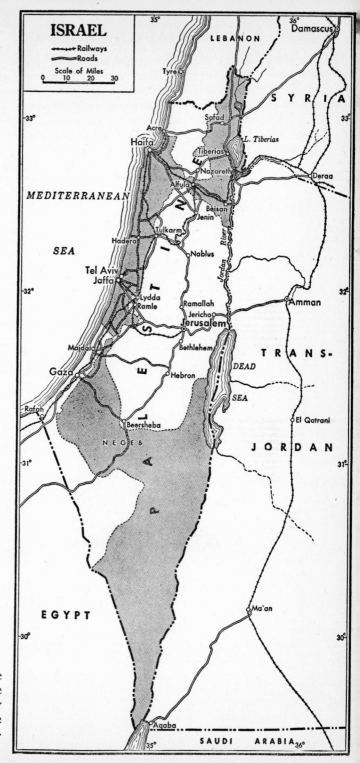

…shaded areas show the …oundaries of the State … Israel as fixed by … resolution of the …nited Nations, No-…mber 29, 1947.

Epilogue

SOME nine months have passed since I wrote the last chapter of these memoirs. I believed then that my task was ended and that the long—perhaps too long—record was complete. But the events which have filled the interval have been of a character which compels me, both on personal and general grounds, to add another word. I have made no change in what I wrote until November 30 of 1947, even where the record "dates": what follows here is a brief review of the extraordinary developments which have intervened.

We accepted the United Nations resolution of November 29 for what it was—a solemn international decision. We assumed—perhaps without thinking very deeply about the matter—that insofar as United Nations action might be needed to implement the decision, such action would be forthcoming; but we also assumed—and here we were on firmer ground —that the main responsibility for implementation would rest with ourselves. For my own part, I felt that the sooner I was in Palestine, the better, and made my preparations accordingly.

For family and other reasons we decided to pay a short visit to London en route, and we were back at our old apartment in the Dorchester on December 23, 1947. There was, it seemed, little political work to be done in England, for the British Government had announced its intention of abiding loyally by the United Nations decision. We settled down to enjoy the company of our children and of a few friends; I attended to some long neglected business affairs. I addressed a meeting at Palestine House, and a small dinner party in aid of the Joint Palestine Appeal; these were my only public engagements. We booked air passage to Palestine for January 25.

Within those few weeks, however, a disturbing change came over the situation at Lake Success, a result of the deteriorating position in London and Palestine. It soon became evident that the British Government placed a peculiar interpretation on its "loyal acceptance" of the United Nations decision. The Assembly of the United Nations had appointed a Committee of Five—known later as the "Five Lonely

Pilgrims"—to proceed to Palestine and begin the implementation of the decision. A Jewish militia was to be created and a Provisional Council of Government set up. If, on the withdrawal of the Mandatory Power Arab opposition developed, the Security Council was to establish an international force; in the meantime the Mandatory was responsible for the maintenance of order. But when, a few days after the meeting of the Security Council, there were Arab attacks on Jewish transports, the Mandatory took no steps. It appeared that the British Government regarded the mere protection of Jewish life as an implementation of partition, and "loyal acceptance" of the United Nations decision did not call for that. The disturbances, which could easily have been suppressed by prompt action, were permitted to spread—a familiar story, this. The Jewish defense forces were at that time still "underground." They had no access to the arms markets of the world. Such arms as they possessed were liable to seizure when discovered. Itself refusing to protect the Jewish community, the Mandatory did not acknowledge the right of the community to protect itself. Haganah convoys were searched, Haganah fighters arrested in the act of defending Jewish lives. "Loyal acceptance" of the decision became, in effect, a process of sabotage.

Nor was it all passive. The Mandatory Power refused the United Nations Committee entry into Palestine, refused to permit the organization of a Jewish militia to take over defense, refused to comply with the Assembly's recommendation to open a port of immigration, refused to hand over any of the Government services to an incoming Jewish successor; it expelled Palestine from the sterling bloc, dismantled the equipment of administration without handing any of it over, and simultaneously allowed the Government services to disintegrate. But while Palestine was closed to the Committee of the United Nations, its frontiers were open to the invasion of irregular Arab forces, which came across the Allenby Bridge on the Jordan, an easily guarded point. Under these circumstances it is not to be wondered at that Arab attacks multiplied. The Arabs now felt that what they could not obtain by argument in the court of the United Nations, they could compel by force of arms.

They were encouraged in this view by the apparent effects of their lawlessness on opinion in the United States and the United Nations. The Jews of Palestine, whose hands were tied by the Mandatory Power, were hastily and superficially adjudged incapable of defending themselves, and the cry arose in certain quarters that only armed intervention by the United Nations—a contingency which became remoter with every passing day—could save the November decision. The Jews were openly accused of having exaggerated their own strength, while underestimating the military power of the Arabs, and of having thus obtained the grant of statehood by what was nothing more nor less than a bluff. On top of all this the United States had established an arms embargo for the entire Near East, an action which seemingly placed Arab aggressors and Jewish defenders on the same footing. Thus a wholly synthetic situation was created which enabled the enemies of the Jewish State to make a last, desperate attempt to force a revision of the United Nations decision.

Toward the middle of January, I was besieged in London by letters, telegrams and telephone calls from friends in the United States. The Executive of the Jewish Agency sent me a formal invitation to return to New York and to co-operate with it in the gathering crisis. I was reluctant to accept. I still nourished the hope that things would somehow straighten themselves out, and I believed I could be more useful on the Palestinian scene. But as the time for our departure approached the telephone calls from New York became more numerous and more urgent, as one responsible friend after another pleaded with me to change my course. One day before the plane was due to leave we canceled the flight, and succeeded in obtaining passage on the *Queen Mary* for January 27. The last two days in London were something of a nightmare. We had arranged to give up our flat at the Dorchester on the twenty-fifth, and the moving man moved in promptly. He chased us from room to room taking carpets from under our feet, cushions from behind our backs, pictures from over our heads, till what had for nine years been our London home dissolved before our eyes and reverted to the hotel suite it really was. And all the while there was a constant stream of telegrams and telephone calls. It was in a thoroughly exhausted condition that my wife and I reached the boat train on the twenty-seventh.

We arrived in New York again on February 4, and on the same day I issued a statement to the press in which I said, among other things: "I am well aware that the implementation of the United Nations resolution raises many difficulties, but these difficulties are as nothing compared with the dangers which would arise if the United Nations policy were to be altered by force. If that were to happen, which I do not believe will, one result would be the decline of the United Nations and a grave blow to the very idea of international authority. Another would be the prolongation of conflict in Palestine. . . . The interests of America lie in the strengthening of the United Nations, in the curtailment of conflict in the Near East, and in the strictest fidelity to the policies to which they are pledged. . . . The steadfast courage of the Jews of Palestine fills me with the greatest pride. They have a right to expect that the civilized world which has endorsed their title to national independence will not leave them in the lurch in the face of a murderous attack which is being openly prepared against them by forces of extremism and violence in the Arab world. . . . The urgent task now is to convince Arab opinion by tangible facts that the Jewish State cannot be prevented from coming into existence. . . ."

The truth is, as all can now see plainly, that these facts really existed, but were being deliberately obscured in a political play. I was profoundly convinced that not only were the Jews of Palestine thoroughly capable of defending themselves, but that the much-touted danger of complete administrative chaos in Palestine, following on the British withdrawal, was an illusion, chiefly created by the British course of action, but belied, in fact, by the soundness of the structure of Jewish life. But it was not easy, in those days, to convince people that the realities of the Palestinian situation were being misrepresented. In Washington it was already being taken for granted that, in deference to the "facts," a fundamental revision would have to take place, and the November decision, if not actually reversed, deferred—perhaps *sine die*. When the Security Council began to discuss the problem at the end of February, the United States leadership was weak. Of the Powers which had supported the November decision, only the Soviet Union still insisted on the assertion of the United Nations authority. The Security Council failed to adopt any resolution for backing up the decision of the General Assembly.

Under these circumstances I obtained an interview with the President of the United States. Unfortunately it was delayed for many reasons, one of them being my ill-health, brought on largely by the strain and pressure of events. By the time I arrived in Washington, on March 18, the adverse tide had apparently become irresistible. The President was sympathetic personally, and still indicated a firm resolve to press forward with partition. I doubt, however, whether he was himself aware of the extent to which his own policy and purpose had been balked by subordinates in the State Department. On the following day, March 19, Senator Austin, the United States representative in the Security Council, announced the reversal of American policy. He proposed that the implementation of partition be suspended, that a truce be arranged in Palestine, and that a special session of the General Assembly be called in order to approve a trusteeship for Palestine, to take effect when the Mandate ended, i.e., on May 15th. In spite of all the forewarnings, the blow was sudden, bitter and, on the surface, fatal to our long nurtured hopes.

The notion of a new trusteeship for Palestine at this late date was utterly unrealistic. Palestine Jewry had outgrown the state of tutelage. Moreover, everything that had made the Mandate unworkable would be present in the trusteeship, but aggravated by the recollection that only a few months before we had been adjudged worthy of statehood. To have accepted this decision would have meant to make ourselves ludicrous in the eyes of history.

In a statement to the press I said, on March 25: "The plan worked out by the Assembly was the result of a long and careful process of deliberation in which the conflicting claims of the various parties were judged in the light of international equity. In order to achieve a compromise between Jewish and Arab national claims, the Jews were asked to be content with one eighth of the original area of the Palestine Mandate. They were called upon to co-operate in a settlement for Jerusalem which set that city's international associations above its predominantly Jewish character. We accepted these limitations only because they were decreed by the supreme authority of international judgment, and because in the small area allotted to us we would be free to bring in our people, and enjoy the indispensable boon of sovereignty —a privilege conferred upon the Arabs in vast territories . . .

"Now some people suggest that the partition decision be shelved because it has not secured the agreement of all parties! Yet it was because the Mandatory Power itself constantly emphasized that the prospect of agreement was nonexistent that it submitted the question to the United Nations. . . . Whatever solution may be imposed will require enforcement. A sustained effort should be made on behalf of a solution twice recommended by distinguished commissions—the Royal Commission and UNSCOP, and now reinforced by the Assembly's authority. I have spent many years laboring at this strenuous problem, and I know there is today no other practical solution, and none more likely to achieve stability in the long run—certainly not the Arab unitary state which the conscience of the world has rejected, or the so-called federal formula which is in fact nothing but an Arab state in another guise, or an impossible effort to impose trusteeship and arrest the progress of the Palestinian Jews toward their rightful independence.

"But for the admission into Palestine of foreign Arab forces no problem of security would have arisen which the local militia envisaged by the Assembly's decision could not have controlled. I shall never understand how the Mandatory Government could allow foreign Arab forces to cross freely by bridge and road into Palestine and prepare in leisure and with impunity to make war against the Jews and against the settlement adopted by the United Nations. I have always paid high tribute to the great act of statesmanship of Great Britain in inaugurating the international recognition of our right to nationhood. But in exposing everything and everybody in Palestine to destruction by foreign invaders the Mandatory Government has acted against its own best tradition and left a tragic legacy to the country's future. . . .

"The Jews of Palestine will have the support of Jews the world over in those steps which they will deem necessary to assure their survival and national freedom when the Mandate ends. I would now urge the Jewish people to redouble its efforts to secure the defense and freedom of the Jewish State. . . ."

In a private letter to the President of the United States, written on April 9, I elaborated these views in detail, adding, in view of the widespread rumours that Palestine would be left by the Mandatory in a state of chaos: "Jews and Arabs are both mature for independence, and are already obedient in a large degree to their own institutions, while the central British administration is in virtual collapse. In large areas Jews and Arabs are practically in control of their own lives and interests. The clock cannot be put back to the situation which existed before November 29. I would also draw attention to the psychological effects of promising Jewish independence in November and attempting to cancel it in March. . . .

"The choice for our people, Mr. President, is between statehood and extermination. History and providence have placed this issue in your hands, and I am confident that you will yet decide it in the spirit of the moral law."

In the swift movement of recent events a great part of the public may already have forgotten how dark the picture looked for us only a few months ago, and how completely it was dominated by the curious notion that the Zionists were "through." Shortly after the reversal of policy in the United Nations the United States delegation, consisting of Senator Austin, Professor Jessup and Mr. Ross, called on us at my hotel and tried to enlist my support for the trusteeship proposal. I must have astonished as well as disappointed them, for I declared bluntly that I put no stock in the legend of Arab military might, and that I considered the intention of Palestine Jewry to proclaim its independence the day the Mandate ended thoroughly justified and eminently realistic. M. Parodi, the representative of France, came to dinner, and renewed the arguments of the American delegation. I had the same answer for him. I added that, given half a chance, the Jews of Palestine would render the world a service by exploding the myth which had been built up round the Arab aggressors. M. Parodi was polite, but obviously incredulous. A few months later, when the issue had been joined and decided, he informed the Jewish representative at Lake Success: "What I thought was Dr. Weizmann's propaganda appears to be the truth."

My strongest protestations I reserved for Mr. Creech-Jones, the British Colonial Secretary, who visited me while I was on my sick bed. Great Britain was in an anomalous position: largely responsible for the failure—up to that point—of the partition decision, but showing no enthusiasm for the alternative proposal of trusteeship. The British view seemed to be that Arabs and Jews should be left to themselves for an unavoidable period of blood-letting. The British clearly anticipated that the Arabs would make substantial inroads on the territory allotted to the Jews, and on the basis of the situation thus created a new solution would be reached, favorable, both politically and territorially, to the

Arabs. It is an astonishing reflection on the relationship of the British to Palestine that they, who had been on the spot for the last thirty years, should have made so false an appraisal of the factors. For either they were really convinced that the Arabs would overwhelm us or else—and this betrayed an even profounder misreading of the realities—they believed that we would ignominiously surrender our rights without so much as a test. Mr. Creech-Jones pleaded that the invasion of Palestinian soil by 7,500 Arabs had taken the Mandatory Power unawares, but there they were and the Jews had to reckon with them. My answer was that we had no intention of evacuating any of the territory allotted to us. It was with the deepest pain that I saw the Mandate coming to an end under circumstances so unworthy of its beginnings, but the fault was not ours. The British had declared that "as long as they are in Palestine they insist on undivided control of the country." One could quite understand that a Great Power should be jealous of its prestige, but Great Britain had not been jealous enough to keep out the Arab invaders. Was that an enhancement of Britain's prestige? And how did it accord with Britain's good name to leave the country in a state of organized chaos? On these points Mr. Creech-Jones was extremely evasive.

The General Assembly of the United Nations reconvened in mid-April. By that time we had something more than protestations to offer, for the realities had begun to emerge. The so-called liberation army of Fawzi Kawakji had been soundly trounced at Mishmar Ha-Emek. In some parts of the country the Jewish forces had assumed the offensive. In an admirable display of discipline and initiative, the *Yishuv* was beginning to erect the pattern of an effective state on the ruins of the Mandatory regime. It created departments of centralized government in areas which the British were progressively evacuating. It was clear that while the United Nations was debating trusteeship, the Jewish State was coming into being.

It had been anticipated that the trusteeship plan would be adopted without difficulty; but within the two months since its proposal, the situation had again altered radically. The session of the Assembly was made notable by the remarkable address of the New Zealand representative, Sir Carl Berendsen, who demanded that the United Nations take a stand on its own decision. "What the United Nations needs," he said, "is not resolutions but resolution." His view won support from Australia and from the countries of Eastern Europe, and from the ever gallant defenders of the Jewish cause from South America, including Professor Fabregat, of Uruguay, and Dr. Granados, of Guatemala, with both of whom I was in close contact. It was at this time, too, that I made the acquaintance of the Secretary General of the United Nations, Mr. Trygve Lie who, within the powers granted him by the Charter, zealously asserted the Assembly's authority. During those crucial days we had many defenders in the public press, foremost among them Mr. Sumner Welles, who wrote a number of impressive articles in the *Herald Tribune*. The *New York Times*, which at best had been always cool to the Zionist program, strongly criticized the United States reversal, and urged that partition be given a chance.

Still, it was hard going. When it became clear in the Assembly that the trusteeship plan could not be adopted, another delaying formula was devised—a "Temporary Truce": both parties were to cease fire, no political decision was to be taken, a limited Jewish immigration was to be permitted for a few months, and in exchange for this transient and dubious security the Jews were to refrain from proclaiming their State in accordance with the November decision. The proposal was to all appearances a harmless one: at bottom it was profoundly dangerous, if only for the reason that every refusal to face the realities of the situation weakened the authority of the United Nations and encouraged in the enemies of the Jewish State the belief that its creation could be prevented.

I was of course in intimate consultation during this period with Mr. Shertok, our chief spokesman at the United Nations and his colleagues. They were thoroughly aware of the dangers which lurked in the truce proposal; but they were also aware that it made a strong appeal to the less determined elements in our own ranks. Perhaps the most telling argument against us was that in proclaiming a Jewish State in the face, apparently, of American disapproval, we should be alienating a powerful friend. Moreover, it needed a certain moral courage to decline a truce when our nascent army in Palestine was still so ill-equipped and the issue apparently still in doubt. Messrs. Shertok, Goldmann and their colleagues felt that at this point my views on the situation would have a considerable effect both within and without our ranks.

On the issue of this truce, as on that of the trusteeship, I was never in a moment's doubt. It was plain to me that retreat would be fatal. Our only chance now, as in the past, was to create facts, to confront the world with these facts, and to build on their foundation. Independence is never given to a people; it has to be earned; and having been earned, it has to be defended. As to the attitude of the United States Government, I felt that many of those who were advising us to ignore the United Nations decision in our favor, and to let our independence go by default, would respect us more if we did not accept their advice. I was convinced that once we had taken our destiny into our own hands and established the Republic, the American people would applaud our resolution, and see in our successful struggle for independence the image of its own national liberation a century and three-quarters ago. So strongly did I feel this that at a time when the United States was formally opposed to our declaration of independence I already began to be preoccupied with the idea of American recognition of the Jewish State.

Many friends and colleagues thought I was being somewhat less than realistic, and tried to dissuade me from encouraging a step which in their opinion could only end in retreat and disaster. They expressed astonishment at what they called my unwonted intransigeance. In Palestine, where the doubts and hesitations which reigned at Lake Success found no echo, there was no thought of relinquishing the rights conferred on us, and by a suicidal act of self-denial refusing statehood; or, if there was any doubt, it was connected with our intentions in America rather than with those of the Palestinian Jews. In the general breakdown of British administration, there was a period when communications between America and Palestine were irregular and unreliable. Our views at the American end were not at all clear to the *Yishuv*. Mr. Ben-Gurion, the chairman of the Jewish Agency Executive, was trying, without success, to ascertain exactly where I stood. In the early part of May, Mr. Shertok left for Palestine to clear matters up, and in the second week of that month I strengthened our contacts with our friends in Washington, and affirmed my intention of going ahead with a bid for recognition of the Jewish State as soon as it was proclaimed. On May 13 I addressed the following letter to the President of the United States:

DEAR MR. PRESIDENT:
The unhappy events of the last few months will not, I hope, obscure the very great contributions which you, Mr. President, have made toward a definitive and just settlement of the long and troublesome Palestine question. The leadership which the American Government took under your inspiration made possible the establishment of a Jewish State, which I am convinced will contribute markedly toward a solution of the world Jewish problem, and which I am equally convinced is a necessary preliminary to the development of lasting peace among the peoples of the Near East.

So far as practical conditions in Palestine would permit, the Jewish people there have proceeded along the lines laid down in the United Nations Resolution of November 29, 1947. Tomorrow midnight, May 15, the British Mandate will be terminated, and the Provisional Government of the Jewish State, embodying the best endeavors of the Jewish people and arising from the Resolution of the United Nations, will assume full responsibility for preserving law and order within the boundaries of the Jewish State, for defending that area against external aggression, and for discharging the obligations of the Jewish State to the other nations of the world in accordance with international law.

Considering all the difficulties, the chances for an equitable adjustment of Arab and Jewish relationships are not unfavorable. What is required now is an end to the seeking of new solutions which invariably have retarded rather than encouraged a final settlement.

It is for these reasons that I deeply hope that the United States, which under your leadership has done so much to find a just solution, will promptly recognize the Provisional Government of the new Jewish State. The world, I think, will regard it as especially appropriate that the greatest living democracy should be the first to welcome the newest into the family of nations.

Respectfully yours,

CHAIM WEIZMANN

On the fourteenth of May the President and his advisers were in constant consultation on the Palestine issue. The Assembly of the United Nations had neither revoked nor reaffirmed its resolution of November 29. In Palestine the British Mandate had only a few more hours to run.* On the same day a historic assembly of the representatives of the *Yishuv* was convoked in Tel Aviv, and proclaimed to the world the rightful independence of the Jewish State, to take effect as of the hour of the termination of the British Mandate.

At a few minutes past six o'clock, American time, unofficial news reached Lake Success that the Jewish State had been recognized by the Government of the United States. The delegates were incredulous, which perhaps was natural at a time when many wild rumors were running through the corridors of the United Nations building. The United States delegation was unaware of any such decision. Finally, after much confusion, Professor Jessup rose to read the following statement issued from the White House:

This Government has been informed that a Jewish State has been proclaimed in Palestine, and recognition has been requested by the Provisional Government itself. The United States recognizes the Provisional Government as the *de facto* authority of the new State of Israel.

This historic statement must be regarded not only as an act of high statesmanship; it had a peculiar and significant fitness, for it set the seal on America's long and generous record of support of Zionist aspirations.

On May 15 a great wave of rejoicing spread throughout the Jewish world. We were not unmindful of the dangers which hung over the new-born State. Five Arab armies were at its frontiers, threatening invasion; our forces were not yet properly organized; we were cut off from international support. But the die was cast. The demoralizing illusions of trusteeship and truce were behind us. We were now face to face with the basic realities, and this was what we had asked for. If the

* It should be borne in mind that Palestine time is seven hours in advance of Washington time.

State of Israel could defend itself, survive and remain effective, it would do so largely on its own; and the issue would be decided, as we were willing it should be, by the basic strength and solidity of the organism which we had created in the last fifty years.

May 15 was a very full day. Recognition was extended to the State of Israel by the Soviet Union and Poland, to be followed shortly by several countries of Eastern Europe and South America. Great Britain remained silent, and I received reports that Mr. Bevin was bringing pressure to bear on the British Dominions and Western Europe to withhold recognition. However, I bethought myself of one surviving author of the Balfour Declaration and addressed a cablegram to General Smuts. This was closely followed by South African recognition.

On this same day, amidst the avalanche of messages reaching me from Tel Aviv, there was one signed by the five Labor Party leaders in the Provisional Government, David Ben-Gurion, Eliezer Kaplan, Golda Myerson, David Remez and Moshe Shertok.

On the occasion of the establishment of the Jewish State we send our greetings to you, who have done more than any other living man toward its creation. Your stand and help have strengthened all of us. We look forward to the day when we shall see you at the head of the State established in peace.

I answered:

My heartiest greetings to you and your colleagues in this great hour. May God give you strength to carry out the task which has been laid upon you and to overcome the difficulties still ahead. Please accept and transmit the following message to the *Yishuv* in my name: "On the memorable day when the Jewish State arises again after two thousand years, I send expressions of love and admiration to all sections of the *Yishuv* and warmest greetings to its Government now entering on its grave and inspiring responsibility. Am fully convinced that all who have and will become citizens of the Jewish State will strive their utmost to live up to the new opportunity which history has bestowed upon them. It will be our destiny to create institutions and values of a free community in the spirit of the great traditions which have contributed so much to the thought and spirit of mankind."

CHAIM WEIZMANN

Two days later, when I was resting in my hotel from the fatigue of the preceding weeks, a message reached me that, according to one of the news agencies, the Provisional Council of State had elected me as its President. I attached no credence to the report, thinking it unlikely that the Council of State, absorbed with a thousand urgent problems, of which not the least were the dangers of the invasion, would have been giving thought to this matter. A few hours later, however, the same message was repeated over the radio and was picked up in the adjoining room where my wife was entertaining friends. Almost at the same moment Aubrey Eban, then one of our younger aides at the United Nations, and at this time of writing the brilliant representative of Israel before that body—and I might add, one of its most distinguished members—came in with some friends from Madison Square Garden, where the Jews of New York were celebrating the establishment of the Jewish State at a mass rally which I could not attend because of ill-health. They brought definite confirmation of the report. That evening my friends gathered in our hotel apartment, and raised glasses of champagne in a toast to the President of Israel.

The next day I received a more detailed report of the proceedings in Tel Aviv. The Minister of Justice, Dr. Felix Rosenblueth, had proposed my election. Mr. Ben-Gurion, Prime Minister and Minister of Defense, had seconded it. He did not conceal the many differences of opinion which had divided us in recent years. He went on, however, to say: "I doubt whether the Presidency is necessary to Dr. Weizmann, but the Presidency of Dr. Weizmann is a moral necessity for the State of Israel." I quote these words, at the risk of incurring the charge of immodesty, only as an indication of the essential unity of purpose which underlay all those struggles of ideology and method which formed part of our movement. But I will not deny that the occasion was one which filled me with pride as well as with a feeling of deep humility. Replying to the notification of my election, I cabled Ben-Gurion:

Many thanks your cable May seventeenth. Am proud of the great honor bestowed upon me by Provisional Council of Government of State of Israel in electing me as its first President. It is in a humble spirit that I accept this election and am deeply grateful to Council for confidence it has reposed in me. I dedicate myself to service of land and people in whose cause I have been privileged to labor these many years. I send to Provisional Government and people of Israel this expression of my deepest and most heartfelt affection, invoking blessing of God upon them. I pray that the struggle forced upon us will speedily end and will be succeeded by era of peace and prosperity for people of Israel and those waiting to join us in construction and advancement of new State.

My first official act as President of the State of Israel, and my last on American soil, was to accept the invitation of the President of the United States to be his guest in Washington and to take up the usual residence at Blair House. I traveled from New York to Washington by special train, and arrived to find Pennsylvania Avenue bedecked with the flags of the United States and Israel. I was escorted to the conference at the White House by representatives of the United States Government and by Mr. Eliahu Epstein, whom the Provisional Government had appointed as its envoy to the United States. In the course of our interview, I expressed our gratitude to the President for the initiative he had taken in the immediate recognition of the new State, and as a gift symbolizing the Jewish tradition, I presented him with a scroll of the Torah. We passed from ceremonial to practical matters and discussed the economic and political aid which the state of Israel would need in the critical months that lay ahead. The President showed special interest in the question of a loan for development projects, and in using the influence of the United States to insure the defense of Israel—if possible, by preventing Arab aggression through United States action, or, if war continued to be forced upon us, by insuring that we had the necessary arms.

The following day I set sail for Europe. It had been my original intention to go again to England for personal and family reasons. I now felt that I was no longer free to do so. Arab armies were attacking Israel by land and from the air; the spearhead of this aggression was the Arab Legion of Trans-Jordan, equipped by British resources, financed by the British Treasury, trained and commanded by British officers. By a particularly bitter twist of historical irony, the main operations of this force were directed against the Holy City. The Hebrew University and the Hadassah Medical Center were under bombardment; Jewish shrines in Jerusalem, which had survived the attacks of barbarians in medieval times, were now being laid waste. Liberal opinion throughout the world, and especially in the United States, was profoundly shocked. I had always believed that an anti-Zionist policy was utterly alien to British tradition, but now an atmosphere had been created in which the ideals of the State of Israel, and the policies of Great Britain, under Mr. Bevin's direction, were brought into bloody conflict. I had no place in England at such a time, and I felt it to be a bitter incongruity that I should not be able to set foot in a country whose people and institutions I held in such high esteem, and with which I had so long and so stubbornly sought to link the Jewish people by ties of mutual interest and co-operation. I decided to arrange my affairs in France; for that country, my wife and I, accompanied by Mr. Ivor Linton, Political Secretary of the London Office of the Jewish Agency, set sail on May 26. From France we proceeded to Switzerland, where I planned to take a much-needed rest before I went on to Israel to assume my duties.

Here, in the quiet of Glion, I write these closing lines to the first part of a story which is not yet half told, is, indeed, hardly begun. Of the crowded events of the last few months, of the first struggles and triumphs of the infant State of Israel, of truces and renewed attacks, of mediation and of old solutions in new guise, I will not speak here. These matters are too close to be evaluated. All that is written here is by way of introduction—one of the many prefaces that may yet be written to the New History of Israel. Its writing has been for me a labor compounded of pain and pleasure, but I am thankful to lay it aside in favor of more active and practical pursuits. If anything I have said should lead the reader to look more understandingly and more kindly on the early chapters of our new history now in the making, I shall feel amply rewarded.

GLION, SWITZERLAND
AUGUST 1948

Index